*The Politics
of Social Services*

The Politics
of Social Services

JEFFRY H. GALPER
School of Social Administration
Temple University

Prentice-Hall, Inc., Englewood Cliffs, New Jersey

Library of Congress Cataloging in Publication Data

GALPER, JEFFRY H.
    The politics of social services.

    Includes bibliographical references and index.
    1. Social service.   2. Social change.   3. Welfare
state.   I. Title.
HV41.G29   361   75-2051
ISBN   0-13-685214-9 pbk.

10 9 8

Prentice-Hall International, Inc., **London**
Prentice-Hall of Australia, Pty. Ltd., **Sydney**
Prentice-Hall of Canada, Ltd., **Toronto**
Prentice-Hall of India Private Limited, **New Delhi**
Prentice-Hall of Japan, Inc., **Tokyo**

Contents

v

Preface

The social services are a political phenomenon. Despite the fact that their political role is not generally understood, the social services nonetheless are active in influencing the values and structures of the social order in ways that best can be understood as political. In fact, an explicitly political analysis of the social services is required to achieve a meaningful understanding of their nature and purpose. One task this book undertakes is to contribute to the development of such an analysis.

Political, as used here, does not imply a concern with electoral or party politics. Though commonly accepted, this is too limited an understanding of that word for our purposes. Rather, *political* implies a concern with the social services as they reinforce the values, institutions, and human behaviors on which our present social order rests or as they challenge those values, institutions, and behaviors. The critical political question, then, is what role the social services play as they support the status quo or as they serve as agents of one or another variety of change.

This question will be asked of the services in many ways. We will need to explore how client problems are interpreted in social service systems, how standards are set for desired outcomes, and how services relate—ideologically and structurally—to other major institutions in the society—for example, the labor market. The concern either for conservation or change stimulates even broader examinations of the views inherent in the social services about the nature of the good life, the good society, and ways of achieving them.

Social service practice that builds on an explicitly political analysis necessarily will be explicitly political. It will be practice that understands and is active in its role in social conservation or social change. It will attempt to provide the very best service in the light of both immediate client needs and the larger need that all of us experience as a consequence of the nature of our society. The second major task of this book is to contribute to the development of such practice.

Some people will consider the nature of the political analysis made here—and the subsequent practice—to be radical; and in many ways, it is. It suggests that the social services, as they presently function, do not and cannot be of great service to clients or to social welfare in general. Furthermore, it describes their limitations as inevitable and logical consequences of the social services' structural and ideological relationships to capitalism itself. The analysis is radical, in this sense, because it roots the problems of the social services in the most fundamental organizational principles of the society.

The practice that is developed is radical, since it suggests that social services will not be of full service to clients and to us all unless their task is seen as a struggle for the creation of a fundamentally changed society and—we believe—for a society organized on socialist principles. We believe that it is impossible to develop a reasonable (i.e., client-oriented, socially useful, personally gratifying) practice in the social services unless that practice is informed by an understanding of the nature of socialism and by strategies and tactics to bring us closer to a socialist society.

The word *radical*, however, is sometimes used to imply extremism or unreasonableness. In this sense, the present analysis is not radical. Although it is not conventional, we believe it to be reasonable. *Conventional* practices and perspectives are the unreasonable element in social services, because they are based on denial and distortion of human need and on self-deceptions about their accomplishments. By contrast, the radical view takes seriously the failures of the services, as it takes seriously and tries to find ways to operationalize the commitment to human services of many social service workers. In working from a socialist perspective, we simultaneously address larger vital issues affecting large populations and express the deepest possible commitment to each of our clients and to the best ideals of the social services. An analysis that points in this direction cannot be considered unreasonable or extreme.

The problems of the social services appear enormous when assessed in such broad-ranging systemic perspectives, and the tasks before us seem overwhelming. The scope of such analysis can lead to pessimism or even temporary paralysis. However, a socialist perspective can finally be liberating and energizing. It is more free of what we see as the inherent pessimism of more conventional thinking and of the futility of the reformist strategies of change to which that thinking gives rise. It points to an approach that makes sense—not only for the moment, but in the long run as well. We have found that the socialist analysis leads to a fuller, and therefore more intellectually satisfying understanding of the services than does the conventional approach. Further, it suggests strategies and responses that are more rewarding and life-enhancing to practitioners than are those stemming from other analyses.

The contradictions in the social services between the surface manifestations of social concern and the deeper reality of human denial are reflected in the lives of social service workers. As social service workers, we are engaged in processes ostensibly designed to help others. In fact, however, we are relatively ineffectual in our efforts to help others. As a consequence, empirical studies have indicated that we become frustrated and cynical as the nature and limitations of our work become clear to us. We typically experience the same kind of denial of our personal needs in our work and our lives in general as do our clients. A radical stance can free us from a commitment to the repressive aspects of our own experience and encourage us to pursue a more consistent endorsement of life-enhancing values.

The socialist analysis addresses the dilemmas of the social services and the contradictory aspects of the lives of social service workers. It does so, hopefully, in an integrated way that is rooted in an understanding of the common, underlying causes of these dilemmas. For these reasons it can clarify and it can energize—even as it vastly enlarges the scope and depth of the tasks before us.

It is my impression that there is a growing number of students and workers in the social services who are aware—at some level—that their work is of marginal use to their clients and of marginal satisfaction to themselves. However, this sense that something is wrong remains unanalyzed and so leads to cynicism or defeatism. It is my hope that this book will be useful to those with that awareness—to clarify what they are feeling, to give it some logical order, and to suggest some alternative directions. If this happens, perhaps those of us who share these commitments can join colleagues, clients, and friends as comrades, brothers, and sisters. At that point, we can do something positive for ourselves and for each other.

Acknowledgments

A number of people have read all or part of the manuscript of this book. My thanks for their efforts and concern go to Leslie Alexander, Paula Bell, Harvey Finkle, Adam Finnerty, Charles Frye, Reynold Levy, Philip Lichtenberg, and Jack Sternbach. To the extent that clear thinking, sanity, and humanity are found in these pages, a good deal of the credit goes to the influence of Harvey Finkle, Phil Lichtenberg, and Jack Sternbach, with whom I shared a collective experience for several years; to the folks involved in the People's Fund of Philadelphia, and to Miriam.

The Politics
of Social Services

1

Introduction

RIGHTIST, CENTRIST, AND LEFTIST PERSPECTIVES
ON THE SOCIAL SERVICES

Criticizing the social services has become so popular an activity in the United States in the 1970s that it sometimes seems a national pastime. As with some other national pastimes, the participants represent a broad spectrum of races, creeds, and ideologies. Among the frequent players are conservative politicians, who use the attacks on services as a way to demonstrate their commitment to traditional values; clients, who speak of the services' failure to meet their needs; social service workers, who are sometimes concerned about the limitations of what they can do to help clients and are often frustrated by their working conditions; and ideologues of all sorts, those who argue that the social services are destructive because they undermine our basic values and those who argue that they are destructive because they support our basic values.

On a more technical level, some of the more commonly suggested sources of the shortcomings of the social services are said to be the absence of an adequate model of social dynamics on which to base intervention;[1] the muzzling of reform efforts by conservative, corrupt, or self-seeking political leaders;[2] the failure of reformers to develop the appropriate coalitions of interest groups to struggle for change;[3] the inherent difficulty of the social service task in the face of the social disorganization that accompanies technology and bureaucratization;[4] the tendency of social policies to disrupt more traditional processes of solving social problems (thereby creating new problems as they meet old needs);[5] and the inevitable inability of social services to meet people's constantly rising expectations.[6] Alvin Schorr, as editor of the official journal of the social work profession, summarized this barrage as it was reflected in attacks on that profession in the early 1970s. He wrote,

> . . . criticism of social work from the Left continues unheeding, even while anti–social work sentiment rises now powerfully from the Right. . . . For at least a little while, we seem likely to be trying to defend ourselves at the same time from charges of representing anarchy and of representing the establishment. We will find little comfort in assuming that, because we occupy some central ground, we must be right. More likely we are entering a chaotic period in which it will be terribly hard to know what we should be doing.[7]

Most of the political debate about the social services has been conducted within a liberal-conservative framework; that is, liberal thought and conservative thought have defined the boundaries of the argument. The liberal position has tended to rest on an assumption that the social services are basically a "good thing" and thus sees the major problem with the services as the absence of enough of them. Although the liberal position contains some criticism of the services and substantial criticism of those that are overtly coercive, "more is better" summarizes a good part of the conventional progressive analysis.

[1] For example, see Kenneth Boulding, "The Boundaries of Social Policy," *Social Work*, 12 (January 1967), pp. 3–11.
[2] This was the dominant thesis used by liberals in assessing the problems of the social services during the Nixon administration.
[3] This has been the argument of those who defend the American version of pluralism as a natural and desirable way to develop social policy.
[4] For example, see Harold Wilensky and Charles Lebeaux, *Industrial Society and Social Welfare* (New York: Russell Sage Foundation, 1958).
[5] For example, see Nathan Glazer, "The Limits of Social Policy," *Commentary*, 52 (September 1971), pp. 51–58; and Edward Banfield, *The Unheavenly City* (Boston: Little, Brown, 1970). This was part of the thought behind Daniel Moynihan's 1969 memorandum to Richard Nixon, counseling a period of "benign neglect" in social policy development. This memo was reprinted in *The Wall Street Journal* (March 13, 1970), p. 26.
[6] See Glazer, "The Limits of Social Policy"; and Herbert J. Gans, "The 'Equality' Revolution," *New York Times Magazine* (November 3, 1968), pp. 36–37, 66–76.
[7] Alvin Schorr, "We Face a Time," Editorial, *Social Work*, 16 (January 1971), p. 2.

Conservatives, on the other hand, maintain that "less is better." The right has long argued that social welfare programs, especially when they involve cash transfers but also when they are of the "softer" variety, undermine initiative, weaken moral fiber, and create imbalance in the workings of the marketplace. Many conservatives saw the New Deal, which represented a major upsurge in social welfare programming in the United States, as a serious diminishing of what they felt to be this country's special greatness. In the 1970s, after thirty relatively quiet years on the social welfare front, the conservative criticisms were revived. For example, Richard Nixon vetoed a national day-care program (contained in the 1972 Child Development Act) partly on the grounds that it would weaken family structure. This updated conservative version is supplemented by extra negativism toward the helping professions that have developed near-institutional status since the 1930s. Conservatives charge that social work, psychology, and psychiatry all pursue fame, fortune, and their own self-interest through the vehicle of social welfare programming.

The analysis herein is developed from a position outside this liberal-conservative debate. It argues that neither more nor fewer services of the current variety would significantly influence the well-being of this country in general or of social welfare clients in particular. This is not meant to question the fact that a quantitatively greater amount of service provision would have the potential to alleviate some human suffering, albeit temporarily and imperfectly. It does suggest, however, that the largest part of our dilemmas cannot be solved by the vehicle of social services as we know them. This leftist position sees the inadequacies of the social services as rooted in the logic of the society as a whole, endemic to the society in its present form, and even functional for the maintenance of current social arrangements. As such, while it recognizes differences in the liberal and conservative positions, it argues that their debate is ultimately unproductive in getting to the issues that must be addressed. Furthermore, it argues that these two positions are more alike than they are unalike in their basic assumptions about human nature and the social order. The left identifies the ideological commonalities in the two positions and criticizes them on similar grounds.

One of the consequences of developing leftist criticism during a period when conservative criticism is on the rise is that it tends to provide ideological ammunition to the forces of the right. The right picks up some of the criticism that the left directs at the social services, but in a way that filters out the left's concern about the support that these social services give to the dominant conservative institutions of the society. As a consequence, what remains is simply a criticism of social efforts to help those in need. This is not at all the socialist position. True, both the left and the right argue that the social services have not much helped those in need, that they have been predicated on a series of inadequate or incorrect assumptions about helping others, have substituted paternalism for self-determination, and have indeed been used as a vehicle for professional self-aggrandizement by social workers, psychiatrists, and others.

But, the right sees the role the social services play in weakening the attachment of individuals to the labor market and in generally undermining traditional values and structures as the root of the dilemmas, while the left sees the dilemmas as being rooted in the services' reinforcement of those very same traditional values. Thus, the left sees the services aligned against the development of collective political struggle through their focus on individual initiative, against the effort of people to dominate rather than be dominated by the market through their reinforcement of the Protestant Work Ethic, and against the nurturance of liberated persons who can help to build a better society through their reinforcement of conforming values and behaviors. As a consequence, where the rightist critique calls for the dismantling of the social services and for a return to what it sees as free market principles and individualism, the leftist critique calls on the services to play a role in organizing people for collective struggle toward the achievement of a socialist society.

Liberals will also attempt to coopt certain elements of the left's position without understanding, or at least without incorporating, the most fundamental parts of it. The leftist criticism that government is not responsive to the needs of citizens is understood or used by the liberal center to buttress its case for electing candidates for the Democratic Party. The leftist struggle for self-determination is transformed into the liberal notion of citizen participation. The analysis of the failure of the social services is converted into an argument about the insufficiency of the social services, and so on.

Characteristically, then, leftist analysis will be taken out of context by the right and the center. They will highlight the fact of criticism without reference to the roots of the criticism and to the radical alternatives these criticisms suggest. But there is no choice. In more progressive political periods, the left will be encouraged to join a common front with liberals to solidify whatever gains are being made. In more regressive political periods, the left will be encouraged to abandon radicalism altogether to help minimize difficulties that the center is experiencing. So if the left abstains or is unable to make gains, the pendulum will shift between rightist and centrist positions.

I firmly believe, as many on the left do, that the ability of the liberal-conservative positions to contain the debate, and surely the utility of that containment for all of us, is passing. The forms may hold on for some while. But these positions simply do not represent our best hopes for

human welfare, and so they must prove ultimately unsatisfying. Therefore, the left can best conduct its struggle for a decent society by presenting the growing numbers of those disenchanted with the sterility of
the old positions with analytical, ideological, and structural alternatives.

OVERVIEW OF THE BOOK

The Theme

The social services in the United States must be examined on several
levels if their nature and role are to be fully understood and if strategies
are to be developed to make the services a useful addition to the struggle
for human welfare. When a multilevel analysis of the services is made,
the following contradiction emerges sharply: the positive social concerns
and the efforts to meet human needs that are represented by the better
impulses of the social services are undermined by the forces which the
social services sustain and reinforce in the society at large. At the same
time that they are concerned about the promotion of human welfare, the
social services buttress values, institutions, and procedures that are destructive to that welfare. The services are products of, and responsive to,
a social order that values economic growth and political stability above
human well-being and that uses social services and the helping professions to preserve and strengthen the ideologies, behaviors, and structures of the status quo. The failures of the social services are rooted not
in their particular shortcomings or specific limitations, but in the fact that
they operate in conjunction with and in support of the same antisocial
forces that they theoretically are organized to mitigate.

This paradox presents more than a small problem for politically conscious and socially concerned social service workers. It suggests that they
must operate in a way that transcends current assumptions and procedures in the social services—they must attempt to create something
wholly new while they are, in many ways, a part of the old. If it is true
that the problems of the social services are determined by internal forces
that are reflective of more pervasive, external realities, then solutions to
social service problems will have to be sought in changes in the whole
society. These changes are of a magnitude that could only be described
as revolutionary. The social service worker concerned with providing
meaningful service to his or her clients, then, has the problem of finding
ways to relate the work of service provision to facilitating radical system
change. New forms of practice must be sought in the relationship of
social service work to revolution. As David Gil has suggested in a lengthy
analysis of social policy perspectives in the United States, "once a thinking person fully comprehends the true situation in America today, he no

longer seems to have a choice but to turn around and join a movement for radical social change, and to ask others to do the same." [8]

The Structure

To understand the contradictory nature of the social services, it is necessary to examine the simplest, most modest facet of the services in the light of progressively larger perspectives. The work of the helping professions must be examined in the context of the role and nature of social services in general. In turn, the social services must be placed in perspective as one of the primary, concrete manifestations of a still larger pattern of institutions and values that can be identified as the welfare state. Finally, the welfare state must be located in the context of the society from which it emanates. [9]

In this book, the analysis begins at the broader level and works down. We begin by looking at the larger set of institutions and processes that represent the welfare state, exploring them in the light of the society in which they develop. The problems in the welfare state and in the social services can be traced consistently to their embeddedness in and indebtedness to the "master institutions which cause the problems," as Gouldner has aptly called them. [10] We will not analyze those master institutions per se in this book. That job has been done well elsewhere. [11] We try here to demonstrate the extent to which the particular problems observed in one sphere are related to the larger issues and are not ad hoc, temporal, or idiosyncratic.

As we interpret the dilemmas of the social services and the social service professions in systemic terms, we suggest that the solutions to these dilemmas must also be systemic. If we accept the premise that the problems of the social services reflect the conservative (that is, system conserving) role of the welfare state in a larger society that is not organized primarily for the sake of human maximization, then we will find no

[8] David G. Gil, *Unravelling Social Policy* (Cambridge, Mass.: Schenkman, 1973), p. 153.
[9] The logic of this argument dictates that American society be analyzed in turn in relationship to world society. This analysis, subsequently, should filter back to further illuminate the specifics of social service practice. Furthermore, alternative practices ultimately must consider social service work in relationship to the larger dilemmas of both this society and other societies. However, the international perspective is not developed consistently in this book.
[10] Alvin Gouldner, *The Coming Crisis of Western Sociology* (New York: Basic Books, 1970), p. 81.
[11] Two useful works, both from a socialist perspective though differing in important respects, are Michael Lerner, *The New Socialist Revolution* (New York: Dell, 1973); and Michael Harrington, *Socialism* (New York: Saturday Review Press, 1970).

solution in either modest reform within the social services or in expansion of existing services by whatever degree. Solutions will be found only through basic or radical change in the whole society.

We try to locate strategic levers in the services by which to work for such changes in the society at large. Social service workers must endeavor to change the services in fundamental ways. However, such fundamental changes will not occur in the social services unless they occur everywhere. We must develop revolutionary theory with relevance to the whole society, and then locate within that theory the contribution that social service workers can make.

The last four chapters of this book develop the kinds of alternatives that can move us beyond the present dilemmas to a more sane and fulfilling society. Several parts of an alternative theory are developed in these chapters. We explore some notions about how a more life-endorsing society might be organized and identify some of the forces at work—especially within the social services—which suggest that these goals are already latent or active themes for many. It is important to remember, for the sake of our own morale, that we are not alone in our efforts to create a radically transformed society.

We also develop some perspectives on strategies—at two levels. The first is that of revolutionary theory for the society as a whole. What models of revolution have been developed or can be developed that would be applicable to the United States in the 1970s, that are feasible, and that have the potential to facilitate the emergence of the kind of society in which we would like to live? Some directions, if not answers, are available.

Second, within the larger perspective of revolutionary possibilities, we explore the contribution that social service workers can make to radical change as they operate within social welfare structures. Such activities, inasmuch as they are designed to contribute to radical change, ought to be consistent with the overall perspective that is developed. Simultaneously, they must be applicable in daily work, in everyday settings. Such theory is also available, though sometimes only in a preliminary way. Both the theory and examples of practice built on it are elaborated.

Finally, we hope to show that the radical analysis does not paralyze. Rather, it suggests options that are sensible and alive and that are strongly infused with democratic and humane values. Although social service workers may not be able to single-handedly bring about a socialist society, they can contribute to its emergence as they serve the true interests of their clients in a meaningful way and as they make their own lives more integrated, productive, and satisfying.

2

The Welfare State:
Description
as Ideology

INTRODUCTION

Social services and the specific social service professions operate largely within the mandates of the national social legislation that determines social policy in the United States. These social policies, taken together as a series of programs, structures, and values, define the extent to which the United States is a welfare state. Although we are not an advanced welfare state as, for example, the Scandinavian countries are considered to be, we are sufficiently involved in social programming to be called a welfare state of some variety.

A general understanding of the welfare state form of social organization is useful, therefore, in attempting to understand the functions and dilemmas of social services. For, as we develop some frames of reference for assessing the overall structure of social policy, we will simultaneously be developing a format for understanding some of the specifics of practice, which in turn forms the basis for connecting alternative forms of practice at the everyday level to the larger questions of social organization.

As we pursue this analysis, we will necessarily explore the welfare state in relationship to capitalism. The welfare state is generally defined in relationship to capitalist processes, that is, as a means to influence and especially to meliorate some of the negative social consequences of the private market. There can be little doubt that capitalism, as a form of economic organization and as a generator of social values and human behavior, is one of the primary factors shaping the society. It makes sense, therefore, to attempt to understand the welfare state in relationship to capitalism, especially in terms of the ways in which welfare state programs modify, interrupt, or humanize capitalist processes versus the extent to which they perpetuate those processes.

On the one hand, this is a straightforward search for structural relationships. In what ways do welfare state programs modify (or not modify) the free play of the marketplace? Has the welfare state introduced (or not introduced) more socialistic processes into the society? To what extent does the welfare state support (or not support) traditional notions of capitalist organization—that is, the wage system and private profit making? As we begin to answer these questions, we will begin to understand more about the welfare state in relationship to capitalism at the level of concrete support or challenge.

On the other hand, the relationship of the welfare state to capitalist society has a more subtle side in the realm of values and ideology. The welfare state, like any institution or set of institutions, is built on and in turn reinforces notions about what constitutes the good life, the good society, and the means to achieve them. These notions must also be explored, especially in light of the extent to which they do or do not replicate and reinforce the beliefs and behaviors on which capitalism rests and depends. In this chapter and the next, both the structural and ideological relationships of the welfare state to capitalism are analyzed.

WHAT IS THE WELFARE STATE?

It is not unreasonable to begin a discussion and analysis of the welfare state by defining the territory being examined. In so doing, however, we immediately confront a problem: it is not possible to make a descriptive statement about the welfare state that is not also evaluative. Furthermore, the inherent evaluative statements present in the most commonly used definitions of the welfare state contain unwarranted *positive* commentary.

To illustrate, the very fact that certain events, processes, and beliefs are labeled "the welfare state" implies that we are in fact discussing phenomena that are concerned with welfare or well-being. We may then be critical of the extent to which human welfare is or is not actually advanced by the welfare state, but we are not encouraged to question the assumption that that is its purpose. However, it is just this assumption that is most in need of critical analysis. We are concerned precisely with the extent to which an increase in social welfare is the purpose of the welfare state and with the definitions of welfare that the welfare state incorporates. We are inevitably presenting the welfare state from a particular point of view. We need to be as conscious as possible about that point of view and how its assumptions influence our thinking.

The framework within which the welfare state is most commonly understood is that of liberal philosophy, or liberalism. This means that the interpretation of the welfare state tends to build on certain assumptions about individuals, the society, and the good life, which can be subsumed under the heading *liberalism*. To clarify how the assumptions and ideology of liberalism influence our understanding about the welfare state, we need first to describe the welfare state as it is most generally understood. We can then consider some key elements of liberal philosophy and explore the ways in which these elements influence that description. We then will be in a position to develop a critical assessment of liberalism as a contribution to the development of a critical assessment of the welfare state itself.

It should not be assumed that the liberal philosophy that informs most thinking about the welfare state is held only by those who would be called liberals in the United States today. As Nathan Glazer has suggested, the welfare state's main premises

> are today hardly less firmly held by conservatives than they are by liberals. In the American context, conservatives will differ from liberals because they want to move more slowly, give more consideration to established interests, keep taxes from going too high. They will on occasion express a stronger concern for traditional values—work, the family, sexual restraint. But on the whole the line dividing liberals from conservatives grows steadily fainter. . . . [One is] hard put to distinguish liberals from conservatives in terms of any naive distinction between those who favor the expansion of social policy and those who oppose it.[1]

In other words, the assumptions of liberalism—as we will present them and as they inform welfare state thinking—cut across and subsume the categories of *liberal* and *conservative* in the United States today.

In the liberal view, one of the most basic ideas underlying the welfare state is "some recognition and implementation of the principle of public responsibility for individual welfare. . . . An adherent to the concept

---

[1] Nathan Glazer, "The Limits of Social Policy," *Commentary*, 52 (September 1971), p. 52. The lack of fundamental disagreement between liberals and conservatives, as it plays out in the welfare state, can be traced to an absence of fundamental disagreement in overall political philosophy between the two. This has been analyzed by Robert Paul Wolff in *The Poverty of Liberalism* (Boston: Beacon Press, 1968), especially Chapter 1, "Liberty," pp. 3–50.

of the welfare state espouses a certain view of the range of society's responsibilities to its members." [2] A belief that the state has some responsibility for the well-being of its citizens is indeed a general principle, one that is so basic that we tend to accept it as a given rather than as a particular social form in a particular historical period. Although a specific welfare program or social service might engender major debate, the underlying principles of public education, of the Social Security system, or of government responsibility for the destitute are not generally in question. Yet the welfare state does represent an important departure from pre–welfare state notions. The general understanding in pre–welfare state days was that intervention by the state for the purpose of influencing the well-being of individual citizens was undesirable and that the achievement of individual well-being was exclusively a private matter. This notion persisted until the passage of the Social Security Act in the mid-1930s. This event is commonly considered the beginning of the welfare state period in our history.

The modern welfare state has a pervasive influence in our lives. All citizens are affected by it in some specific life activity—whether it be going to public school or receiving Social Security benefits upon retirement.[3] All are influenced as well as by a variety of side effects of the welfare state. For example, all citizens have some relationship to government-created housing or to public programs of income maintenance, either through personal inclusion or in reaction to the forces and populations generated by these programs.

At its broadest, the welfare state is said to include all government functions that lead to intervention in the society for the sake of securing human well-being, with the exception of military activity. More specifically, it often is identified as those government interventions that are concerned with medical care, housing, education, cash transfers (such as public welfare or veteran's benefits), and the personal social services (such as mental health programs, day-care, or physical rehabilitation programs).[4]

---

[2] Nicholas Regush, *Welfare: The Social Issues in Philosophical Perspective* (Pittsburgh: University of Pittsburgh Press, 1972), p. 150.

[3] The number of persons receiving benefits directly from income transfer programs alone was approximately 60 million in 1972. See *Studies in Public Welfare: Paper No. 1, Public Income Transfer Programs: The Incidence of Multiple Benefits and the Issues Raised by Their Receipt,* James R. Storey for the Subcommittee on Fiscal Policy, Joint Economic Committee (Washington, D.C., Government Printing Office, 1972), p. 1.

[4] Some of the issues raised in trying to identify the specific boundaries of the welfare state are discussed by Martin Rein in "The Boundaries of Social Policy," *Social Policy* (New York: Random House, 1970), pp. 3–20; Kenneth Boulding, "The Boundaries of Social Policy," *Social Work,* 12 (January 1967), pp. 3–11; and Alfred J. Kahn, *Social Policy and Social Services* (New York: Random House, 1973), especially Chapter 1, "The Terrain: General Social Services," pp. 11–34.

A formal definition of the welfare state from the liberal perspective identifies it as a

> modern, democratic Western state in which the power of the state is deliberately used to modify the free play of economic and political forces in order to effect a redistribution of income. The welfare state, furthermore, is a "legal state," with laws protecting "rights," and establishing legal procedures for the protection of these rights.[5]

The key idea in this definition is the attribution to the welfare state of a social purpose—that of representing the public pursuit and extension of social values through public law. This occurs through the creation of specific social welfare programs that impose social values concerning people's rights to certain minimum standards of living on otherwise unfettered economic forces.

In quantitative terms, welfare state programs are frequently understood as being roughly equivalent to the United States government's public Social Welfare Expenditures (SWEs). These include social insurance, other public income-maintenance programs, public education, public housing, and medical care, as well as such personal social services as child care, child development programs, homemaker programs, big brother and big sister programs, parole and probation, family planning, information-advice-referral and advocacy programs, programs for the neglected, dependent, and disturbed, and so on.[6] In fiscal year 1970–1971, SWEs were $170.8 billion, or about 17 percent of the Gross National Product of that year.[7] (If private SWEs of $72.3 billion that year are included, total SWEs were 23 percent of the GNP.)[8] Of this amount, the personal social services have been estimated at about $10 billion, or $50.00 per capita.[9]

THE PAST AND FUTURE OF THE WELFARE STATE

Part of the prevailing understanding of the welfare state concerns its past and future. Here too assumptions of a political nature are embedded in descriptive material. There is no single way to understand the emergence or project the future of something as complex as the welfare state.

---

[5] Charles I. Schottland, "Introduction," in Schottland (ed.), *The Welfare State* (New York: Harper & Row, 1967), p. 10.
[6] Kahn, *Social Policy and Social Services*, p. 3.
[7] Cited in Kahn, *Social Policy and Social Services*, p. 35.
[8] *Ibid.*, p. 37. Private SWEs include items such as personal expenditures for medical care or rehabilitation and private charity.
[9] *Ibid.*, p. 35.

Any interpretation of its development will inevitably reflect particular ideologies and political perspectives, just as any definition of it will represent a subjective position.

In the liberal view the welfare state is considered a natural and inevitable response to various societal changes that contain the potential to disrupt social stability and impair individual well-being. These underlying pressures are frequently thought of as industrialization and urbanization.[10] The welfare state in its broadest dimensions (as opposed to specific policy and program alternatives) is interpreted as an inevitable development inasmuch as it is not considered representative of a particular series of choices. Rather, it is considered to reflect a continuous unfolding of logical and necessary responses to social developments, predetermined by society's major values and institutions and "animated by men's commitment to the activist fulfillment of their transcendental values."[11] In this view, industrialization and urbanization create various social problems that lead to social unrest and sometimes to mass organization as a response to this unrest. To contain these pressures, welfare state programs emerge; thus, social unrest has acted as a kind of triggering device.

In one such analysis, the welfare state was interpreted as "in part at least a concomitant of the decline of the large, extended 'welfare family.'"[12] The word concomitant, in its dictionary definition, suggests "an accompanying or attendant condition."[13] The use of this word to describe the genesis of the welfare state implies that an automatic process is occurring. In this analysis, extended family networks are disrupted in the face of urbanization and industrialization. On the basis of a presumed basic social requirement that the functions once performed by the extended family should continue to be performed, a public mechanism develops in conformity with the overriding social values the society is presumed to share.[14]

[10] More specifically, analysts look to such factors as the comparative size of national income, share of income necessary for industrial development, or changes in family structure. For an example of this line of thought, see Asa Briggs, "The Welfare State in Historical Perspective," European Journal of Sociology, 2 (1961), reprinted in Schottland, The Welfare State, pp. 38–39.

[11] Alvin Gouldner, The Coming Crisis of Western Sociology (New York: Basic Books, 1970), p. 182, discussing and critiquing the views of Talcott Parsons. Parsons's theories provide important sociological support for this school of historical interpretation.

[12] Briggs, "The Welfare State in Historical Perspective," p. 45.

[13] Webster's New World Dictionary, Second College Edition (New York: World Publishing Company, 1970).

[14] This problem of historical interpretation is discussed in John Goldthorpe, "The Development of Social Policy in England, 1800–1916," Transactions of the Fifth World Congress of Sociology, 4 (1962), pp. 41–56; and Dorothy Wedderburn, "Facts and Theories of the Welfare State," in Ralph Miliband and John Saville

This view appears again in the writings the late Richard Titmuss, an influential and thoughtful analyst of the welfare state. As Wedderburn has argued, Titmuss, in his *Essays on the "Welfare State,"* analyzes the welfare state as the collective recognition of socially determined needs in which society is presumed to share a uniform vision, a common basis of self-interest, and the possession of an automatic mechanism for actualizing that vision.[15] The welfare state represents the unraveling of an inner plan in a deterministic and inevitable fashion as society organizes to meet its basic needs under changing conditions.

Similarly, Wilensky and Lebeaux postulate a series of problems that society must solve or conditions with which it must deal to continue to function. Their book, *Industrial Society and Social Welfare,* perhaps the most widely read interpretation of the welfare state in the United States, is organized to explain how social integration is achieved in the society.[16] In part, their answer is that social integration is a consequence of broadly shared values and goals. From this perspective, developments in the society at large and in the welfare state in particular are manifestations of an essentially integrated society's problem-solving impulses.[17] As Titmuss does, Wilensky and Lebeaux postulate not only commonly shared values (which are observable in the welfare state, which does enjoy wide approval), but also common ultimate interests; that is, they argue that inasmuch as people have come to accept certain social forms, it must follow that all persons' best interests can be served by those forms. They recognize that the welfare state may be inadequate in practice (Titmuss is likewise anything but complacent about the welfare state in practice,

(eds.), *The Socialist Register* (London: Merlin Press, 1965), pp. 127–146, also reprinted in Milton Mankoff (ed.), *The Poverty of Progress: The Political Economy of American Social Problems* (New York: Holt, Rinehart and Winston, 1972), pp. 190–206. Also useful is John Carrier and Ian Kendall, "Social Policy and Social Change—Explanations of the Development of Social Policy," *Social Policy,* 2 (July 1973), pp. 209–224.

15 Wedderburn, "Facts and Theories of the Welfare State," assessing Richard Titmuss, *Essays on the "Welfare State"* (London: Unwin University Books, 1958).

16 Harold Wilensky and Charles Lebeaux, *Industrial Society and Social Welfare* (New York: Russell Sage Foundation, 1958).

17 A recent report of the Social and Rehabilitation Service of the Department of Health, Education and Welfare on the role and nature of the social services reflects the view of society as representing a shared value system, of which the services are a part, and is congratulatory about this fact. It states that "in American society, the community norms are those of the middle class which, even though it has variety, has limits. Most people who work in the social services are middle class and, therefore, are fairly good proponents of these community values." Dorothy Daly, Martin Loeb, and Frederick Whitehouse, "The Social Services and Related Manpower," a paper commissioned by the Social and Rehabilitation Services, Department of Health, Education and Welfare (Washington, D.C.: Government Printing Office, 1971), p. 8.

though he is less critical of the welfare state as a social form). Hence, elaborating their well-known distinction of residual and institutional conceptions of welfare (welfare as an emergency system which comes into play only if and when the market and family break down versus welfare as a front line, routinized function of modern industrial society), Wilensky and Lebaux write,

> As the residual conception becomes weaker, as we believe it will, and the institutional conception increasingly dominant, it seems likely that distinctions between welfare and other types of social institutions will become more and more blurred. Under continuing industrialization all institutions will be oriented toward and evaluated in terms of social welfare aims. The "welfare state" will become a "welfare society," and both will be more reality than epithet.[18]

Again, in introducing a case example on juvenile delinquency, they write,

> The social problem of juvenile delinquency in many ways provides the best illustration of the theme of this book so far: that the technological changes of industrialism lead to changes in the structure of society: these societal changes, in the context of American culture . . . produce or intensify concern about social problems, which creates a demand for welfare services.[19]

Consistent with this interpretation of the historical development and nature of the welfare state is the postulation of a future welfare society. An important component of this vision is a belief in the permanence of the welfare state form of social organization. Wilensky and Lebeaux, as indicated, suggest that the "welfare state" will become the "welfare society." [20] This society, presumably the end point of the development of the "institutional" point of view of welfare, is characterized as one in which

> Social welfare becomes accepted as a proper, legitimate function of modern industrial society in helping individuals achieve self-fulfillment. The complexity of modern life is recognized. The inability of the individual to provide fully for himself, or to meet all his needs in family and work settings, is considered a "normal" condition; and the helping agencies achieve "regular" institutional status.[21]

The future of the welfare state, in the liberal view, involves institutionalizing the welfare state into a potpourri of specific services. This notion of the welfare state's future accepts as givens the basic institutions and dynamics of the society as they now exist. Following this logic, we must

[18] Wilensky and Lebeaux, *Industrial Society and Social Welfare*, p. 147.
[19] *Ibid.*, p. 181.
[20] *Ibid.*, p. 147.
[21] *Ibid.*, p. 140.

look for ways to create special structures, outside of work and family, to help people meet needs which those critical institutions do not meet. The larger problems of the society will be managed by a permanent and extensive apparatus, separate from the major institutions, but subservient to them. The liberal theory of the welfare state projects a future which is essentially an intensification and elaboration of present patterns. In this view, the welfare state develops and matures in symbiotic relationship with the forces of production which first foster the need for a welfare state and then use the welfare state programs to enable people to "solve" problems in such a way that they continue, in Wilensky and Lebeaux's terms, to participate in the "culture of capitalism." [22]

In the view of social work planners, social work will be heavily involved in the future development of the welfare state. In Kahn's formulation,

> The first-line challenge is the invention of those social institutions, arrangements and services that meet the new circumstances and support the child-rearing, socialization, and interpersonal experience patterns deemed essential. If primary group relationships are valued, these social inventions should concentrate on them.
>
> These are not theoretical abstractions; they are generalizations referring to a process in which social work is engaged but needs to go further—group programs for adolescents, new camping and cultural activities for family units and adolescents, new forms of day-care or nursery service, informal kaffeeklatsch and baby-sitting centers in deprived areas, many services for senior citizens, from Friendly Visitors and home helps to "meals on wheels," and so on.[23]

This kind of thinking represents a conceptualization of both the welfare state and the social work of the future which, some hope, will be heavily involved in the delivery of ever more elaborate social services as part of the larger welfare state complex.

[22] *Ibid.*, p. 41. This view conforms to a notion of the future development of the United States which Jerry Rubin has described as the prevailing belief that "history is over." Jerry Rubin, *Do It!* (New York: Ballantine Books, 1970), p. 87.

[23] Alfred J. Kahn, "The Societal Context of Social Work Practice," *Social Work*, 10 (October 1965), p. 152. Kahn's vision has found specific expression in a social services bill proposed by the National Association of Social Workers. See "NASW's Proposed Draft Bill: 'Social Services Amendments of 1972,'" *NASW News* (February 1972), p. 9. While the bill has not enjoyed much legislative success as of this writing, the vision it represents does enjoy some popularity, as witnessed by a recent grant of $190,000 to Kahn and his associates for a cross-national study of social services from the Office of Research and Demonstration, Department of Health, Education and Welfare. See "Cross-National Study of Social Services," *Newsletter*, The Alumni Association of the Columbia University School of Social Work (Summer 1973), p. 2.

THE LIBERAL FRAMEWORK

Why have we identified these descriptive qualities and theories as characteristic of a liberal perspective? In several important ways, as we will see, the welfare state represents a concrete manifestation of the ideals of liberalism. Both liberalism (as political philosophy) and the welfare state (as social invention) operate in a symbiotic relationship of challenge to, but fundamental acceptance of, the values and structures of capitalism. As ideology, liberal philosophy serves to justify and validate the welfare state's relationship to capitalism. In the remainder of this chapter, we explore the ways in which the liberal perspective infuses the conventional interpretations of the welfare state. Our discussion is structured around key elements that define the liberal position, notably, a commitment to capitalist economics and to competitive individualism.

The Welfare State and Capitalist Economics

In the liberal view, the welfare state is accepted as a basically desirable way to meet human needs and to organize the society to respond to the problems of urbanization and industrialization. The particular programs and benefits of the welfare state are juxtaposed to the vacuum that would exist if industrialization and urbanization proceeded in the absence of welfare state arrangements. From the liberal perspective, welfare state programs seem to represent real if limited responses to people in need. From this vantage point of immediate relief to human suffering, the welfare state is counted a desirable social invention.

The welfare state is further understood as representing an infusion of social values into a society largely dominated by economic values. How has the economic power of capitalism been challenged or mitigated? In the liberal view, this challenge was organized through liberal forces. In Arthur Schlesinger, Jr.'s, formulation, liberalism has been "the movement on the part of the other sectors of the society to restrain the power of the business community." [24]

There have, in fact, always been forces challenging capitalism, and these have been important factors in our history. However, one could hardly say that labor, progressive, or socialist organizations have ever developed the willingness or strength to force fundamental changes in the nature of capitalism. Consequently, to understand how the welfare

[24] Arthur Schlesinger, Jr., *The Age of Jackson* (Boston: Little, Brown, 1946), p. 505.

state has emerged, one must suggest that processes were at work above and beyond these progressive forces, for example, wars that created new social needs and opportunities or an economic surplus that became available for social uses. Simultaneously, liberal theorists suggest that capitalism has social tendencies embedded in it and that an undying antagonism between progressive forces and capitalism is a historical relic. The welfare state emerged, they suggest, as the most demanding periods of capital accumulation passed and as capitalism was more able to respond to a broader range of social needs.

What is important to understand in this context is that liberalism is a philosophy that is supportive of and consistent with capitalism. It is generally acknowledged that the development of liberal philosophy was stimulated, in large part, by the development of capitalism.[25] In turn, liberalism has served as capitalism's official ideology. The individual freedom of action required in a capitalist system led to a philosophy of human affairs which glorified the vigorous pursuit by each individual of a personal vision of well-being. The liberal idea was and continues to be linked to a competitive notion of economic life. As Dorothy James has suggested,

> Individualism and materialism have been twin pillars of liberal thought over the three centuries since John Locke's work first appeared. Whatever differences may have developed between liberals on the question of which functions were legitimate for government, all . . . assumed that men had an inherent right to seek private ends, that individuals must be free to have and use private property.[26]

Liberal thought has been and is fundamentally accepting of the notion of private property and its accumulation and, therefore, is fundamentally accepting of capitalism. Liberals may wish to modify capitalism, or to intervene in its processes for the sake of greater equality, but their views do not entail a fundamental critique of capitalism itself, or lead to visions of or programs for a socialist society.

Consequently, liberalism takes capitalism and capitalist notions of the good life as givens and then assesses the welfare state in terms of compensation for some of the economic overzealousness of capitalism. Since liberalism asks relatively little of the welfare state, it is relatively easily satisfied. However, the liberal view of the welfare state does not contend with the limiting possibilities for individuals and for the society which are rooted in capitalism itself. For example, the liberal view may point to what

[25] Harry K. Givertz, *From Wealth to Welfare* (Stanford, Calif.: Stanford University Press, 1950), p. *viii*.
[26] Dorothy Buckton James, "The Limits of Liberal Reform," *Science and Society*, 2 (Spring 1972), pp. 311–312.

it sees as the welfare state's concern for individual well-being, but it does not question the nature of that well-being. In our society today, well-being tends to be understood as economic well-being rather than as social, psychological, or spiritual well-being. So, in suggesting that the welfare state promotes well-being, the liberal persective is putting economics first and, moreover, assumes a view of economics rooted in the opportunity to compete rather than in concerns for economic equality. The liberal definition of the welfare state, consequently, is basically congratulatory and uncritical of the welfare state's underlying assumptions. It does not explore or criticize the bedrock on which the welfare state builds, namely, a commitment to an economic system organized around the private control of capital.

Irving Howe, in his introduction to *The Radical Papers*, identifies a critical problem in efforts to understand the development of the welfare state. He writes,

> It would be hard to say to what extent the welfare state is the result of a deliberate attempt to stabilize capitalist society from above, so that it will avoid breakdown and revolutionary crises; to what extent it is the outcome of relatively autonomous economic processes; and to what extent it is the partially realized triumph of the struggle of masses of men to satisfy their needs.[27]

We have suggested that, in the liberal view, the welfare state is seen largely as the outcome of autonomous processes, partially stimulated and guided by progressive forces. The welfare state seems to conform very well to the model of social development inherent in liberal thought. It represents a relatively gradual unfolding of social processes and is based, by and large, on a consensus about the good life.[28] The welfare state has not been the outcome of cataclysmic events, although the periods of unrest in the 1930s and 1960s were surely precipitants and shapers of its development. The liberal view does not see progress as coming about through revolutionary changes, but rather through the gradual humanization of existing arrangements. By and large, these modifications, in the case of the welfare state, are thought to be in a progressive direction. This is consistent with liberalism's view that society is steadily improving. Inasmuch as the welfare state can be said to represent a positive advance in the society's concern for public well-

---

[27] Irving Howe, "Introduction," in Howe (ed.), *The Radical Papers* (Garden City, N.Y.: Anchor Books, 1966), p. 6.

[28] As opinion polls have generally discovered, most people have seen and continue to see the welfare state as representing a public expression of their own best self-interest. See Lloyd Free and Hadley Cantril, *The Political Beliefs of Americans: A Study of Public Opinion* (New Brunswick, N.J.: Rutgers University Press, 1967); and Regush, *Welfare.*

being, liberal theory can claim to explain and understand its growth. If it does not point in the direction of heightened well-being, then liberalism has no vision of how the good society can be achieved. Liberalism presupposes a basic faith in social institutions as they are and in the fact that they can be gradually transformed into better versions of themselves. Otherwise, it has no notion of progress.

In general, then, the first key element in liberal ideology that influences interpretations of the welfare state is the fundamentally benign attitude that it encourages toward capitalism. The liberal view of capitalism assumes that capitalism can be modified, made responsive, and humanized by the pressure of various interests and that the welfare state is, in fact, a manifestation of that responsiveness. In the next chapter, therefore, we will need to look especially at the way in which the welfare state does relate to capitalist institutions and at the extent to which it has modified and humanized those institutions as the liberal model postulates.

The Welfare State and Individualism

The second key element in liberal philosophy that infuses thinking about the welfare state is its commitment to individualism. Consistently, the welfare state is described as representing "a recognition and implementation of the principle of public responsibility for individual welfare." [29] As we have reason to be critical of the liberal assumptions about the possibilities of capitalism, so we have reason to be critical of its assumptions about individualism. Here, as a prelude to further analysis, we want to identify the nature of individualism and its centrality to liberal thought.

The liberal view rests essentially on a "commitment to a set of methods and policies that have as their common aim greater freedom for individual men." [30] That is, liberalism is essentially a highly individualistic philosophy. It assumes that collective well-being consists of and derives from the summation of individual well-beings. It is true that modern liberalism has developed in a collectivist direction, of which the welfare state is an important manifestation. [31] However, the fundamental liberal idea continues to be that of individualism, although this notion is tempered by the belief that each individual's pursuit of his or her self-

[29] Regush, *Welfare*, p. 150.
[30] David Sills (ed.), "Liberalism," *International Encyclopedia of the Social Sciences* (New York: Macmillan and Free Press, 1968), p. 276. Useful discussions are L. T. Hobbhouse, *Liberalism* (New York: Oxford University Press, 1964); and C. B. Macpherson, *The Real World of Democracy* (Toronto: CBC, 1965).
[31] See Allen Grimes, "Introduction," in Hobbhouse, *Liberalism*, pp. 1–8; and Givertz, *From Wealth to Welfare*, especially Chapter 12, "The Welfare State: One Variant," pp. 230–258.

interest can best be supported by public interventions on behalf of groups of people. This does not imply that liberalism, in its more collectivist form, is socialism. At least in theory, "liberalism [retains] its distinction from socialism in taking for its chief test of policy the freedom of the individual citizen rather than the strength of the state." [32]

The key to modern liberalism is said to be its concern for individual opportunity.[33] So, in the liberal view, liberty does not consist of the achievement of any particular concrete outcomes for the whole society. Nor is liberalism particularly concerned with assuring specific outcomes for individuals, since it presumes that each individual will pursue his or her own version of self-interest vigorously and rationally, given the opportunity. As a consequence, the concern of collective intervention is to assure each person sufficient freedom of expression and a sufficient base of physical well-being to permit active pursuit of that person's self-interest. As Norman Podhoretz has suggested, in taking exception to some criticisms of liberalism's shortcomings,

> Liberty [which Podhoretz sees as the essential commitment of the liberal] is not everything. Like everything else in the world, it is what it is and not something else. It is not, for example, equality. Nor is it "distributive justice." Nor is it "community." [34]

In assessing the welfare state, then, we must look at the ways in which it is built on these notions of individualism. The analysis and critique of individualism which we develop in the next chapter will be useful in helping us to uncover the limitations of the welfare state as a response to the human situation in the present period.

SUMMARY

We have suggested that there is no value-free way to describe the welfare state. In order to identify our general area of concern, therefore, we described the welfare state in the terms in which it is most commonly understood. We suggested that the frame of reference that this description utilizes is that of liberal philosophy, and we characterized that philosophy as rooted essentially in commitments to capitalism and individualism. In the next chapter, we describe specific manifestations of these commitments in the welfare state and analyze the resulting dilemmas.

[32] J. A. Hobson, *The Crisis of Liberalism* (1909), reprinted in Alan Bullock and F. W. Deakin (eds.), *The British Liberal Tradition* (London: Adam and Charles Black, 1956), p. 190.
[33] *Ibid.*
[34] Norman Podhoretz, "Liberty and the Liberals," *Commentary*, 52 (December 1971), p. 6.

3

The Welfare State: Counterculture or Corporate Liberalism?

INTRODUCTION

Liberalism's assumptions that institutions of the welfare state modify and humanize capitalist processes and that competitive individualism is an appropriate base from which to maximize individual and social well-being do not survive close scrutiny. The liberal analysis serves the ideological function of justifying the welfare state and the social order which it represents and supports, but it does not adequately portray the nature and function of the welfare state and obscures the radically different kinds of social arrangements we must pursue if we hope to achieve a more decent society.

Viewed without the ideological filter of liberal interpretation, the welfare state emerges as a series of programs and policies organized to meet a limited and distorted notion of human needs, within a framework of support for capitalist institutions and values. Rather than the logical and inevitable unfolding of social welfare aims in a capitalist society, the welfare state represents a historically specific form of social organization that has emerged as a result of the continuing ability of capitalist institutions to mold and transform human needs and social struggles within the logic of capitalist requirements.

We will demonstrate this in two ways. First, we examine and analyze some of the structural relationships of the welfare state and capitalism. Second, we seek to understand and critique the role that liberal ideology plays in justifying the welfare state.

THE WELFARE STATE AND ECONOMIC LIFE

By reviewing some aspects of the history of governmental intervention into public economic and social life we can begin to uncover the patterns of government involvement in the society. We can explore the extent to which government's social welfare interventions are structurally and ideologically similar or dissimilar to its interventions in nonwelfare areas. It is not difficult to see that the non–social welfare interventions, despite their multifaceted rationales, have been structured to stabilize and reinforce a system of private enterprise and have neglected or overridden human values. When social welfare interventions are examined, we readily observe a developed ideological screen that suggests that their primary role is meeting human needs. But, ultimately, their common purpose with other government intervention becomes clear. This in turn illuminates the particular roles the welfare state has played in relationship to capitalist institutions and the particular choices it has represented in the development of our social order.

Robert Heilbroner has identified three general periods in the history of government intervention into the economy.[1] The first began with the Colonial era. Government monies were made available through the colonies to private interests for the development of roads, canals, railroads, and schools. While it is not possible to quantify these inputs, because of the lack of adequate record keeping at the time and because of the loss of relevant documents, Heilbroner concludes that it is likely that they were as formidable and crucial for their time as federal intervention is in our own time.

In the second period, which he locates as stretching from the Civil War to the New Deal, government activity developed in the direction of vigorous intervention in a wide variety of regulatory capacities, as exemplified by the Federal Reserve System, the Federal Trade Commission, and the Interstate Commerce Commission. Government was motivated by its desire—and the desire of major industrialists—to regulate otherwise

[1] Robert L. Heilbroner, "Phase II of the Capitalist System," *New York Times Magazine* (November 28, 1971), pp. 30, 76–90.

uncertain markets and unstable competitive conditions. Far from being resisted by the dominant economic interests (as has often been assumed when government is interpreted as a disinterested party regulating economic interests in the name of overarching principles of social justice), these interventions were welcomed, encouraged, and perhaps instigated by corporate leaders. They had the effect of controlling competition, and they produced the kind of environment that was becoming increasingly important for big business, namely, predictability and stability.[2]

The third phase witnessed government's taking a central role in trying to achieve acceptable levels of employment, growth, and well-being. This is the period in the United States which we identify with the welfare state. The critical point, for our purposes, is to understand that the welfare state phase of government intervention was not a major departure from earlier roles government had played. It was, rather, an extension of the general thrust of government's efforts to rationalize, stabilize, and generally involve ever larger parts of the social order in a growing, interlocking network. Inasmuch as it is fairly clear that the logic of that network up to the time of the welfare state phase was the logic of big corporations, we are encouraged to wonder what, if anything, might have altered that logic as it became extended to social welfare programming.

As will be seen, many of the programs identified as welfare state measures have employment and economic stability and growth objectives at their root. This should come as no surprise in the light of the forces that gave rise to major federal inputs into social welfare programming in the 1930s. On the one hand, social programming was a logical extension of other government efforts during that period to mobilize a prostrated economy. It became clear to Roosevelt and big business leaders that welfare measures were not an encroachment on capitalist prerogatives, but could serve as a much-needed stimulus to consumers' ability to purchase. On the other hand, to business interests, government welfare measures were a preferable alternative to the more radical alternatives being advanced by Huey Long and his followers, by the Townsendites, by the Communist Party, and by various progressive forces throughout the country.

The involvement of big business interests in social welfare planning has been extensive. The welfare state should not be judged by the company it keeps, but it is useful to examine the corporate sources of its support and the corporate inputs that have shaped its policies, as one way to under-

---

[2] John K. Galbraith, in *The New Industrial State* (New York: Signet Books, 1968), has documented the extent to which the "technostructure" requires general stabilization of all conditions of production and sales as a foremost necessity of operation.

stand the relationship of social welfare to capitalism and to document our thesis of social welfare as handmaiden to capitalist logic.

Historians Gabriel Kolko and James Weinstein have demonstrated the extent to which big business, in the pre–welfare state, Progressive Era years, supported and benefited from the variety of regulations and reforms of that period.[3] These regulations and reforms were important forerunners of current welfare state programs. Business's goal, in pursuing these reforms, was stability and predictability, and liberal reform was seen as a "means of securing the existing social order." [4] In fact, the organizations in which big businesses were involved helped to develop labor and welfare programs as a preferable alternative to independent and potentially less controllable union activity. Their overall goal was to achieve higher degrees of integration of labor and business in order to reduce the likelihood of autonomous political action by labor. These corporations, in the Progressive Era, "were developing the new liberal-or-progressive ideology of the welfare state." [5] That is, they were beginning to arrive at the point of view, brought to fruition through the welfare state itself, that welfare programming could be so molded as to be a social and ideological ally of private enterprise. Corporate leaders were seeing that these kinds of social institutions did not represent "creeping socialism," but were a logical and desirable extension of the capitalist perspective into ever-widening arenas of the society. This is not to suggest that they were in the forefront of these struggles, pursuing some subtle Machiavellian scheme. Rather, as demands arose from various sectors of the society, corporate interests came to understand that these demands could be met in a fashion consistent with their overarching concerns for profit and predictability.

For example, Weinstein has demonstrated the logic that led advanced corporate interests to support the introduction of workmen's compensation. The National Civic Federation, one of the leading organizations of big business interests of the time, threw its support behind it because it clearly saw workmen's compensation as an alternative to both the growing socialist movement and to employer liability laws that threatened to make manufacturers liable for suit by injured employees. Further, it was a way to demonstrate to labor business's social concern.[6] As George W. Perkins of International Harvester and the U.S. Steel Corporation argued at the

---

[3] Gabriel Kolko, *The Triumph of Conservatism* (New York: The Free Press, 1963); and James Weinstein, *The Corporate Ideal in the Liberal State: 1900–1918* (Boston: Beacon Press, 1968).
[4] Weinstein, *The Corporate Ideal in the Liberal State*, p. xiii.
[5] *Ibid.*, p. 55.
[6] *Ibid.*, Chapter 2, "Leadership in Social Reform: Workmen's Compensation," pp. 40–61.

Tenth Annual Meeting of the National Civic Federation in 1909, Harvester's plans for compensation, as for profit sharing, pensions, and illness and accident insurance, were not motivated " 'out of pure philanthropy, but by purely business spirit. [The idea was] that the plans would so knit [the company's] vast organization together, so stimulate individual initiative, [so] strengthen and develop the espirit de corps,' that it would enable the company to increase its earnings." [7] With the concerted aid of the National Civic Federation and the business interests that made up its membership, and in opposition to much of organized labor and those socialist organizations that saw the movement as a further tying up of labor with the logic of an expanding corporate society, all but six Southern states had compensation laws by 1920. By that time, the federal government had amended its earlier legislation to include all civil employees in compensation programs.[8]

Business's conception of its self-interest, as expressed in its concern for welfare programs, has not substantially changed since the Progressive Era. In the important case of income maintenance, big business interests are substantially involved in promoting social welfare reform. For example, in 1967 Nelson Rockefeller, then Governor of New York, convened an elite group of economic advisors to consider some possibilities for welfare reform. Their recommendations were as progressive as those of the welfare state bureaucrats who spoke on the matter in that period. These men, part of a conference commemorating the 100th anniversary of the New York State Board of Social Welfare, made a series of recommendations about income maintenance programs which included replacing the existing system of public welfare with an income maintenance system, possibly a negative income tax, establishing a system of uniform national standards for public welfare, and providing a floor below which no state could fall and no person be expected to live.[9] This is not an isolated example of big business's interest in welfare reform in the current period. In 1969, one of the major government inquiries into the issue of poverty in the last thirty years, the President's Commission on Income Maintenance Program rec-

---

[7] *Ibid.*, p. 46, citing George W. Perkins at the *Tenth Annual Meeting of the National Civic Federation,* New York, November 22–23, 1909 (New York: National Civic Federation, 1910), pp. 144–149.

[8] *Ibid.*, p. 61.

[9] *Report from the Steering Committee of the Arden House Conference on Public Welfare,* Appointed by Governor Nelson Rockefeller, Commemorating the 100th Anniversary of the New York State Board of Social Welfare, 1967, p. 12. The group included Joseph Wilson, Chairman of the Board of Directors, Xerox Corporation; Joseph Block, Executive Director, Inland Steel Company; John Coleman, Senior Partner of the New York Stock Exchange Firm of Adler, Coleman and Company; Gilbert Fitzhugh, Chairman of the Board of the Metropolitan Life Insurance Company; Arjay Miller, Vice-Chairman of the Ford Motor Company; and others.

ommended a variety of reforms, many similar to those of the Arden House Conference called by Rockefeller.[10]

In both of these cases, leaders of the largest corporations in the United States were heavily involved in promoting welfare reform. Their concern did not focus on the inadequacy of welfare as a financial support system, however, as witnessed by their recommendations for very low levels of family support. They were concerned with the need for uniform national systems of income maintenance that could stabilize troublesome segments of the population and relieve strained state and local government finances. Both of these groups were convened during periods of broadening social unrest, inner-city riots, and the formation of organizations of welfare clients. While the men involved may not have objected to explicit repression as a response to these developments, they recognized that government interventions in the form of a relatively inexpensive national income maintenance program were more to their benefit. These observations begin to suggest the extent to which welfare state programs have enjoyed the support of the very interests they claim to challenge. However, we need also to explore the *outcomes* of welfare state programs in terms of their relationship to capitalist interests.

The liberal interpretation of the welfare state rests on the belief that the welfare state will modify the workings of the marketplace. In turn, this rests on the belief that the government will intervene in the economy in the name of transcendent principles of social justice. The data about the economic base and impact of social welfare programs do not support these notions. Welfare state programs have served the needs of private capital and have done so in a wide variety of ways.

One of the ways in which social welfare has supported capitalist needs is through the role it plays in offering direct opportunities for the investment of capital. Welfare state programs, despite their government sponsorship and their collective ideology, provide outlets for the investment of private dollars and, consequently, for private profit making. Public programs are so organized that government finance, that is, public monies, provides an extensive and dependable source of profit for private enterprise.

For example, Medicaid and Medicare and the public housing programs are not programs of socialized service provision. The government does not

---

[10] President's Commission on Income Maintenance, *Poverty Amid Plenty: The American Paradox* (Washington, D.C.: Government Printing Office, 1969). The Chairman of this Commission was Ben Heineman, President of Northwest Industries. Commission members included D. C. Burnham, Chairman of Westinghouse Electric Corporation; J. Henry Smith, President of the Equitable Life Assurance Society of the United States; and Thomas J. Watson, Chairman of the Board of the IBM Corporation.

provide medical care or housing. Rather, it finances the purchase of these services by consumers. The services themselves continue to be provided by private suppliers. Public housing is actually publicly financed housing, which is built by and which thus enriches private developers. Medicare is publicly financed medicine, provided by private practitioners who still make their profit. The introduction of new programs in social welfare areas does not necessarily alter the typical capitalist patterns of provision of service to consumers. What it often does is to stabilize and supplement payment and profit to providers for services rendered and, as recent scandals in both housing and health care programs have revealed, often for services not rendered.

The Medicare program, for example, has resulted in some improved health care to the elderly. However, its effectiveness has been diminished because, to a large extent, these public dollars went to higher salaries for doctors. From 1966 to 1968, Medicare and Medicaid accounted for an average increase of after-tax income of approximately $3,200 to each physician in the United States.[11] The program served, in part, to provide higher payment to doctors for services they would have previously provided in any case, rather than leading to more or better care for the elderly.

In the case of federal urban renewal programs, designed in part to improve housing conditions for the poor, direct government financing and tax advantages have resulted in tremendous windfalls for builders. For example, in a typical scenario,

> The builder buys an urban renewal site for, say, $1 million, and plans a $10 million apartment project. He gets a Section 220, FHA-insured mortgage for something around $10.8 million (90 percent of replacement value of land and buildings, plus a 10 percent builder's profit). This leaves him with only $200,000 of his own capital in the project. And the potential for gains on this small equity investment is tremendous: After deducting interest (say $56,700 at 5¼ percent) and mortgage amortization (at, say 1½ percent annually, or about $162,000) from an estimated net income before depreciation of 10 percent, or $1.1 million, the builder-sponsor is left with pretax income of $371,000. After corporate income tax, the net income is about $178,000—a yield of almost 90 percent on his cash investment.[12]

[11] Bruce C. Stuart and Lee A. Bair, *Health Care and Income*, Research Paper No. 5, State of Michigan, Department of Social Services, Lansing, Michigan, April, 1971, p. 44. See also Theodore R. Marmor, "Why Medicare Helped Raise Doctor's Fees," *Trans-action* (September 1968), pp. 14–19. For a more technical explanation, see Martin S. Feldstein, "Econometric Analysis of the Medicare Program," in *Benefit-Cost Analysis of Federal Programs*, Joint Economic Committee, Congress of the United States (Washington, D.C.: Government Printing Office, 1973), pp. 182–199.
[12] *Architectural Forum* (July 1962), p. 103, cited in Charles Abrams, *The City Is the Frontier* (New York: Harper & Row, 1965), p. 110.

In addition, depreciation, accelerated depreciation, and tax shelters can reduce builders' taxes on earned income, especially in the early years of the project, to practically nothing.

In the case of public welfare, business is again paid to provide services. For example, businesses receive a direct subsidy from manpower programs for welfare recipients they hire to fill jobs. In addition to this direct subsidy, the welfare program serves as an indirect subsidy to businesses by allowing them to pay wages on which people could not otherwise live. Other welfare benefits, such as health care, day care, and food stamps, further encourage businesses to pay a nonliving wage. Is business castigated for exploiting welfare clients? On the contrary, it is highly praised for its public-mindedness in bringing the welfare population into the "world of work."

Business is given a variety of other indirect subsidies by the welfare program. For those businesses least able to provide long-term stable employment, at adequate wages, with responsible employee benefits, the welfare system becomes a support to their continued marginality. Rather than be forced to develop a fringe benefit system, for example, the marginal employer releases workers during periods of lower productivity or during difficult economic periods, leaving the worker to the welfare system. For example, for the marginal employer, the Aid to Families of Dependent Children Program (AFDC) serves functionally as an equivalent to the maternity leave benefit provision of more substantial industries. It is known that welfare clients generally work prior to being on welfare, often work while on welfare, and will work again when they are off welfare.[13] Rather than conceptualize welfare as a system apart from the market, it makes more sense to view the welfare system as a poor man's or, more often, a poor woman's, unemployment insurance. Welfare programs have been assigned the task of coping with those persons or groups who are not of prime use in the productive process. These programs become, in Gouldner's terms, "strategies for the disposal and control of useless men . . . [The] transition to a welfare state . . . implies a greater involvement of the state in developing and managing the disposal of the 'useless.'"[14] The same concept, depoliticized and couched in acceptable professional terms, sees social work as "the technology whose central idea is the delivery of social services to control dependency."[15]

[13] See Martin Rein, "Barriers to Employment of the Disadvantaged," in Rein, *Social Policy* (New York: Random House, 1970), pp. 374–414; and Mildred Rein and Barbara Wishman, "Patterns of Work and Welfare in AFDC," *Welfare in Review*, 9 (November–December 1971), pp. 7–12.

[14] Alvin Gouldner, *The Coming Crisis of Western Sociology* (New York: Basic Books, 1970), p. 76.

[15] Charles Atherton, "The Social Assignment of Social Work," *Social Service Review*, 43 (December 1969), p. 421.

In the same vein, the low benefits and punitive quality of welfare assistance help to assure a supply of workers for the least desirable, lowest paid jobs in the market by making even poor work preferable to welfare for many. For example, in 1970 approximately 60 percent of four-person, inner-city families in the United States had gross earnings of less than $7,000.[16] Similarly, in 1966, out of a total labor force of 50 million people, approximately 8 million, or 16 percent, were full-time workers earning wages that put them in the low wage bracket.[17] This means that they did not earn enough at full-time work to cross over the official U.S. government poverty line. Keeping welfare benefit levels always lower than even these meager wages forces this vast army of workers to remain in financially exploitative work. Neither their particular employers nor the society at large is challenged on the fact that we do not seem able to provide jobs at a living wage for all who want them. In this way, the welfare system serves a more hidden but still vital role in support of capitalist interests.

The welfare state, then, rather than representing, as in the liberal view, the deliberate intervention of the state to modify the free play of economic forces to effect a redistribution of income, is better understood as the intervention of the state to support economic growth and stability, presuming a definition of social well-being that is limited to economic well-being. The welfare state is not a counterforce to economic interests. It is their ally and support, serving in a form that has tended to obscure its underlying functions from those who hope to find in it a humanizing social influence. Every welfare program can be demonstrated by direct or indirect linkages to be based on the assumption of and support for a private market and the principles of the private control of capital.[18]

We ought not to leave the impression that this is a government secret, hidden from the populace. A fitting conclusion to this section is some comments justifying welfare state programs, contained in a document prepared in 1966 by the Department of Health, Education and Welfare, entitled *Social Development: Key to the Great Society*. In the opening pages, Ellen Winston, then U.S. Commissioner of Welfare, prefaced a plea for more social welfare spending with a bow in the direction of the prevailing powers. She argued that "what is good for the social

---

[16] William Spring, Bennett Harrison, and Thomas Vietorisz, "Crisis of the Underemployed," *New York Times Magazine* (November 5, 1972), p. 48, citing a 1970 Census Bureau Employment Survey.

[17] U.S. Department of Commerce, "Year 'Round Workers with Low Earnings in 1966," *Current Population Reports*, 58 (April 4, 1969), p. 6.

[18] A review article of interest on these issues is Clauss Offe, "Advanced Capitalism and the Welfare State," *Politics and Society*, 2 (Summer 1972), pp. 479–488.

development of all people becomes good for the economy." [19] In support, she highlighted the fact that "every dollar spent to alleviate poverty has a quick turnover," and that the support of people in need is a form of investment in the society.[20] Clearly, the pursuit of social welfare goals is couched within the values of a society that justifies its social welfare activities in terms of their economic impact.

THE WELFARE STATE AND THE COMMITMENT TO INDIVIDUALISM

Liberal ideology, as we suggested earlier, is rooted in a commitment to capitalist economics and to individualism. It is through its commitment to individualism that the welfare state serves as ideological support for capitalism. Having previously discussed the structural links between the welfare state and the private control of capital and pursuit of profit, we must now discuss the ways in which these links are justified, politically and theoretically, from the welfare state perspective.

Menscher has identified the welfare state's commitment to individualism in suggesting that

> Governments in England and America, whatever the party in power, continued the established policies of social legislation. Some set the limits of social support more narrowly, but on the whole all would agree with Mary Follett that social legislation was in support of individualism "because it is legislation for the individual." This position was clearly stated by contemporary British Liberal leadership: "We argue that welfare is actually a form of Liberty inasmuch as it liberates men from social conditions as truly as any governmental or personal coercions." Some twenty years earlier, Harold Macmillan of the Conservative party had said in much the same vein, "We are seeking to discover what is the minimum basis of material welfare and security that man must enjoy if he is to maintain his physical efficiency and increase his liberty." [21]

As Menscher suggests, welfare state programs, despite their collectivist appearance, are based on individualistic notions. That is, while they represent government interventions on behalf of the whole popula-

[19] Ellen Winston, "Economic Progress and Social Welfare," in *Social Development: Key to the Great Society*, Welfare Administration, Department of Health, Education and Welfare, Publication 15 (Washington, D.C.: Government Printing Office, 1966), p. 2.
[20] *Ibid.*
[21] Samuel Menscher, *Poor Law to Poverty Program* (Pittsburgh: University of Pittsburgh Press, 1967), p. 332. The Follett quote is from Mary P. Follett, *The New State* (New York: Longmans, Green, 1918). The "contemporary British Liberal leadership" is Elliot Dodds, "Liberty and Welfare," in George Watson (ed.), *The Unservile State* (New York: Macmillan, 1957), p. 17. Macmillan's comments are from Harold Macmillan, *The Middle Way* (London: Macmillan, 1938), p. 27.

tion, or on behalf of certain groups in the population, their nature makes them consistent with the liberal notion that government policy is desirable only to the extent that it strengthens the power of the individual in his or her quest for well-being, in conformity with the standards of the society at large. Welfare state interventions tend not to establish specific goals or outcomes in terms of social accomplishments, for example, amount of income redistributed or number of jobs created. Rather, welfare state programs are concerned with rehabilitating individuals, providing disabled or retired individuals with income, educating individuals, controlling individuals considered to be deviant, resocializing those who have gone astray, and so on. Kahn's enumeration of the three general tasks of the social services illustrates this quality in welfare state programs. According to Kahn, their role is "to strengthen and repair *family and individual functioning,*" to "provide new institutional outlets for *socialization, development and assistance,*" and to "develop institutional forms for new activities, essential to *individuals, families and groups. . . .*" [22]

Examples of this pattern abound. Health programs, like Medicare or Medicaid and proposals for national health insurance, operate within a model of enabling private citizens to be more effective in competing for a share of the goods offered by the private medical market. [23] Similarly, antipoverty programs have attempted to enable the poor to compete more equally with others by nudging them into the mainstream of society. The War on Poverty and the categorical assistance programs focused their interventions on training, social services, casework treatment, and so on. They did not establish and would not have had any mechanism to accomplish specific goals for the national redistribution of income.

In addition to focusing on the individual in terms of the goals of service, welfare state programs also focus on the individual in the process of delivering services. Welfare state programs tend to distribute benefits on an individual basis. Consistent with the liberal belief in individualizing each person's negotiation for a share of the total resources of the society, clients enter a negotiation process with benefit systems, on the basis of which their personal benefit allotments or treatment programs are determined. The means test further assures that the undeserving will not be given resources paid for by others.

---

[22] Kahn, *Social Policy and Social Services,* p. 16 (Italics added.)
[23] For example, see *Analysis of Health Insurance Proposals Introduced in the 92nd Congress,* Committee on Ways and Means, August, 1971 (Washington, D.C.: Government Printing Office, 1971).

Individualism and Social Welfare

As a philosophy, individualism has some attractive qualities. It identifies individual well-being and its pursuit by each of us as core values in the society. It carries this belief in its suggestion that each person is normally the best judge of what is in his or her own best self-interest and that people want to and will pursue their own best self-interest as their first priority in life. It assumes, therefore, that people are rational, clear-minded, and self-motivated. By way of illustration, these ideas find expression in the Code of Ethics of social work, a key profession in welfare state programming. This Code affirms social work's belief "in the dignity and worth of human beings [and] respect for individual differences." [24] Social work ethics are concerned as well with individualization of service and of entitlement to benefits and with the struggle for self-determination, now more often in a group than an individual context.[25]

These notions of the nature and pursuit of individual well-being are limited, however, both in their ability to understand what the nature of individual well-being is and in their prescriptions for its achievement. To develop this argument, we draw out and assess some key assumptions underlying the commitment to individualism and show the ways in which these assumptions play out in social welfare programming.

Individualism and Self-Determination

As stated above, a critical assumption of individualism is that each of us is the best judge of his or her own best self-interest. In welfare state programs, this principle finds expression in the liberals' emphasis on the provision of cash versus the provision of direct service,[26] on vouchers to maximize client choice in the selection of social services or educational facilities, and in the furor created when a theorist or program advocates the imposition of particular behavioral standards on clients.[27]

In fact, at a basic level, the most broadly accepted goal of social welfare programs may be seen as enabling people who are not judged

[24] "Profession of Social Work: Code of Ethics," *Encyclopedia of Social Work* (New York: National Association of Social Workers, 1971), Volume I, p. 958.
[25] "Ethics in Social Work," *Ibid.*, p. 324.
[26] An overview of this debate is found in Kahn, *Social Policy and Social Services*, pp. 112–118.
[27] For example, witness the liberal reaction to the assumption of personal incompetence of the poor found in Edward C. Banfield's *The Unheavenly City* (Boston: Little, Brown, 1970).

to be in a position of self-determination to attain a position where they can be self-determining. That is, programs concerned with economic dependence attempt to provide either direct cash grants or training and counseling, so that economically dependent persons will be in a position to enter the mainstream of economic life and function as autonomous, self-determining individuals. Mental health and physical rehabilitation programs identify self-determination as a key standard against which to measure their success. Even public housing programs and medical programs for the aged are promoted on the basis of the support they provide for maximum self-determination for the family or individual. And certainly within the social welfare professions like social work or the rehabilitation specialties, client or patient self-determination is a key plank and a guiding principle for practice.

The concern for self-determination seems to have a democratic ring of freedom about it. However, it is not truly sustaining of a deep commitment to freedom. This is little understood because we are so caught up in the more limited options normally before us: the typical alternatives of "individual free choice" versus the imposition of specific behavior patterns from a central authority. Of these choices, liberal individualism indeed seems preferable. But, we have not considered and experimented with the critical third option that is available to us, namely, *collective self-determination*. If we extend the notion of collective self-determination from the social to the economic realm, we begin to outline the dimensions of a democratic, communal socialism. (This will be explored in a later chapter.) It is not surprising, therefore, that a capitalist society encourages us to focus more narrowly on individualism versus dictatorship as the only choice available.

At the very least, the assumption that each of us is the best judge of his or her own best self-interest fails to contend with the possibility that any one of us might not accurately assess the essence of his or her situation. We might make wrong choices for ourselves because of inadequate or inaccurate information or because of faulty thinking based on general distortions in assessing our overall situations. A liberal society attempts to deal with this problem through an emphasis on education, so that each of us will have as much knowledge and decision-making ability as possible. In this context, education is seen as a device to shore up the individual in his or her private dealings with the society.

However, even if we diagnose our situations accurately, without wrong information or general distortions, our conceptions of what we are and what we need—that is, our conceptions of our own best self-interest— still have important social determinants. People understand themselves and assess their needs partly through interaction with others. Individualism, however, implies that our conceptions of our needs are privately determined, as autonomous processes in each of us. This assumption that people are free to determine their own needs in a private fashion means isolating people from one another in their efforts to cope with the influence of prevailing public values. It is possible, but difficult, to reach alternative conceptions of one's needs on one's own, but, more often, private need determination means acceptance of the public definition of private needs. Individualism denies this, and in practice the assumption of individual need determination means *not* examining prevailing social definitions of what people should and will need.

Individualism, then, as a key element in liberal philosophy, misinterprets the way in which people come to understand who and what they are and need. It fails to see that our so-called private decisions are, in fact, the translation into our private lives of public values. In a society organized on capitalist principles, it is not surprising that the liberal version of self-determination has led many individuals to internalize capitalist values at the same time that they believe themselves to have assessed these values independently.

The larger dilemma of self-determination is directly reflected in social welfare areas. For example, the majority of persons who are on welfare want to work if they can.[28] For most of these people, however, working means joining the ranks of the working poor. Most of us have so internalized the society's commitment to work that to see ourselves as being self-determining we must work, even if this means being nearly enslaved at demeaning, dehumanizing jobs for pay that is not life-sustaining. Encouraging self-determination within a welfare state context often means encouraging people's independence from controlling welfare programs in order to free them for dependence on a controlling labor market. Welfare state programs accept and express conventional social definitions of self-determination, in that way creating an illusion of choice for the client of the social welfare program and encouraging the client in the belief that self-determination is gained, when in reality only the mode of oppression has changed.

A similar case can be made for every social welfare effort to free clients for autonomous activity. We must challenge and help clients to challenge the range and depth of choices available to all of us collectively. Otherwise, helping people to be more free to seek alternatives is simply to encourage them to choose their own brand of oppression in a society that does not make joyous and liberating options available for most of us. Thus far, this has been the welfare state's model of practice. In this way, the welfare state has created an illusion of freedom and choice at the

---

[28] See Leonard Goodman, *Do the Poor Want to Work?* (Washington, D.C.: The Brookings Institution, 1972).

same time that it has kept people linked with and committed to capitalist values and institutions.

Individualism and Self-Aggrandizement

In addition to assuming that people can and should define their needs in a personal and private way, individualism also operationalizes the belief that people want to be, will be, and should be, self-aggrandizing in their behavior. Though it is given other names and is circumscribed by various rules and regulations, selfishness is the expected and desired norm of liberal society.[29] In the welfare state, for example, many programs are designed to give people support, training, or coercion to enable them to "get ahead." But, "get ahead" of whom? The very notion of pursuing well-being implies improving one's competitive advantage with others.

It does seem to be the case that people, by their nature, try to solve the problems that face them. However, individualism has a particular notion of this process in that it views people, in their problem-solving roles, as competitive and even as mutually antagonistic. It views individual problem solving as essentially unsocial activity. Furthermore, this is not subject to criticism. Self-aggrandizement is desirable because it is seen as the route by which people can achieve the things that will make them happy. Competitive behavior is not criticized because it is seen as an inevitable part of the human condition and not as a matter about which there is choice.

However, it is self-defeating to view each individual's self-aggrandizing behavior as a desirable method to achieve well-being. In the first place, the social situation of modern society is exceptionally dense. Each individual's life is so enmeshed in the lives of all of us that there is little free zone in which one person can pursue social welfare in the absence of a relationship to others. To this extent, the notion of a privately pursued social welfare is illusory and anachronistic. Possibly it represents a lingering wish for an earlier time when people could more easily strike out on their own frontier. More likely it also reflects the reality that cooperative approaches to well-being are quite difficult to pursue in our society because of the very real ways that we have become antagonistic and destructive to one another. Consequently, we pursue autonomy with such vigor because it has come to represent not only its own positive qualities, but also a compensation and substitute for a healthy and creative social interdependence of which our society is relatively barren.

---

[29] See Sheldon S. Wohlin, *Politics and Vision* (Boston: Little, Brown, 1960), Chapter 9, "Liberalism and the Decline of Political Philosophy," pp. 286–351.

Furthermore, when one of us does come out ahead in the struggle with the rest of society for a larger share of available resources, his or her achievement is not complete. Just as our perceptions of our needs have social determinants, so too our ability to meet our needs has a critical social component. People need to have a positive relationship with one another to experience a sense of social well-being. If we achieve our successes in a competitive relationship with others, we will need to be on guard against them for fear that they will try to take our gains from us. We will view others with suspicion, and that suspicion will not be entirely unfounded. We will necessarily assume a guarded and un-complimentary view of others that is destructive to the achievement of important human values, namely, community, human warmth, and social integration. The self-aggrandizing pursuit of individual well-being, then, must necessarily lead to the achievement of limited conceptions of over-all well-being, since it takes so little of the human situation into account.

The route to autonomy and self-determination, as promoted by social welfare programming, is personal self-development to better enable the one individual, or a select group of individuals, to compete with all the others. The consequences are precisely those we would predict: welfare state programs have in fact stimulated bitter competition among various sectors of the society, for example, welfare clients and the working poor or racial groups who have struggled with one another for greater say in the community boards of various social agencies. Because the consequences of this intergroup competition are so profound, and because it is so charac-teristic of welfare state programming and the larger liberal reformist approach to change within which that programming is formulated, we have devoted the whole of a future chapter (Chapter 5) to the issue.

Individualism and Human Nature

As individualism postulates self-aggrandizement as the logical and even optimal way to meet human needs, so it argues that such behavior is the inevitable consequence of human nature. Individualism encourages a competitive capitalistic ethic. It attempts to justify this ethic by assuming that mutual competition is inevitable in human society, that each must be in conflict with all.[30] It postulates capitalism not only as a superior eco-nomic form but as the logical social extension of the human personality.

In *Civilization and Its Discontents*, Freud argued that the functioning of the society as a harmonious whole requires the suppression of impulses and needs in the individual.[31] According to Philip Lichtenberg, this part

[30] See Philip E. Slater, *The Pursuit of Loneliness* (Boston: Beacon Press, 1970).
[31] Sigmund Freud, *Civilization and Its Discontents* (Garden City, N.Y.: Double-day Anchor Books, n.d.).

of Freud's thought is based on a conception of self-social disparity.[32] It assumes that the individual achieves satisfaction essentially as a "closed system that opens minimally to the outside world."[33] The self-directed actions of the child and, consequently, the adult are the most satisfactory actions to the individual, but they are antagonistic to other-directed or social activity. By its very nature, therefore, the striving for individual well-being conflicts with the possibilities of cooperative relationships.

However, Lichtenberg has demonstrated the way in which the notion of self-social disparity misunderstands the process by which satisfaction is achieved by the child and leads to unfortunate social consequences. Those children raised in a manner that leads to what we understand as the best ideals of mental health are raised in a cooperative relationship with their world, or in a condition of self-social unity. If, however, antagonistic and destructive patterns of social organization dominate the child's development, then these patterns will have to be imposed on the child and will produce adults who are antagonistic to their environment. They will be antagonistic because their earliest experiences so patterned them and because they will continue to seek the childhood satisfaction they failed to achieve, but in the distorted fashion to which they became accustomed as children.

Individualism, then, is based on a view of human nature in which people are seen to be, inevitably, mutually antagonistic. If people are that way in fact, it is as a consequence of particular destructive ways in which they were raised. But these ways are supportive of the particular social order in which we now live, and the negative consequences of individualism for human well-being matter little to a society organized with corporate profit as the central measure of social welfare and private wealth as the primary measure of personal well-being.

The propaganda of the welfare state and the mechanics of specific social welfare programs reflect these limited views of human nature. Characteristically, the welfare state encompasses a view of people as essentially passive in relationship to larger social forces and issues, while exceptionally active in pursuing their more individualized agendas. It distrusts people to take actions that are simultaneously the best actions for themselves and for the society. In one sense, its logic is correct inasmuch as the destructive nature of the social order forces people, when they act on their own behalf, to act against the social order. But, welfare state logic is incorrect when it suggests that this conflict is natural and inevitable.

[32] Philip Lichtenberg, *Psychoanalysis: Radical and Conservative* (New York: Springer, 1969).
[33] *Ibid.*, p. 18.

For example, welfare programs build in powerful compulsions for individuals to work, on the assumption that they might not work if they were not forced to do so. At the same time, all evidence indicates that people want to work and will work if they are given any opportunity to do so. In other words, the assumption is that some people will not want to be responsible participants of the social order as a consequence of the human tendency to want to get something for nothing. This assumption is made despite the available evidence and in the face of the fact that our society is so organized that large numbers of people cannot work even if they wanted to.

Social policy is based on a deep distrust of human nature. As former President Richard Nixon remarked in one of his more widely quoted press conferences,

> The average American is just like the child in the family. You give him some responsibility and he is going to amount to something. If, on the other hand, you make him completely dependent and pamper him and cater to him too much, you are going to make him soft, spoiled, and eventually a very weak individual.[34]

Nixon, reflecting a strong dimension of thought in public policy, operated on the basis of a fundamental belief that to fully meet people's basic needs is to corrupt them. People will act, in Nixon's view and in the view of the mandates of policy, more out of need to overcome deprivation than on the basis of an experience of satisfaction and of rewarding previous encounters with the world or in conjunction with the needs of the larger social order.

At the same time, the overriding goal of each of us is assumed to be personal and private comfort. This finds reflection in the welfare state emphasis on cradle-to-grave security. Alternative views of people as seeking growth, self-actualization, experience, and adventure are not part of this conception, with the exception that capitalism has a limited and antisocial notion of people as being competitive and striving. In Gunnar Myrdal's approving phraseology, people growing up in advanced welfare states are "like domesticated animals . . . with no real conception any longer of the wild life."[35] Simultaneously, people are envisioned as fragile and insignificant. Society, by comparison, is pictured as a juggernaut, consisting of powerful forces easily capable of demolishing the meager psy-

[34] Interview with Richard Nixon, November 5, 1972, as reported in the *New York Times* (November 10, 1972), p. 20.
[35] Gunnar Myrdal, *Beyond the Welfare State* (New York: Bantam Books, 1967), p. 73. A valuable essay on some aspects of Myrdal's views on the welfare state is Paul A. Baran, "Social and Economic Planning," in Baran, *The Longer View* (New York: Monthly Review Press, 1969), pp. 236–246.

chic resources of individuals and the structural resources of the family. While this description may contain some accurate elements, the disturbing aspect of the welfare state conception is that this view of people is seen as inevitable and, therefore, desirable.

For example, in a typical formulation, Kahn has suggested that

> The complexities of modern society "have created a need for the organized provision for many aspects of life that in simpler societies were governed by custom or by the family." Included are measures to aid the helpless members of society, particularly institutional care, foster home care, home helps, recreational facilities, neighborhood centers. Families in the disorganized or in the more normal categories at times require guidance in career choices, home-management advice, and personal assistance in matters of family relationships.[36]

If public policy manifests an uncomplimentary view of people in general, it holds a doubly uncomplimentary view of women in particular. For example, the Aid to Families of Dependent Children program (AFDC) imposes an enormous range of behavioral constraints on women. Since, as suggested earlier, AFDC assumes the functional role of an unemployment program for a marginally employed group of working people, in this case, women, we might compare it to unemployment insurance. Unemployment insurance, which does not focus particularly on women, is free from behavioral constraints beyond those concerned with ensuring that the client actively seek employment. AFDC, however, says that a woman with a man available to her, or "in the house," is not eligible for benefits. If a woman lives with a man, she loses her autonomy and is assumed to be part of a unit with him. In other words, the women's unemployment compensation program (AFDC) attempts to control more of a woman's total existence, while the man's unemployment program limits its concern to the man's effort to become reemployed.

The manner in which the AFDC program operates to strengthen the image of women as dependent and servile alerts us to welfare state policies and procedures with potential impact on all women. Because the AFDC program identifies a population for whom a wide variety of life conditions are determined by public policy, it spotlights the values which are held and operationalized by the welfare state. Public policy for the whole population of women supports the subservient status of women in family life. Thus, in many states, married women do not have independent legal

---

[36] Alfred J. Kahn, "Social Services in Relation to Income Security: Introductory Notes," *Social Service Review,* 39 (December 1965), pp. 381–89, reprinted in Paul E. Weinburger (ed.), *Perspectives on Social Welfare* (London: Macmillan, 1969), p. 217. Internal citation is Ida C. Merriam, *Social Services Provided by Social Security Agencies,* Members of the I.S.S.A. (ISSA No. XV/V/I: Geneva: International Social Security Association, 1964), p. 4.

status. In the everyday course of events, we may not be attuned to these aspects of public policy. We are alerted to look for them, however, by the more visible policies affecting the lives of AFDC mothers.

In general, then, the welfare state conforms rather consistently to the limited and uncomplimentary views of human nature which are latent in liberal thought. In so doing, it is destructive to us in a number of ways. It encourages us to believe that behaviors which are the product of a particular social order and particular historical circumstances are instead a reflection of innate human qualities. It focuses on the negatives of human behavior and ignores the opposite qualities which have managed to survive in the society. It leads to programs and procedures that build on these negative assumptions and so reinforces them in the manner of a self-fulfilling prophecy. And finally, it discourages the pursuit of radically different possibilities for the society since it claims inevitability. In spite of this, we have argued that welfare state programs rest on a faulty understanding of the human situation.

Individualism and Democracy

A final consequence of individualism is its failure to provide a basis for the strengthening of democratic processes in the society. Inasmuch as individualism focuses on individual self-aggrandizement, it is not a philosophy that encourages any one person to be concerned about the whole society. In this way, individualism has given ideological support to undemocratic tendencies in the society, by both justifying and obscuring our failure to develop social structures that would permit all citizens to have maximum input into decision making in the areas that effect them.

Individualism leads to a theory of society as an ad hoc conglomeration of self-seeking individuals. The well-being of the whole, it is assumed, will emerge from the ensuing interplay. However, individual units, when aggregated, develop system principles, and these principles in turn influence the well-being of individual units. This is simply another way of saying that when people interact closely with one another, they develop social values and social institutions that are, in many ways, more than merely a sum of the parts. Liberal philosophy has not developed, in theory or practice, ways for individuals to collectively influence the overall shape of the society. Rather, individuals are encouraged to be relatively passive in determining the nature of the policies and programs that affect their lives. Clearly, overall decisions get made in any society. In the absence of explicitly democratic and participatory principles, those who make the decisions will be those who have been most successful (as liberalism defines success) in getting to the top of the various decision-making hierarchies.

In part, liberalism deals with the authoritarian and nonparticipatory decision-making patterns that emerge through a mystification of the extent to which specific patterns of control operate. Liberalism prides itself on not establishing blueprints for individuals which dictate their lives.[37] It encourages a distaste for societies in which national goals, whatever they may be, are clearly specified. Individualism thus helps assure that society will not be egalitarian because it leaves decision making in a region that is not explicit and is easily controlled by particular interests in the name of particular economic and social values.

In its welfare state manifestation, this pattern finds expression in programs that shape the relationship of individuals to the social order in such a way that individuals are helped and managed so that they will play an "appropriate" role in the large scheme of things. Human need is not the prime concern, but simply another element to be accounted for within a larger priority system. Maintaining the established order requires placing high value on stability, predictability, and the interchangeability of parts. Individuals, a potentially weak link in this chain, must be made to conform to this pattern. As Galbraith has suggested, "It is the essence of planning that public behavior be made predictable . . . that it be subject to control." [38]

Examples are found in a number of programs of the welfare state, for instance, public housing or the Model Cities programs. In these cases, public policy involves a fairly large expenditure of public funds, program areas that are quite sensitive politically, and a planning process that is complex, multifaceted, and highly intertwined in a conglomeration of bureaucracies, local governments, and political forces. Government policy, operating in such a dense arena, must be, from the planners' perspective, well thought out, highly rational, and carefully modulated and negotiated to satisfy the multitude of interests involved. These programs, however, affect human lives, and those affected may have their own special ideas about how and toward what ends they would like these programs to operate. Their potential is great, as the least predictable, least manageable element in a complex planning process, to cause disruption in the overall plan.

Citizen-participation components have been structured into these welfare state programs partly as a response to this possibility. They illustrate one mechanism by which the welfare state attempts to fit people into a complex scheme. Citizen participation is a version of a fundamentally democratic idea, namely, that people should make the decisions about matters that influence their lives. However, the purity of that idea has

---

[37] Harry K. Givertz, *From Wealth to Welfare* (Stanford, Calif.: Stanford University Press, 1950), p. 230.
[38] Galbraith, *The New Industrial State*, p. 326.

been diluted to the point where citizens in the welfare state are some-times invited in an advisory capacity to make inputs into the decision-making processes. Citizen participation, rather than being seen as the basis of policy, has become another program element.

Admittedly, there are many citizens in this country, which makes allowing everyone to directly control everything rather unwieldy. None-theless, the central planning idea of the welfare state assumes certain larger system imperatives that can be modified only slightly but that do have some margin for citizen input. At the same time, citizen participation creates some sense of responsibility and inclusion and helps provide a democratic veneer and ideological overlay in a process that is often planned in a centralized way.

Why are welfare state programs not controlled by citizens and communities, instead of being "participated in" by them? Presumably, welfare state planners would respond that people cannot have everything they want, and that people would want things that did not make sense from a systems perspective, that is, from the perspective of the total plan. One must ask, then, why is there such a disjuncture between what people would want, if they had their way, and what they can get? Are people essentially unreasonable in their needs and demands? Possibly they have been made so by deprivation. On the other hand, perhaps it is the case that our system is indeed organized so that it cannot come as close to meeting human needs as it might or should. To give people free rein to express their needs and to structure programs to meet their needs would violate too many of the imperatives of the present organization of our system. People cannot be trusted to exercise control. While it is possible to argue that human nature is such that people are essentially antisocial, it is just as possible to argue that people are essentially very social. What could be interpreted as antisocial behavior in welfare state terms might be social behavior seeking expression but thwarted by the antisocial, antihumanitarian structures of the welfare state.

The welfare state, then, attempts to control people's behavior in order to encourage their regulated and "responsible" participation in the system. It views people as manageable and structures its policies and programs to help ensure that they will be so. At the same time, the elaborate control structures established by welfare state programs are an acknowledgment that people have a drive, resilience, and quest for self-actualization that do not lead to their easy acceptance of such control.

SUMMARY

We have attempted in this chapter to lay the groundwork for a critical understanding of the functions of the social services. We have done so by assessing some aspects of the welfare state as a whole, especially in relationship to the structures of capitalism and its ideology, liberalism. We have argued that the welfare state can best be understood as a support system for capitalist institutions and that liberal ideology serves the function of both obscuring and justifying this relationship.

In the next chapter, this pattern of analysis continues at the more specific programmatic level of the social services that play out, in daily practice, the larger ideological, political, and economic functions of the welfare state.

4

The Political
Functions
of the Social Services

THE SOCIAL SERVICES IN POLITICAL CONTEXT

The general philosophy of the welfare state is concretized through the creation of social policies at the federal level and is eventually operationalized through the provision of the specific social services. Consequently, these services represent a direct link to a larger political philosophy and are strongly influenced by that philosophy. To understand the full meaning and purpose of the social services, therefore, it is necessary to see them both in their own light and in the light of the larger context within which they function.

When we make this dual analysis, the following contradiction in the social services emerges sharply: the social services deny, frustrate, and undermine the possibilities of human liberation and of a just society, at the same time that they work toward and, in part, achieve greater degrees of human well-being. The social services represent the larger duality of liberalism and of the welfare state as we have drawn these out in the previous two chapters. They express concern for individual and social welfare, but they do so in a form shaped by limited and distorted values and structures and, thus, ultimately undermine the pursuit of human welfare.

One half of this duality is the fact that, whatever else they do or do not do, public welfare programs do provide resources to people who would otherwise have less. Mental health programs alleviate psychological distress for some of their clients. Those social service workers who struggle to meet human needs and feel that they make some progress in doing so are not fools or charlatans. On the contrary, their commitment to their clients and the real help they are sometimes able to provide represent that part of the welfare notion that has remained true to the concept of welfare.

However, social services do not operate in a vacuum. They are established within a political and economic context. This context, we believe, acts to subvert the welfare concept by organizing the role of the social services so that they support and reinforce conformity, among both clients and workers, to the very institutions and values that generate the problems to which the services were addressed in the first place. The services mirror in their internal structures and procedures the kinds of people-denying orientations contained in the larger society. Thus, as they succeed in achieving their mandates, they succeed in denying the greatest potential for life and joy in their clients.

We have two purposes in the sections that follow. First, we explore and illustrate some of the ways in which the social services contain the denial of their own best ideals. Their intimate relationship with people-limiting dynamics in the larger society and their internal absorption of people-denying values are also examined.

Second, we suggest that these patterns are neither accidental nor amenable to piecemeal reform. The services function in a symbiotic relationship with the major institutions of the society because, like the welfare state policies of which they are a manifestation, they are generated by the need to shape and contain social reform efforts within the logic and requirements of a capitalistic society. They contain people-denying values because these are consistent with the logic of our major institutions. Were the social services to pursue a fuller notion of human liberation, the consequences would be revolutionary. For example, if mental health agencies single-mindedly devoted themselves to helping people become mentally healthy, they might well encourage people in the view that the proper role of a mentally healthy person in a mentally unhealthy society is to be revolutionary. Such outcomes would create tensions between those facilities and their larger support systems, to say the least. The problems we identify are resolvable by nothing short of a radical change in the society as a whole.

REGULATING CLIENT BEHAVIOR

The social services foster particular behavior patterns in clients both as a condition of usage and as a consequence of service. These patterns require clients to accept behaviors and roles for themselves in which they accommodate themselves to conservative visions of the good society and the good life. These visions perpetuate liberalism's notions of justice and decency, but deny clients the fullest possibilities of their own well-being. In this section, some of the major ways the social services encourage this kind of self-denying conformity in clients are discussed.

Social Services and the Labor Market

In the previous chapter, we explored and found unconvincing the liberal thesis about the nature of the welfare state. That thesis argued that the welfare state represents a humanistic modification of market forces by progressive state intervention. It saw the welfare state as an alternative to the market and to market principles. We argued that the liberal view captures only the rhetoric of this nation's social policies. The reality is that welfare state programs have been so organized that, in practice, they support and nurture market institutions.

One of the ways in which this occurs is through the role the social services play in channeling people into the labor market, thus serving as a support to that market. Once we realize this, it becomes harder to argue that the services can be seen as an alternative system for people who have failed to maintain themselves through labor market participation. Policy developments in the mid-1970s emphasize this pattern. As the 1973 rule revisions to the public assistance regulations put it,

> Families and individuals must be free to accept or reject services. Acceptance of a service shall not be a prerequisite for the receipt of any other services or aid under the plan, *except for the conditions related to the Work Incentive Program or other work program under a State Plan approved by the service.*[1]

To many, this observation will be neither a surprise nor a source of distress. After all, in a society in which work must be done, and which is organized according to marketplace principles, it is to be expected

[1] Proposed Rule Making, *Federal Register*, HEW, SRS, "Service Programs for Families and Children and for Aged, Blind or Disabled," Volume 38, Part II, February 16, 1973, p. 4609. (Italics added.)

that people will work and that systems will be developed to encourage them or force them to work when, for any reason, they are not willing or able to work. From this perspective, the existence of a social service network is a preferable alternative to a Spencerian notion of the survival of the fittest in which those not able to work would simply be allowed to fall by the wayside.

In criticizing the social services as a labor market support, we do not mean to imply that work itself is inherently undesirable. Even if it is true that we are entering an age of nonscarcity or of postscarcity in which work, as we know it, will not be required for our maintenance, we will still have the obligation to relate ourselves to the larger society in some way that facilitates the survival and maximization of that society. In other words, in a better world, work in its present form might be abolished, but we would still require individuals to contribute to the larger whole in some fashion. Contrary to the present reality, the ideal situation would be one in which the individual's maximum contribution to the society as a whole would be, simultaneously, exactly that person's maximum contribution to his or her own self-development. In a truly humanized society the ideal toward which we would strive would be the elimination of the duality between actions which primarily benefit the individual actor and those which benefit others. The work of the society would not be dehumanizing or exploitative of the individuals who perform it, but would facilitate their development as people.

It is around this issue that the role of the social services in shaping clients' work behavior must be criticized. The social services are organized within the context of a society that defines its well-being in terms of economic growth and has its primary expectation of the individual his or her maximum contribution as a worker or as a facilitator of workers to economic growth. This contrasts sharply with the potential of our society. We may always recognize the need for economic achievement, but we can learn to see that achievement as fostering conditions which encourage human fulfillment.

In our own society today, the struggle for economic growth produces neither equitable nor humanistic outcomes. We do not function on the basis of a social view of the meaning of work, and even in our limited economic view we distribute the rewards of satisfying work and high pay inequitably. For many workers, work is a means to an end, the end being leisure time at high levels of consumption.

To the extent, therefore, that the social services buttress the labor market, they move people into a relationship with the means of production that ensures their exploitation as producers and, eventually, as consumers. This is the basis of the criticism in our observation that the social services are structured to service the labor market. If work fit the model that serving oneself and serving others were identical processes, then the social services might happily function to reinforce the labor market. Inasmuch as work is, at present, exploitative of workers, inasmuch as it turns human beings against themselves, we need to try to understand as fully as possible the way the social services, which we hope would represent life forces and energy for the liberation of people, have come to represent the opposite.

The income maintenance provisions of the Social Security system, in some of their facets, provide an illustration of the process by which human needs are met in this society within a market framework. This system represents a social policy response to some rather basic human needs for retirement security and for protection against death of the primary wage earner in a family with dependents. While these needs exist in every society, the need for public involvement is exacerbated in an industralized society in which more traditional mechanisms for meeting these needs are disrupted. In the United States, it took the crisis of the mid-1930s, with its extraordinary economic dislocations, to bring such a system into existence. The Society Security system obviously operates in close relationship to the market. Receipt of Society Security benefits is contingent on the worker's past participation in paid employment in the labor force. Reforms in the system have so modified it that receipt of Social Security benefits has required progressively less firm attachment to the market, though the principle of prior labor market attachment has been retained. Presently, however, even persons with a rather casual prior relationship to the labor force are entitled to some benefits.

Nonetheless, the Social Security system both compensates for the inadequacies of the labor market and ties people more firmly to it. A recent development in this program is illustrative. In 1972, the Senate Finance Committee began to plan for the provision of higher pension benefits to the lowest paid workers in the labor force.[2] On the surface, this seemed like a liberal and generous act and a further departure from rigorous actuarial calculations of benefit entitlement. However, the underlying realities highlighted other motivations. Among these realities was the fact that nearly all of the estimated 340,000 persons to be immediately affected by this provision were persons who were receiving supplemental welfare benefits as well as Social Security benefits. (A total of 1.2 million persons receive benefits from both programs.) These Social Security amendments, therefore, actually served to shift the financing of some portion of the supplemental welfare benefits to the

[2] "Big Pension Rise for Lowest Paid Gains in Senate," New York Times (March 28, 1972) p. 9; and "Major Provisions of Senate Bill on Social Security and Welfare," New York Times (June 14, 1972), p. 32.

Social Security system. They also made an estimated 93,000 people ineligible for Medicaid.[3] These provisions, in other words, did not necessarily result in increased benefits for recipients. That part of the recipients' benefits received from welfare would now come from Social Security, and many would no longer be at a low enough income level to be eligible for welfare. Furthermore, since public welfare is financed from the more progressive income tax and Social Security from the less progressive payroll tax, the shift would mean that lower paid workers, in general, would pay proportionately more for their future benefits under the new arrangements. What the welfare state giveth, the welfare state taketh away.

In addition, the same provision encouraged the lowest paid segment of the labor force to remain faithfully at work, in that it proposed disproportionately rewarding more stable low wage workers. The provision suggested, in other words, that if people remain at low paid work for long periods of time, they will be able to count on marginally more generous retirement benefits. This proposal attempts to encourage the loyalty of a segment of the work force which might otherwise have little motivation to work steadily and stably. The admitted need of low wage earners for retirement income beyond that which they could normally provide for themselves is acknowledged. Simultaneously, this need is met in a way which encourages workers to buy into the system, and into a level of the system that ensures their marginal financial existence both as active workers and as retirees.

A second example of the use of social services as a labor market adjunct is the provision of day-care services. We have generally not had a substantial public day-care program in the United States. Some relatively few facilities have been provided through the welfare program, and a brief, nonwork-related effort was undertaken, and then largely pha ed out, during the War on Poverty years.

In 1971, a coalition of forces surfaced with legislation to establish a broad network of day-care facilities as a part of a $2-billion-a-year package of child-development legislation.[4] This legislation was passed by both houses of Congress, but was vetoed by Richard Nixon, then president. At the same time, a day-care program, oriented toward custodial care rather than child development passed with congressional and presidential blessing as part of welfare program revisions. To pressure welfare mothers to work, apparently not so much out of a need for labor as a need to reduce the welfare rolls and as a warning to others not to leave their jobs, an

---

[3] "Social Security Rise Becomes a Nightmare for Many Elderly," *New York Times* (October 3, 1972), p. 16.

[4] For a brief review, see "Child Development Plan Vetoed," Notes and Comments, *Social Service Review*, 46 (March 1972), pp. 108–111.

$800 million network of child-care and day-care center facilities for children of low income working mothers was envisioned.

The 1973 crackdowns on social service expenditures also reflected these priorities. Social services which had been provided to a relatively broad range of clients, from a base in public welfare programs, were increasingly restricted only to current welfare clients. One of the few exceptions to this restriction was day care, but only "in the case of a child where the provision of such services is needed in order to enable a member of such child's family to accept or continue in employment or to participate in training to prepare such member for employment." [5] (Death or abandonment by the mother is a further exception, later stated.)

The message is clear. We will have a day-care program in this country if and when it serves the purpose of making welfare recipients or others work, but not if and when its primary focus is simply the healthy development of children. The provision of services for children is used as a tool to reach the real target, the welfare recipient. Moreover, we must keep in mind that forcing welfare recipients to work speaks as well to a far larger number of the working poor who otherwise might find welfare an attractive alternative to work.

These examples only scratch the surface. The fact that patients in mental hospitals have been exploited for the work they could perform while institutionalized has recently come to public attention once again.[6] The variety of ways in which the public welfare system has attempted to pressure clients to work, both in the past and present, has been widely documented.[7] Similarly, for a variety of social service programs, a return to work status might well be taken as the operational definition of success. Mental health programs and alcoholic treatment centers, juvenile delinquency prevention services, and physical rehabilitation workshops come to mind. Recreation programs often have as a stated purpose the inculcation of disciplined attitudes toward work. The value of work and of being a good worker is a cornerstone of the value system of this country, and it has been adopted all too uncritically by the social services. Of course, it would be politically suicidal for the social services to represent themselves as being against the work ethic. Because the services do not understand or address the radical possibility of encouraging a different kind of work—a personally and socially useful work—they have been left in the position of encouraging the typical patterns of work as we have known them. This has not been of the fullest service to clients.

[5] Proposed Rule Making, p. 4613.
[6] "Suit Asks Department of Labor to Halt Alleged Peonage in Mental Institutions," *New York Times* (March 14, 1973), p. 21.
[7] This dynamic is reviewed in Frances Fox Piven and Richard A. Cloward, *Regulating the Poor* (New York: Vintage Books, 1971).

The Social Services and Social Conformity

The emphasis on work is not the only way in which the services attempt to shape client behavior in conformity with prevailing conservative values. In all programs, a variety of notions about the ways in which people are expected to behave are structured into the rules and regulations. It is very difficult to think of any social service which is available to people simply as a consequence of their human existence.

Public welfare offers an embarrassing wealth of case material. Undoubtedly because welfare involves the direct distribution of cash and, consequently, is involved in competition with the other major cash distribution mechanism, the labor market, its clients are especially subject to behavioral control.[8] Welfare regulations have been used to shape client behavior in every area of life. Regulations attempt to control sexual conduct, family relations, market purchases, the household budget, registration for work and work training, the right to privacy, and so on. To a large extent, being on welfare means a loss of control over one's life. Decisions are made for the welfare client in his or her role as consumer, provider, parent, and citizen.[9]

A recent development in welfare, the "brownie-point system," made these dynamics more explicit. Welfare clients, in the several states where this program was implemented, were required to "earn" welfare benefits by accruing points. These points were garnered by meeting certain behavioral mandates—so many points and, consequently, so many dollars, for registering for work, for taking one's children to the doctor, for serving as a cub scout or brownie troop leader, and so on.[10] The efforts to control welfare clients' behavior continue to escalate, as illustrated by the massive

[8] Hagith Shlonsky has argued that the distribution of any money or in-kind benefit that would influence the prevailing stratification system will operate on the basis of the principle of minimums as opposed to the principle of optimums. The welfare system does have a potential influence on the stratification system and operationalizes the principle of minimums through behavioral constraints, as well as other mechanisms. This is a useful distinction, though it minimizes the extent to which the adequate provision of any social service would have such an influence. Shlonsky's argument is developed in "Welfare Programs and the Social System," *Social Service Review*, 45 (December 1971), pp. 414–425.

[9] See, for example, Carol Glassman, "Women and the Welfare System," in Robin Morgan (ed.), *Sisterhood Is Powerful* (New York: Vintage Books, 1970), pp. 102–115; Betty Mandell, "Welfare and Totalitarianism," Parts I and II, *Social Work*, 16 (January 1971), pp. 17–26; and 16 (April 1971), pp. 89–96; and Julia B. Rauch, "Federal Family Planning Programs: Choice or Coercion?" *Social Work*, 15 (October 1970), pp. 68–75.

[10] See " 'Brownie Point' Welfare," Notes and Comments, *Social Service Review*, 46 (March 1972) pp. 111–113.

efforts to force welfare clients to work,[11] the renewed efforts to develop birth control programs to curtail potential welfare roll increases,[12] and the increased concern about addicts on welfare which has resulted in plans to curtail benefits to addicts who do not accept treatment.[13] Cloward and Piven have highlighted the role of the social services in socializing clients into an acceptable political stance. They argue that passivity and/or conformity are encouraged by conditional benefits with inadequate, if any, procedures for appeal and by the general debilitation and demoralization of the welfare way of life.[14]

These dynamics in the welfare program are both relatively well known and of wide concern. As such, they may obscure the extent to which such conditions operate in other programs. For example, the receipt of Social Security benefits requires registration of the individual with the government (the Senate Finance Committee, at one point, suggested that this occur when a child entered the first grade),[15] regularized work with a registered employer, and retirement at a specific age on penalty of benefit reduction or complete benefit loss. Similarly, institutional child care in the United States has been and continues to be heavily motivated "by a concern for idleness, lack of productivity, presumed moral depravity, and the protection of society," [16] with a consequent impact on the services provided. The use of the various behavior-modification techniques likewise makes the behaviors valued in clients more explicit. This was clearly the case in a report of a social service program in a public school system where self-discipline and conformity were encouraged through a token-economy system, a point-exchange system, and a chart system.[17] Day hospitals for formerly hospitalized mental patients likewise use the positive notion of the therapeutic community "to reactivate the patient's ability to behave

[11] "Major Provisions of Senate Bill on Social Security and Welfare," *New York Times* (June 14, 1972), p. 32.

[12] "Wider Birth Curb Aids Backed by Senate Panel," *New York Times* (June 8, 1972), p. 53.

[13] "Senate Panel Moves to Cut Off Relief Funds for Some Addicts," *New York Times* (June 1, 1972), p. 10.

[14] Richard Cloward and Frances Fox Piven, "The Professional Bureaucracies: Benefit Systems as Influence Systems," in Murray Silberman (ed.), *The Role of Government in Promoting Social Change*, Proceedings of a Conference, Arden House, Harriman, New York (New York: Columbia University School of Social Work, 1965). A similar theme is developed by Matthew P. Dumont in "The Junkie as Political Enemy," % *The Journal of Alternative Human Services*, 1 (July 1974), pp. 16–25.

[15] "Major Provisions of Senate Bill on Social Security and Welfare," p. 32.

[16] James K. Whittaker, "Group Care for Children: Guidelines for Planning," *Social Work*, 17 (January 1972), p. 52.

[17] H. G. Wadsworth, "Initiating a Preventive-Corrective Approach in an Elementary School System," *Social Work*, 15 (July 1970), pp. 60–66.

responsibly and thus to become capable of maintaining himself independently in the community. Such independence implies the ability to earn a living or at least contribute to his maximum potential."[18]

A classic demonstration of these dynamics was provided by Kingsley Davis who argued that individualism and an array of values associated with the Protestant Ethic are inherent in the concept of mental health as pursued by the mental health movement as he observed it in the 1930s.[19] The characteristics of the Protestant Ethic, as he described them, are democracy (in the sense of favoring equal opportunity to rise socially by merit rather than birth), worldliness, asceticism, individualism, rationalism and empiricism, and utilitarianism.[20] The mental health movement, as he was able to demonstrate, utilizes this value schema as its standard of mental health. Consequently, mental health is defined as the active pursuit of a career, the engagement in competition within the rules of the game, the focus on "wholesome" recreation (asceticism) and on purposeful activity in general (utilitarianism). Individualism is reinforced by focusing on the person as responsible for his or her own destiny, the definition of the ultimate good as the satisfaction of individual needs, and the assumption of human behavior as understandable in terms of individuals abstracted from their society.[21] Inasmuch as the values of the Protestant Ethic are intimately tied to the values and behaviors of a capitalist society,[22] Davis's analysis suggests that the mental health professions operate to reinforce values and behaviors supportive of capitalism.

In a specific case, Leichter and Mitchell examined the kinship patterns that were reinforced by the family caseworkers in New York City's Jewish Family Service.[23] Although the clients, mostly of Eastern European origin, rarely reported problems with kin, caseworkers, from their perspective, consistently saw a wide array of problems in family patterns and acted vigorously to deal with them. The client population operated within their traditional network of extended family relationships, and the workers saw this as destructive to the nuclear family and as an inducement to maintain immature dependency patterns. The workers saw health as lying in the direction of breaking kinship ties and establishing closed nuclear families, and they focused their casework intervention on achieving these

[18] Pascal Scoles and Eric W. Fine, "Aftercare and Rehabilitation in a Community Mental Health Center," Social Work, 16 (July 1971) p. 79.
[19] Kingsley Davis, "Mental Hygiene and the Class Structure," Psychiatry, 1 (1938), pp. 55–56. Reprinted in Herman Stein and Richard Cloward (eds.), Social Perspectives on Behavior (New York: Free Press, 1958), pp. 331–340.
[20] Ibid., p. 332.
[21] Ibid., p. 333.
[22] Max Weber, The Protestant Ethic and the Spirit of Capitalism (New York: Scribner's, 1958).
[23] Hope Leichter and William Mitchell, Kinship and Casework (New York: Russell Sage Foundation, 1967).

ends. Consequently, a more typical middle-class kinship structure was reinforced. The consequences were twofold. At the least, a sustaining and gratifying pattern of family relationships was weakened. Additionally, as nuclear family patterns were established, the ties of these persons to capitalist structures were reinforced.

The extended family potentially violates the Protestant Ethic and the capitalist values of individualism and self-reliance in the same way that the commune and the counterculture represent such threats. The fewer the nonmarket supports on which the individual or nuclear family can rely, the more they are forced to maintain themselves within the market structures. This means engaging in regular work and not engaging in behaviors that might jeopardize job security. It seems unlikely that the workers of New York's Jewish Family Service saw themselves as agents of capitalism. Nonetheless, the values that they had internalized and that they expressed in their professional practice were values that derive from and reinforce the kind of isolationism, individualism, and conformity which are supportive of capitalist society. The Leichter and Mitchell case study, consequently, serves as a specific illustration of what Walter Miller has identified as social work's intolerance of class differences and its concern with eliminating those lower-class behaviors that are not seen as functional or useful within the dominant value schemes of the society.[24]

Finally, we should not overlook one of the most obvious, but one of the most important, ways in which the social services carry a message about the behavior that is expected of adults. This message is contained in the fact that the social services are rarely funded at an adequate level. This is so obvious that we may tend to overlook its significance. One cannot escape the reality of this country's wealth, yet social service programs generally operate on marginal budgets. Whatever reasons are presented publicly for this fact, a clear implication is that public services are simply not high-priority items in our society. The message is that people who cannot make it in the private market cannot really count on a public support system for much help.

A few figures will help make this point. It is true that the total amount of funds devoted to social welfare expenditures in the United States has increased over time. Social welfare expenditures (SWEs) as a percent of Gross National Product (GNP) rose from 11.8 percent in 1965 to 16.9 percent in 1971.[25] Over the past thirty years, this pattern has been consistent. However, much of this growth reflects local community input into education, which is included in the government's overall index to welfare

24 Walter B. Miller, "Implications of Urban Lower Class Culture for Social Work," *Social Service Review*, 33 (September 1959), pp. 219–236.
25 Alfred M. Skolnick and Sophie R. Dales, "Social Welfare Expenditures, 1970–1971," *Social Security Bulletin*, 34 (December 1971) Table 4, p. 9.

state expenditures. It also reflects the Social Security program, which is paid for directly by workers through a generally regressive tax. When expenditures for education and for Social Security are taken out of the Social Welfare Expenditure figures, SWE as a percentage of GNP went from 4.5 percent in 1949 to 3.1 percent in 1959 to 4.8 percent in 1970. The figures and consequently the measure of this nation's concern for public service look quite different from the more rosy picture of growth and commitment that is usually painted.

REGULATING SOCIAL SERVICE WORKERS

As social service workers control clients as a function of the services they provide, so too are they controlled by the conditions of their work. These controls foster discipline in workers, encourage the acceptance of hierarchical and authoritarian structures, and create passivity and dis- engagement from others. It is necessary to impose on these workers the kinds of controls to which production workers are more easily subjected as a function of their basic conditions of work, inasmuch as the workplace is one of the key institutions in which values of conformity and obedience are inculcated. In part, this occurs as a result of fairly straightforward indoctrination, as occurs when professional workers are encouraged to feel that it is inappropriate to unionize. More subtly, however, it occurs as a result of the assumptions of work that are rarely explicit, but are im- plicit in the daily realities of work. There are several reasons why it is important that the behavior of social service workers be shaped through their agencies.

In the first place, as the number of social service workers grows, they become a more significant part of the total work force in the United States. The growing size of this population makes clearer the dimensions of the problem. In 1900, 4.3 percent of all working people were professional or technical workers. In 1960, 11.1 percent, and in 1970, 14.4 percent were in this category.[26] In 1960, they represented approximately 7.5 million work- ers. In 1970, 89 percent of all professional and technical workers were salaried. Within the category of professional and technical workers, 136,000 persons were social welfare and recreation workers, 1.7 million were elementary and high school teachers, and 1.1 million were health workers. In other words, almost 39 percent of the people in this important category of workers were in job classifications largely embraced within

[26] *Historical Statistics of the United States: Statistical Abstract of the United States, 1970* (Washington, D.C.: Government Printing Office, 1970), p. 74. These figures and those in the remainder of this discussion on labor force composition are analyzed in Albert Syzmanski, "Trends in Class Structure," *Socialist Revolution,* 2 (July–August 1972), pp. 101–122.

welfare state bureaucracies. Not included in these figures are 4.3 million clergymen, 1 million dieticians and nutritionists who often work in social welfare settings, and 180,000 college teachers. Furthermore, service workers have increasingly become proletarians; that is, the proportion of professionals and technical personnel who function as entrepreneurs has been decreasing steadily since the turn of the century, while the total number of people in these job categories has increased.

Another reason why service workers must be monitored is that they are often asked to perform as workers acts that might violate their deeper impulses as people. In order to ensure that workers will perform as required by the social services, they must be pressured, propagandized, or molded into conformity with the role requirements of the job. The social service worker's situation creates some problems of control because accountability is less easy to achieve than in some other kinds of work and because social service workers have, as part of the aura of professionalism, an ideology that values autonomous activity.

However, social agencies have generally mastered the problem of control. They are assisted, in the case of more highly trained workers, by the fact that such workers are less likely than others to be conscious of the extent to which they are not autonomous. The ethics of professionalism encourage such workers to adopt the self-image of independent practitioners. In order to maintain this myth, however, it is necessary for these workers to ignore certain realities of work, especially concerning the lack of input into policy decisions affecting the nature of the services provided and, consequently, the nature of their work. In many respects, professional workers are technicians whose practice requires some latitude. Caseworkers in the more elite private agencies, for instance, have some trappings of autonomy, such as an office, a secretary (shared), dictating machinery, (often) middle-class and respectful clients, and a decent salary. These enhance a feeling of well-being, self-respect, and autonomy. The organizer or planner may have even more discretion over work conditions, such as the daily schedule, and may hobnob with higher status professionals, politicians, and business people. On the other hand, all of these activities take place within a framework that the worker has had little hand in shaping. In many agencies, workers have virtually no control over their assignments and certainly no officially sanctioned input into evaluating the assumptions on which their work proceeds.

Self-regulation, then, is a key to the control of many of the more highly trained workers. However, they are not the majority of the social service work force.[27] In fact, in social work, the trend is toward greater use of less

[27] Over 80 percent of direct service positions in public and voluntary social agencies are staffed by workers without professional social work degrees. See Frank M. Loewenberg, "Toward a Systems Analysis of Social Welfare Manpower Utilization Patterns," *Child Welfare,* 49 (May 1970), pp. 252–253.

highly trained personnel, accompanied by increased routinization and structuring of the task of the job. The social work function in public welfare, for example, has been divided into the social service functions, which the smaller number of elite trained workers perform, and the cash eligibility functions, which the eligibility technicians perform. The mental health aide in mental health settings and the army of nurses, technicians, and aides in hospital settings perform routine tasks, while the trained worker does the more complex social casework.[28] For these workers, it is clear that employment in a service setting shares much with employment in more routinized production settings: control is maintained by the more traditional methods of rigidly enforced hours of work, closely monitored sick leave, watchful supervisors, narrow job definitions, and so on.

For both groups, work is generally structured in hierarchical fashion. The social work tradition of supervision ensures a lifetime of boss-worker relationships extending before the worker. One escape is to rise in the hierarchy. The supervisor continues to be supervised and controlled, but in turn can supervise and control others. However, the pressure to rise in the hierarchy, as a mark of one's worth and as a response to the pressures at the line level, give rise to devaluation of the immediate tasks of the line worker—a devaluation which both the line worker and the agency share. The realization that the major rewards come from rising hierarchically as opposed to excelling horizontally is bound to undermine the effort to do the best possible job at the line level.[29]

We have suggested that social services can presently be of very little assistance to people. It is likely that the workers who provide these services will experience some sense of the limited impact of their work. To the extent to which this awareness leads to feelings of powerlessness or to resignation and cynicism, workers will be easily managed and dominated in their work settings; they will be unlikely to feel that any actions they might take would make much positive difference. Cynicism and resignation, as opposed to anger that turns to rebellion, maintain the status quo. Cynicism is reinforced when the worker, feeling inadequate in the face of the human crises that are part of everyday work, finds no sense of crisis and urgency in the agency or profession. Cynicism also flourishes when

28 For a discussion of the extent of these developments in welfare, see R. C. Agento, "Behavioral Expectations as Perceived by Employing Agencies," *Public Welfare*, 28 (Spring 1970) pp. 209–213. For the mental health field, see R. L. Barker and R. B. Briggs, "Perspectives on Social Work Manpower in Service Delivery Approaches," in T. Carlson (ed.), *Social Work Manpower Utilization in Mental Health Programs* (Syracuse: Syracuse University Press, 1969), pp. 15–24.
29 Bertha Reynolds, a social worker whose life and work were informed by Marxist thinking, has identified in her autobiography the suspicion with which she was regarded when she attempted to return to direct practice after a distinguished career as teacher and author. See *An Uncharted Journey* (New York: Citadel Press, 1963), especially Chapter 15, "Pause in Transit," pp. 231–242.

the worker's performance, which the worker may consider inadequate, is viewed as satisfactory and even helpful by the agency supervisors and is rewarded by promotion.

As a consequence, social service workers typically do not seek hierarchical advancement as a way to find the satisfaction lacking in working directly with clients,[30] and are likely to become cynical about the possibilities of being helpful to others. The few empirical studies that have been done on worker attitudes corroborate this point. Wasserman studied welfare workers for a two-year period, beginning with their entry into the welfare system, and found them to be in severe conflict.[31] The workers saw supervision as oppressive bureaucratic control. They had to break rules to try to do a marginally better job for their clients. Breaking rules led, in turn, to feelings of guilt and anxiety. Over time, they became desensitized to their clients' needs and grew increasingly cynical. They were quite aware that they could not do much to help their clients, and they saw their primary options as either leaving the agency or attempting to move up in its hierarchy.

On the other hand, in a study conducted in the early 1960s, Billingsley found that the 110 caseworkers he studied in two private family casework agencies tended to be oriented more toward carrying out agency policies and procedures than toward what they themselves saw as the needs of their clients and the mandates of their profession. While the consequences for the workers were not specifically explored in the study, some degree of cynicism or, at the least, some loss of sensitivity to others would seem to be unavoidable.[32]

Similarly, a research team of the Social and Rehabilitation Services (SRS), Department of Health, Education and Welfare, reviewed nine empirical studies on the effects on initial entry into the social welfare and rehabilitation fields and found the impact on the worker to be primarily negative. The dominant worker responses were disillusionment, loss of

[30] This is reinforced by the advice given the worker in the professional literature. For example, a prominent casework theoretician has written that, when agency policies are unfair, unwise, or unnecessary, a desirable course is to try to work for change in policy, recognizing that workers can bring about improvements in policy and its administration, or at least can try to keep things from getting worse, "especially at the supervisory and higher administrative levels." Florence Hollis, *Casework: A Psychological Therapy*, 2nd ed. (New York: Random House, 1972), p. 144.
[31] Harry Wasserman, "Early Careers of Professional Social Workers in a Public Child Welfare Agency," *Social Work*, 15 (July 1970), pp. 93–101; and "The Professional Social Worker in a Bureaucracy," *Social Work*, 16 (January 1971), pp. 89–95. An excellent journalistic account of one man's brief and painful career as a welfare worker is Phil Tracy's "Working for Welfare," *The Village Voice*, in four parts: February 24, 1972; June 22, 1972; June 29, 1972; and July 6, 1972.
[32] Andrew Billingsley, "Bureaucratic and Professional Orientation Patterns in Social Casework," *Social Service Review*, 38 (December 1964), p. 407.

idealism, and loss of interest in staying in the field.[33] While specific causes of these reactions were not analyzed, the report did suggest that the lack of accomplishment of the field in general "may increase the amount of cynicism among workers and decrease the extent to which they will continue to emphasize service goals as opposed to self-serving goals in their behavior." [34]

Saucier studied worker turnover in an empirical analysis of the Franklin County Welfare Department, Columbus, Ohio.[35] Of the 233 caseworkers, 72 percent left the agency within a 26-month period between 1967 and 1969. While the conditions of work were not the primary focus of the study, it was observed that 50 percent of the workers' time was involved with paperwork and only 20 percent in direct communication with clients or in collateral interviews.

The Social and Rehabilitation Services' study of manpower cited above extensively analyzed the problem of high turnover among social welfare personnel. Some underlying problems in the field are highlighted by their findings. Their conclusion was that

> A standard or acceptable rate of turnover of Social Welfare and Rehabilitation Services workers, based on a smattering of opinions and data on rates of turnover among professionals in other fields, is estimated to be between 10 per cent and 15 per cent per year. By this standard, the amount of turnover in the Social Welfare and Rehabilitation Services field overall can be characterized as excessive, for it seems about double the acceptable rate.[36]

In their analysis, "much turnover is . . . attributable to efforts (often fruitless) to locate a professionally more challenging and rewarding position." [37]

Ullman et al. reported on a survey of over 600 National Association of Social Work (NASW) hospital-based social workers and 500 NASW social workers not in hospital practice.[38] (Hospital-based social workers represent approximately one-sixth of the entire NASW membership.) Of the hospital-based workers, only 45 percent could say they were

[33] Social and Rehabilitation Services, Department of Health, Education and Welfare, *Overview Study of the Dynamics of Worker Job Mobility*, National Study of Social Welfare and Rehabilitation Workers, Work, and Organizational Contexts, Research Report No. 1 (Washington, D.C.: Government Printing Office, 1971), Table 1, p. 30.

[34] *Ibid.*, p. 89.

[35] Anne Saucier, "The Qualifications and Activities of Caseworkers in a County Welfare Department," *Social Service Review*, 45 (June 1971), pp. 184–193.

[36] Social and Rehabilitation Services, *Overview Study of the Dynamics of Worker Job Mobility*, p. 50.

[37] *Ibid.*, p. 126.

[38] Alice Ullman et al., "Activities, Satisfaction, and Problems of Social Workers in Hospital Settings," *Social Service Review*, 45 (March 1971), pp. 17–29.

generally very satisfied with their work, as opposed to only somewhat satisfied or dissatisfied.[39] The hospital-based and nonhospital-based groups, taken together, reported approximately similar levels of dissatisfaction with specific aspects of work, with 75 percent reporting heavy workloads, 72 percent reporting inadequate community resources for referral, and 56 percent reporting little or no promotional opportunity, as serious or moderate problems in their work.[40] No data were reported on the extent to which workers felt they were effective. It seems unlikely, however, that they would feel they were making a major impact, given that they are overworked and that they do not have adequate community resources to supplement their in-house activities. Specific studies of worker response in dealing with health problems of the poor [41] and with mentally disabled clients in a public welfare setting [42] do illustrate how pessimistic many service workers become.

Finally, the services reinforce the larger patterns of social control by their discriminatory responses to female and black workers. The social services have been no exception to the rule that women and blacks have the lower level jobs in the professional hierarchies and get less money than white males for similar jobs. The situation of the female workers in social work has recently been reviewed by Scotch, who found patterns of discrimination against women in social work in salaries, promotions, and job opportunities.[43] The salaries of male social workers are higher than those of females and have risen proportionately faster. More males than females have achieved administrative positions, have published professional articles, and hold honorific and leadership positions in professional organizations. Inasmuch as the service professions support discriminatory practices regarding minorities and women in the profession, they help to support the larger patterns of exploitation in the society.

Thus, the general message to the client that is contained in the fact of underfinanced, inadequate, and inappropriate services is also a message to the worker. The worker is providing social services to people who have, for some reason, failed to contain within themselves the symptoms of our social crisis. The worker knows how poorly provided for these clients

[39] *Ibid.*, Table 5, p. 23.
[40] *Ibid.*, Table 6, p. 24.
[41] Lois Pratt, "Optimism-Pessimism about Helping the Poor with Health Problems," *Social Work,* 15 (April 1970), pp. 29–33.
[42] Arthur Segal, "Workers' Perceptions of Mentally Disabled Clients: Effect on Service Delivery," *Social Work,* 15 (July 1970) pp. 39–46.
[43] C. Bernard Scotch, "Sex Status in Social Work: Grist for Women's Liberation," *Social Work,* 16 (July 1971), pp. 5–18. See also Janet Saltzman Chafetz, "Women in Social Work," *Social Work,* 17 (September 1972), pp. 12–18; and Martha Williams, Liz Ho, Lucy Fielder, "Career Patterns: More Grist for Women's Liberation," *Social Work,* 4 (July 1974), pp. 463–66.

are. The message must necessarily be that if the worker does not remain properly at work and properly within the accepted standards of behavior, he or she might someday be forced to accept the very kind of inadequate service being provided to present clients. The social service worker knows better than anyone, save clients, that the social services are not what they claim to be and that making it on one's own in the market is the nearest one can come in our society to having security.

THE SOCIAL SERVICES AND THE COMPETITION FOR SCARCE RESOURCES

The United States is marked by significant inequalities in the internal distribution of nearly all its resources. By every measure, we are a wealthy nation, and just as clearly our wealth is so distributed that a small fraction of the population receives an overwhelmingly disproportionate share of it. We are so used to hearing the figures that their full meaning can escape us. Nonetheless, it remains a measure of this country's distorted priorities that the top 20 percent of the families in the United States receive over 40 percent of the income of all families and the top 20 percent of all individual units receive over 50 percent of the income for all individual units.[44] This maldistribution creates the potential for discontent and hence for political instability. Unless most people in the country can be convinced that inequalities are nonexistent or, if existent, are inevitable or desirable, they might try to take a larger share of the available resources for themselves. For them to do so would, of course, threaten the established order of the society.

A variety of possibilities suggest themselves as mechanisms for maintaining social stability in the face of both absolute and relative levels of deprivation. The most effective technique is to convince people that inequalities do not exist or are not as great as they really are. In fact, there is a great deal of propaganda to the effect that the United States is a classless society. Those inequalities that do exist are assumed to reflect individual abilities rather than institutionalized or class-based patterns of distribution. Furthermore, it is argued that some inequalities are inevitable in any society and are productive as a stimulus for individual effort. Inequalities also lead to the accumulation of capital, to investment, and, thus, to national economic growth. However the facts are presented, the general problem is the same—to encourage people to accept or at least to live with significant inequalities in the society.

[44] These figures are for 1967. U.S. Department of the Census, *Current Population Reports*, Series P–60, No. 59 (April 18, 1969), Table 25, p. 24.

The social services face a similar problem. They are one of the types of resources that the society has at its disposal and that must be distributed in accordance with the political mandates under which other resources are distributed. That is, we must ration them so as to obscure the fact that the amounts of resources being distributed are meager, so that awareness of inequities in the distribution of social services is minimized, and so that challenges to the overall order of the society are diffused. The social services are in fact distributed in a manner that meets these political requirements. In this section, the variety of ways in which this occurs are examined.

Maintaining Class Antagonisms

One of the most significant political outcomes of the social services and, from a conservative perspective, one of the most functional outcomes, is that they lead to exacerbation of tensions and divisions among sectors of the population. Social services tend to provide benefits on narrowly selective dimensions. The result is that some people, who are essentially similar to those who do receive benefits, do not receive benefits, because of shades of difference in their income, residence, age, sex, race, or health. Subsequently, these groups tend to view one another as the primary obstacles to receiving needed services, and competition among groups consisting of equally exploited people is established.

These divisions occur on at least two dimensions. First, the poor must place greater reliance on public social services, and, second, there is competition among the poor for control of those services. In each case, need for and competition over scarce resources establish internecine warfare, which can only benefit the more advantaged segments of the population who have the private resources to permit them to stand above these conflicts.

One of the outcomes of the development of a more elaborate welfare state structure has been to exacerbate the mutual antagonisms of the working poor, the blue-collar workers, the lower middle classes, and the welfare population.[45] This reflects the first of the divisions created by the patterns of service distribution. The lower middle classes are often not eligible for public service programs such as medical care, income supplements, housing supports, and so on. At the same time, they are able to purchase adequate services on the market only with the greatest difficulty. Close at hand are the poor who receive public assistance, seemingly without expending any effort to achieve that self-reliance so prized

[45] See Peter Binzen, *Whitetown, U.S.A.* (New York: Vintage Books, 1970); and Louise Kapp Howe, *The White Majority* (New York: Vintage Books, 1970).

by the lower middle classes. The outcomes are antagonism and the subsequent failure of groups like the National Welfare Rights Organization to organize the working poor and the unemployed into coalitions with welfare recipients. This antagonism, while having some basis in reality, is misplaced in that it ignores a more appropriate dimension for political struggle: the extent to which the United States has a dual system of publicly financed services, one for the poor and one for the middle and upper classes.

The services for the poor are the public social services. Expenditures for these programs are usually highly visible and often subject to political attack since they are expenditures on behalf of a group that tends to be politically unpopular, socially scapegoated, and relatively unable to mount a counterattack. At the same time, those with money to purchase private social services are subsidized in these purchases through the tax system. For example, tax deductions for medical expenses and mortgage interest are a public subsidy to those who are able to buy medical care or private housing. So, for example, the poor rely more heavily on the Social Security system for retirement income than the nonpoor, some of whom are able to save for retirement through a private pension plan. Yet, the private system represents a public expense of approximately $1 billion a year in taxes foregone as a result of the tax deduction privileges built into that system.[46] Similarly, public expenditures for medical care programs which primarily benefit poor people need to be weighed against tax deduction privileges for medical expenses of which middle- and upper-class people are more likely to make use. In 1970, total gross budgetary costs for Medicare and Medicaid were $4.6 billion, while tax deductions for private medical care and private health insurance in that year resulted in $3.2 billion in taxes foregone by the federal government.[47] Likewise, in 1962, the federal government spent approximately $820 million for housing for poor people, while in the same year it spent approximately $2.9 billion in subsidies for housing for middle- and upper-income people.[48] Private charity contributions to the poor must be weighed against the value of those contributions to the people who claim them as tax deductions, and so on. Even the dependency allowance system in the tax codes encourages this pattern. The AFDC mother may receive as little as $20 per month in welfare benefits for an additional child, or

[46] President's Committee on Corporate Pension Funds and Other Private Retirement and Welfare Programs, *Public Policy and Private Pension Programs* (Washington, D.C.: Government Printing Office, 1965), p. *vii*. See also Jeffry Galper, "Private Pensions and Public Policy," *Social Work*, 18 (May 1973) pp. 5–12.
[47] Joint Economic Committee, Congress of the United States, *The Economics of Federal Subsidy Programs* (Washington, D.C.: Government Printing Office, 1972), p. 38, Table 3–4, and p. 206.
[48] Alvin Schorr, *Explorations in Social Policy* (New York: Basic Books, 1968), p. 24.

$240 per year. The person who earns $50,000 per year and deducts the standard deduction of approximately $700 per year for each dependent will avoid over $350 of taxes per year with an extra child, since he or she will be at the 50 percent tax-bracket level. The poor person gets a government grant for another child of $240 per year, and the wealthy person gets a grant of $350 per year.

This reflects the generally perverse effect of the tax system on these patterns of income versus benefits. The higher the income of the taxpayer, the more he or she benefits from a given deduction. While the poor person may claim a $675 deduction for an additional dependent, the actual savings of taxes will be no more than 10 percent of this amount. That is, if taxable income is reduced from $4,000 to $3,325, tax is reduced from $400 to $332, or by $68.00. On the other hand, if taxable income is reduced because of an extra dependent from $75,000 to $74,325, tax may be reduced from $37,500 to $37,162, or by $338.00. The same pattern prevails for deductions for medical expenses, mortgage payments, and so on.

The reality is that public financing undergirds a great deal of the social services for all classes and, in fact, does not benefit the poor to the exclusion of, or more heavily than, the nonpoor. Nonetheless, the poor serve as a scapegoat for the lower middle and middle classes. That the financial stress felt by working people is not based on the relatively small expenditures for welfare programs is a logical argument, but it is weak in the face of the hysteria that is encouraged by politicians and the press. The dual social service system obscures important commonalities among welfare recipients and working people and isolates them from one another. Those benefiting most from public financing—the wealthy—escape the most bitter condemnation, or else become targets of far less hostile populist appeals for tax reform. The middle and lower classes go to the boards over the spoils.

Similarly, there is competition among recipient populations for welfare state goods and services and for the control of welfare programs. Grassroots political organizing around services often takes place along racial and ethnic lines. In the absence of a class analysis, this has had the effect of turning blacks, Puerto Ricans, and white ethnic groups against one another in the poverty program, the Model Cities Program, and in numerous struggles for community control of social services.[49] These struggles among oppressed groups deflect attention from the common enemy and permit the continued allocation of small amounts of resources to these programs, since each group sees the problem in terms of com-

[49] For the case of Model Cities, see Melvin B. Mogulof, "Black Community Development in Five Western Model Cities," *Social Work*, 15 (January 1970), pp. 12–18.

petition with and victory over other groups in an essentially similar condition.

The isolation of poor people from one another is reinforced by the manner of benefit distributions in welfare programs. As Cloward and Piven have pointed out, benefits are generally distributed individually, in a manner which inhibits aggregation of clients.[50] Complex procedures encourage individualized negotiations around eligibility. The structure and arrangements of benefit receipt encourage clients to assume a highly individualistic perspective on the problems, which does not lend itself to unified political action.

Two recent experiences in the city of Philadelphia illustrate these dynamics. An interesting mechanism was developed in Philadelphia in the early 1970s to ration one valuable resource—placement in a progressive high school within the public school system. This program, the Parkway School, utilized a city-wide lottery as a device to select students. The effect of this device was to focus a great deal of attention on the mechanisms of choice, on the gambling aspects of the lottery, and on the hope of beating out the other contestants. If the payoff did not come, only chance and other eager parents, not the political system, could be blamed. Consequently, the lottery focused attention away from the reality that the city was offering a very limited quantity of desirable resources and was otherwise offering mediocre educational services. John Cohen, a psychologist of gambling, has identified the general political phenomenon that operates in such cases. He writes,

> In the context of a competitive culture, the idea of luck may serve as a convenient stabilizer, convenient, that is, to the "lucky ones," at the same time stultifying initiative and independent thinking. Daily emasculation of the reflective processes of millions, whose horoscopes are cast in the daily press, produces a politically pliable mentality that sees the futility of social intervention if everything is foreordained by the stars.[51]

Another plan with potential for stimulating competition among the have-nots was recently developed by the Philadelphia Housing Authority. "Good" public housing tenants will now have an opportunity to move to more preferable public housing units as they become available.[52] A "good tenant" is defined as one having no record of trouble with other tenants. As the tenants themselves will be the judges in these matters, and a favorable rating of one tenant will reduce the possibilities of other tenants

---

[50] Cloward and Piven, "The Professional Bureaucracies."
[51] John Cohen, *Chance, Skill and Luck: The Psychology of Guessing and Gambling* (Baltimore: Penguin Books, 1960), p. 190.
[52] "City to Reward 'Good' Tenants in Its Projects," *The Philadelphia Inquirer* (October 26, 1971), p. 12.

moving up the ladder, this plan reinforces the competition of the poor with one another. It is interesting that a city housing administration which has not been noted for its concern for tenant self-determination has suddenly proposed a scheme for self-determination in one facet of its operation. In true colonial fashion, those with power and those who control the resources permit self-determination at a very distant point in the chain of events, under a set of circumstances that assures that self-determination will be, in the long run, an additional mechanism to weaken organized opposition.

This mutual alienation of people and of classes of people is facilitated, often unwittingly, by the social planner whose job is ostensibly to develop criteria for the most rational possible use of existing welfare state resources. In the process, the planner rationalizes and professionalizes some mechanism for distributing scarce resources to competing groups. In the name of rationality, equally valid claims on resources are set against one another, and discriminations are made among competing groups. This process occurs whenever communities or groups apply for funding within the framework of a larger social policy as, for example, in Model Cities, day care, drug treatment, and so on, and within the limits of some overall pool of funds allocated to that category of program. The planner, in these circumstances, professionalizes a process of discrimination despite his or her conscious intentions. In the case of the advocate planner, the worker's role is defined as ally to a community or group. All too often, the reality is that the planner's effort to get "more" of anything for one segment of the community results in a reduction of the resources available for some equally needy group that is without the good fortune of a planner to serve it.

Substituting Services for Hard Resources

The substitution of inexpensive social services for more vital and critical services is another mechanism by which we make do with scarce resources and simultaneously deflect greater political consciousness. Fully meeting people's needs in any area of service would entail not only more expense than the society is prepared to allow, but, as we have argued, would require a radically altered society. As an alternative, the social services function to encourage people to redefine their needs and their views of what a solution to their problems entails, so that inexpensive and politically accommodating services can replace expensive and politically disruptive services. Hence, the counseling components of social service programs tend to receive more support than those which involve the distribution of harder resources like money, jobs, and houses. This occurs despite continued and substantial evidence that social services cannot take the place of the more substantial goods and resources that people need.[53]

This process began the first time that the moral influence of the Charity Organization Society friendly visitor was offered to the poor in the place of cash assistance.[54] Since that time, the social services have continued to be offered as a substitute for the critical structural changes that our society requires.[55] In the face of a job market that has fairly consistently demonstrated its inability to provide sufficient employment for all, the society has offered job training to the poor and social services to welfare clients. In the face of our inability and/or unwillingness to make our school system responsive to the needs of all, we have tacked on a Head Start program to help children cope with the poor programs they will experience.[56] In the face of society's inability to deal with the repressive psychological realities of the society, an elaborate network of mental health facilities has been developed.

On the one hand, then, we offer the social services, which have a primary focus on changing people, as a substitute for policies dealing with the structure of the society which has created the people's problems. This is relatively less expensive economically and politically than the massive redistribution that would be required for structural changes, and it keeps the focus on the individual as the target of intervention.

On the other hand, those services we do offer are a conservatized and warped version of services that would adequately meet people's needs. Job training services typically train people for low-status, low-paid, low-mobility employment in marginal industries. Sewing-machine operators and beauty parlor technicians come to mind.[57] It is not unreasonable to assume that a training program that trained for decent work would

[53] Among the more recent data are two excellent studies of welfare clients and of juvenile delinquents. These are Edward J. Mullen, Robert M. Chazin, and David M. Feldstein, "Services for the Newly Dependent: An Assessment," *Social Service Review*, 46 (September 1972) pp. 309–322; and William C. Berleman, James R. Seaberg, and Thomas W. Steinburn, "The Delinquency Prevention Experiment of the Seattle Atlantic Street Center: A Final Evaluation," *Social Service Review*, 46 (September 1972) pp. 323–346.

[54] Roy Lubove, *The Professional Altruist* (New York: Atheneum, 1969), p. 15.

[55] Some commentary is offered by Alvin Schorr in two editorials in *Social Work*, 14 (January 1969), p. 2; and 14 (April 1969), pp. 2 ff.

[56] See the discussion in John M. Romanyshyn, *Social Welfare: Charity to Justice* (New York: Random House, 1971), pp. 366–367.

[57] For example, in 1971, clerical, service, and machine workers constituted 43 percent of MDTA (Manpower, Development and Training Act) trainees. Of the remainder, 13 percent were in the professional-technical-manager category, 16 percent in construction related work, 7 percent other, and 21 percent unknown. These data are from the *Manpower Report of the President, 1972* (Washington, D.C.: Government Printing Office, 1972), Table F–7, p. 267.

require decent inputs. Instead of providing such inputs, we substitute low-level goals which are less expensive to achieve and which do not threaten the established stratification patterns. Likewise, we do not rehabilitate drug addicts by the adequate provision of life supports that would make drug use unnecessary. Rather, we lock them up, narcotize them with methadone, or do counseling. Similarly, we do not help the mentally ill move toward their own liberation; we maintain them on drugs. The social services, then, have functioned as a substitute, and a poor substitute at that, for the more fundamental kinds of policies and changes required in the society.

Intake and Referral

In a number of ways, we parcel out limited social services with a veneer of rationality and objectivity. We try to make do with inadequate resources, while creating the impression that those with proper claims on resources can have these claims met. Each of the discriminatory mechanisms we employ is rationalized on a variety of grounds and so is not always understood as a discriminating mechanism by workers or by clients, though more often clients know full well that they are simply being shut out, regardless of the rationale.

Two of these mechanisms are the social service functions of intake and referral. As we would expect, they are not generally understood in this way by those who staff them. Intake is seen, in professional terms, as serving the function of determining the extent that agency resources and client need match and as preparing the client for further use of the services. Elaborate diagnostic categories have been developed to assess clients, and on this basis precise discriminations are attempted. However, when intake is examined in the light of its role in resource distribution, it becomes clear that it serves in part to screen out some number of clients to prevent overload of the system, thus ensuring that the agency will be more successful with those cases it does accept.[58]

The rationale for this process from within the profession generally concerns the desire of the profession to use itself with the population group with whom it feels most effective. The client populations so selected will have the most chance of using a service well. One effect of this process is that the population so selected is likely to consist of those persons already somewhat advantaged. The capacity to make use of help is itself a mark of strength. This process of selecting those clients most able to use a service leads to a systematic neglect of those who may be most in need

[58] See David Hallowitz and Albert V. Cutter, "Intake and the Waiting List: A Differential Approach," *Social Casework*, 35 (December 1954), pp. 439–445.

of help.[59] It also leads to a higher probability that the service will be able to demonstrate higher success rates. Intake, therefore, both excludes the most needy clients and builds in the higher success rate required by the service structure to strengthen its competitive hand in the struggle with other services for funding.[60]

Referral, likewise, takes the pressure off the service system, but in a somewhat different manner. The client is taken into the service structure and is given a referral which is itself defined as a service. The nature of that service is that the client is sent elsewhere for service. Referral, in professional terms, is something more than a shove out the door. It may involve a diagnostic intake interview, an advance contact with the service structure at the receiving end, and some discussion with the client about the referral. Inevitably, some number of clients will get lost in the transfer, some will never get into the service structure to which they are sent, some will get in and will be referred out again, and some will get sent to services that do not exist or that exist in name only. An analogy is the parking problem in most large cities: there are never enough spots for all in need, but at any one time some cars are cruising the streets, looking. Referral is a way of dealing with clients in need without really dealing with them. Whatever its ostensible justification, it serves the function of rationing scarce social service resources to a population that needs more services than are available.

Similarly, waiting lists serve a number of functions for social agencies. They permit social agencies to deal with more people than they can actually serve. At the same time, as Perlman suggests, a waiting list may

> stand as a reminder to board and community that more people need help than the agency can accommodate and that, therefore, it needs more money to employ professional staff. . . . One may also wonder whether some prestige has become attached to an agency's having a waiting list. Not only is a waiting list a declaration that casework service is in great demand, but it

[59] See Martin Rein, "The Social Service Crisis: The Dilemma—Success for the Agency or Service to the Needy?" *Trans-action*, 1 (May 1964), pp. 3–8; and Elaine Cumming, *Systems of Social Regulation* (New York: Atherton Press, 1968), p. 122. These findings were anticipated by the work of Lichtenberg, Kohrman, and Macgregor, who found that families which were more healthy initially were more highly motivated to seek psychiatric care in a child psychiatry clinic than were families which were initially less healthy. See especially Chapter 10, "Mental Health Rankings and Motivation," in Philip Lichtenberg, Robert Kohrman, and Helen Macgregor, *Motivations for Child Psychiatry Treatment* (New York: Russell and Russell, 1960), pp. 190–194.

[60] A more frank discussion of these functions of intake than is usually found in the literature, from a period when these rationalizations were somewhat less overlayed with professional jargon, is found in Emil Steger, "Intake Policies in Family Case Work," *National Conference of Social Work*, Boston (Chicago: University of Chicago Press, 1931), pp. 189–197.

duplicates the usual pattern of private psychiatric and psychoanalytic intake.[61]

Stigmatizing Services

There are a variety of additional ways employed to ration services. Making the receipt of services unpleasant surely helps to dissuade some number of eligible and needy people from using them. The stigmatizing effects of public welfare are not inevitable concomitants of an income distribution system. They are built into the intake processes and the ongoing conditions of benefit receipt, and they serve as one of the ways that eligible persons are discouraged from becoming clients.

Another mechanism employed to keep people away from services is keeping services a secret. The systematic publishing of information on Social Security through employers and the mass media, in comparison with the absence of information on the availability of public welfare, should tell us that selective processes of information dissemination are at work.[62] People are also kept out by rigid eligibility criteria, including age (old age assistance and Social Security), sex (AFDC, in large part), residence (welfare residency laws [until the courts declared them unconstitutional] and such devices as mental health catchment areas [limited by geographic boundaries], target populations, service districts, and the like), income, and others.

Maintaining High Client Turnover

Finally, social services are rationed by bouncing—moving people who are recipients of services out of the service system as quickly as possible. A number of mechanisms for bouncing are utilized. For some services, like Unemployment Insurance, the straightforward device of a set number of weeks of eligibility is employed. For welfare, demands for behavioral conformity are made on the client, and clients are dropped from the service if these demands are not met. In mental health centers, elaborate rationales have been developed for emergency short-term service, after which the client may have to enter another network to continue treatment. In each case, some professional-rational-scientific overlay is developed for

[61] Helen Harris Perlman, "Some Notes on the Waiting List," *Social Casework*, 44 (April 1963), p. 201.

[62] It is estimated that approximately one-half of those eligible for public welfare are not recipients. See Dorothy Buckton James, *Poverty, Politics and Change* (Englewood Cliffs, N.J.: Prentice-Hall, 1972), p. 42. Even programs ostensibly designed with outreach purposes are often undermined if they prove too successful. For an example of one case and a description of the general phenomenon, see Stanley S. Brody, Harvey Finkle, and Carl Hirsch, "Benefit Alert: Outreach for the Aged," *Social Work*, 17 (January 1972), pp. 14–23.

a process of exclusion. These mechanisms enable the service system to come closer to giving an appearance of meeting need. In reality, the function served is the rationing of a scarce resource in such a way that the underlying reality of scarcity is obscured in a barrage of regulations and professional rationales.

SUMMARY

In this chapter we have reviewed some of the political functions of the social services. We have observed that these functions are to encourage conformity and conservatism in both clients and social service workers and that the services help to maintain a larger political climate hostile to social change.

In each example, we have suggested that these problems are not anomalous, incidental, or transient. They are the logical consequence of the fundamental purposes served by the social services. It follows that these problems will not be amenable to piecemeal reform efforts from within the social services. They must be solved by addressing the larger social issues that give rise to the specific problems.

In other words, we have suggested that a reformist approach will not be adequate. The problems are too intimately connected with the whole fabric of the social order. In the next chapter, this aspect of the situation of the social services—the inadequacy of reformism—will be explored.

5

Social Reform:
The Liberal Response

We have, thus far, explored some of the limitations and contradictions in the social services and in the social policies and the underlying liberal values in which they are rooted. We have discussed the ways in which these problems prevent the social services from making a significant contribution to human welfare.

The radical analysis of these dilemmas is, of course, not widely accepted at present by those in and around social welfare programs. However, the particular criticisms we have made of the specific limitations in the services tend to be widely known and, frequently, widely shared. Many observers are fully aware of the low levels of financial support provided by income maintenance programs, of the coercive aspects of social services, of the failure of various rehabilitation programs to rehabilitate, and so on. The conventional perspective on the services is not complacent or cold-hearted. It acknowledges problems, and it attempts to deal with them. In this chapter, the nature of the strategies to which the conventional approach gives rise will be explored. These strategies are identified under the general heading of reformism or social reform, in contrast to the radical change or revolutionary change strategies that derive from the radical perspective.

We suggest that the reformist approach to social change cannot be successful in solving the basic problems that we face. Nor can it achieve even the relatively modest goals it sets for itself. The fundamental reason for this failure is that reformism accepts, works within, and ultimately supports the very values and institutions that must be challenged and changed if we are to develop a humane society. The ways in which reformism is self-contradictory need to be more widely understood so that change efforts by social service workers can transcend these limits.

THE NATURE OF REFORMISM

Reformism is not a very precise term, although it is sufficiently precise to enable us to identify a category of change activity and strategy. To define reformism, it will be useful to suggest at the outset a number of things that it is not.

Reformism is frequently equated with incrementalism. This is the notion that planned change in a society will and should occur through modest changes, each a small departure from previous practice. However, incrementalism ought not to be taken as a defining characteristic of reformism. With very few exceptions, all change, including change that could be called revolutionary, consists of relatively small departures from previous practice. There are very few moments in history at which large changes have been made at one instant. Revolutions themselves are as often the public and symbolic recognition of a variety of changes that have taken place in the society over time as they are the moment at which the change actually occurs.

This will be all the more true as the idea of revolution becomes more consistent with the kinds of concerns for change that some radicals are now developing. Revolution is increasingly being seen as more than the overthrow of those in power and as more than the replacement of a particular aspect of a system. Rather, it is coming to be understood as a change in culture, psychology, and organizing principles as well as in economics and political forms. In this light, revolutionary change will necessarily have many incremental aspects. Radical change strategies conceptualize and utilize incremental changes quite differently from the way that reform strategies do. Nonetheless, the incremental nature of change efforts does not necessarily distinguish reformism from other approaches.

Radicals who do not understand the necessarily incremental nature of radical work may disparage their own efforts when the results are not cataclysmic. They may feel frustrated and untrue to their visions and commitments. It is important for radicals to realize that, by and large, only small changes are possible at any one time. It is the nature of these changes, as well as their "size," that distinguishes them from reformism.

Reformism also ought not to be equated with strategies of change that are nonmilitant or peaceful. Some efforts at reform, historically and currently, have been quite militant and have utilized conflict and even violence as a strategy. For example, union struggles for higher wages may be militant and may involve violent conflict, but they are not, as a consequence, revolutionary. Similarly, black-power advocates whose militance is directed toward developing black capitalism have not always understood that militance and radicalism are separate dimensions of change efforts. One has to do with tactics and style, the other with underlying analysis and goals. They may or may not be associated with one another.

In addition, reformism ought not to be characterized as a strategy that is "reasonable"—in contrast to radical change which has been labeled unreasonable. Many of the reformist efforts to change social policies have been quite unreasonable in their assumptions about what people are like and in their projections of the ways in which a decent society should be organized. The appeal to reason has too often been an appeal to compromise principles of social justice and human dignity for the sake of some more easily achievable but unfulfilling or destructive outcomes.

Finally, reform efforts cannot be distinguished by their feasibility. Most reforms are much diminished between their first expression and their final realization. Nonradical though reforms may be, they are fought bitterly by conservative forces and are often badly compromised, belying any notion that reformism is a strategy of change that is defined by its feasibility. What equating reform with feasibility has meant in practice is that reform, like politics, has come to be seen as the art of the possible. However, what is considered possible often bears remote resemblance to desirable change and should not be graced with the label of reform.

What then are the distinguishing characteristics of reform? Reform can be identified as an approach to change in which the range of change that is attempted is bounded by the major structures and values of the society as they exist at that moment. In its dictionary definition, *reform* is "a movement aimed at removing political or social abuse," or an effort "to make better by removing faults or defects," or by "putting a stop to abuses or malpractices or by introducing better procedures."[1]

[1] *Webster's New World Dictionary*, 2nd ed. (New York: World Publishing Company, 1970)

The superstructure, or the fundamental nature of what exists, is not challenged by reformism. Reformism seeks change and improvement within the boundaries of what is.

We have suggested that the critical dimensions for understanding "what is" are the structures of capitalism and the ideology of liberalism. As a consequence, we find reformers supporting the right of each individual to an education or to a job, fighting for more adequate welfare benefits or for greater citizen input into policy making. We do not generally find these struggles rooted in questions about the nature of the political and economic purposes served by education, the need to redefine the nature of work, or the question of direct democratic control of our institutions.

Reformism is closely linked with the political forms of pluralism. As reformism in the United States is associated with capitalism and liberalism, so is pluralism, which has been called "the heart of liberal ideology in the Western world.[2] In the pluralist model of social organization, society is assumed to be composed of reasonably independent groups which have voluntary and overlapping memberships. Public policy, accepted as binding on all, emerges as a result of the interplay of these groups and the agreements worked out among them. Government's role is to assure access of all groups to the bargaining arena and to act on "the common denominator of group concurrence."[3] The pluralist vision sees government as referee between competing and antagonistic groups. It defines government's role as arbitrating the processes of group struggle over the relative shares of the society's resources that each group will have at its disposal. As such, the pluralist model accepts and builds on a competitive model of social organization. The limitations and contradictions of reformism and of pluralism stem from these roots.

A CRITIQUE OF REFORMISM

The Reformist Dilemma

Reformism creates what must be a painful dilemma for the reformer. In the face of a society beset by an enormous number of very critical social and economic problems, the reformer engages in a series of discrete efforts to ameliorate some aspect of the total problem and does so without an analysis or strategy that connects the specific effort to a solution to the totality of problems. The reformer often seems to be in

[2] "Pluralism," in David Sills (ed.), *International Encyclopedia of the Social Sciences*, Volume 12 (New York: Macmillan and Fress Press, 1968), p. 164.
[3] *Ibid*. Also found in Theodore Lowi, *The End of Liberalism* (New York: Norton, 1969), p. 71.

the rather frustrating position of choosing from a shopping list of alternative projects. When the effort in any one direction is exhausted, or proves too exhausting, a new problem area and a new project are carved out from a revised list of priorities.

This is not meant to suggest that the committed reformer ought to be condemned for his or her errors or failures. Rather, the reformer must be admired for the good intentions that are often a part of the reform effort and for the dogged pursuit of social ideals in the face of a good deal of evidence suggesting that such activity is not socially productive. Rather than see reformers as part of the problem, as some radicals tend to do, we must recognize that reformism represents an enormous source of energy that could be productive if it were freed from the self-defeating analysis and strategy that binds it.

That the reformist impulse represents unusual energies is demonstrated by the persistence of reform efforts in the face of the special difficulties of reform—difficulties that are in many ways more frustrating than those faced by the radical. One of these is the reformer's rather arbitrary point of engagement in the matrix of social problems, which must lead to some feeling of whimsy in the choice of activity. A radical analysis points to underlying causes and unifying themes in the approach to social problems and social change. Whatever the particular point of entry, the radical is always trying to reach the more basic dynamics and more basic strategic levers for change in the whole society through the particulars with which he or she is engaged. The reformist approach tends to be more ad hoc. For example, the reformer may get involved with trying to effect a change in leadership of a given institution, in a particular policy, or in a specific program. Whatever effort is undertaken, other equally pressing problems are left unexplored, and few, if any, connections are projected between the one effort and others. The radical engages in particular struggles also, but does so with an eye toward creating greater political consciousness and political organization in the process, with the long-term aim of changing the system that produces the particular problems.

Another problem reformers face is that they so often fail to achieve even the relatively modest goals they set for themselves. The fact that trying to establish a social services program for the elderly in a public housing project will not lead to structural change in the society does not make it very much easier to establish that program. That reformers continue to engage in reform efforts that are inevitably limited and yet quite hard to achieve is a measure of the persistence of the human drive for a more decent world.

Reformist solutions are typically formulated from an abstract appreciation of the history of efforts to deal with the problems under consideration. The liberal philosophy in which reformism is rooted does not contain a developed vision of the good society or a means for achieving such a society. As a consequence, reformism tends to focus on the moment, on ongoing processes, and to see the future as being simply an elaborated version of the present. This has the effect of imposing a limited optimism on what seems to be the reformer's rather basic pessimism and skepticism. The reformer is pessimistic in that he or she accepts the fact that reform efforts are unlikely to make a significant impact on the neglect, alienation, and destruction in the society. The social worker, for example, may feel good about helping a client or about reducing or humanizing some bureaucratic red tape, but is unlikely to be under the illusion that these activities are a fundamental link in any grand movement for social change. Hence the basic pessimism and skepticism. On the other hand, reformers often claim that a particular reform represents a critical breakthrough in a given problem area. Such claims can only be based on historical myopia. The history of reform efforts suggests that most reforms are the updated or not even updated revivals of earlier efforts that did not prove useful.[4]

For example, welfare policies have gone through repeated cycles of loosening and tightening the requirements for eligibility, of integrating and then separating the provision of social services for welfare clients from cash allocations, of reducing the welfare rolls through a "no-nonsense, get-tough approach" to a rehabilitation approach.[5] Typically, the 1962 public assistance amendments were described as "momentous" and as a "landmark." [6] So too were the 1967 amendments which piggy-backed efforts at forcing welfare mothers to work onto the earlier effort to casework people off the welfare rolls. More recently, the Family Assistance Program was touted with the same assurances that it, too, was a "new departure that will find a solution for the welfare problem." [7] Similarly, as Joseph Fried has described for our national housing programs,

> The history of federal efforts in behalf of the nation's ill-housed families has been a history of rhetorically impressive promises followed by singularly

[4] An exception may be those reforms that are based on technological developments, such as new drugs to treat mental patients or addicts or electronic data-processing equipment to monitor parolees or welfare clients.
[5] Samuel Mencher's *Poor Law to Poverty Program* (Pittsburgh: University of Pittsburgh Press, 1967) rewards the reader's careful attention by providing an opportunity, in the income maintenance case, to observe this recurring pattern in detail.
[6] U.S. Congress, Committee of Ways and Means, *The President's Proposals for Welfare Reform, 1969* (Washington, D.C.: Government Printing Office, 1969), p. 94.
[7] See the account in Gilbert Steiner's *The State of Welfare* (Washington, D.C.: The Brookings Institution, 1971), pp. 36 ff.

unimpressive performances, of intricate programs long on solemnly avowed goals but short on the first thing needed to achieve them—money.[8]

Beginning with the Housing Act of 1949, cited as a "legislative landmark," we have had a notoriously monotonous history of "new departures." The Omnibus 1968 Housing Act was "the instrument that at last would provide a breakthrough in home production and services." [9] In 1971, the *Third Annual Report on National Housing Goals* suggested that "the outlook is the brightest in years." [10] And so it goes.

Perhaps this should be interpreted simply as a reflection of basic optimism. Perhaps it is, in part. However, it is also a reflection of an inability to see that "new programs" do not solve the basic dilemmas of the society and shows a blindness to the inevitability with which these solutions have been tried and rejected in the past. And yet, the reformer has few alternatives. Committed to seeking changes in the society, aware in some ways of the society's agonies and his or her own disaffection, the reformer struggles on. But in the absence of a radical analysis and radical program, the reformer is committed to repeating efforts that have failed in the past.

Furthermore, it is typical of reform activity, especially when undertaken by middle-class or professional people, to deal with the problems of some group of people other than their own. The altruistic nature of such efforts is even more impressive in light of the fact that reformers tend to isolate their efforts to help others from problems in their own lives. Reformers believe that solutions lie in changing some particular aspects of the way the society works. This assumes that the system can work adequately for some, though it fails for others. For example, if the issue is the distribution of society's material resources, the reformer might suggest that many get enough, though some do not. If the reformer is among those who gets enough, he or she will see the problem as principally affecting those who do not get enough. The commitment to create change will be a concern for others and their well-being, not a concern for oneself in any direct sense.

In contrast, the radical tends to feel more personally implicated in the problem, whatever it is. For example, the radical analysis of the problem of economic injustice suggests that all people are treated as commodities in our society and, consequently, that all are affected by the problem of economic exploitation. Poverty is part of the same prob-

---

[8] Joseph P. Fried, *Housing Crisis, U.S.A.* (New York: Praeger, 1971), p. 60.
[9] "Lag in Housing Spurs a Drive to Alter Law," *New York Times* (March 22, 1971), p. 1.
[10] *Third Annual Report on National Housing Goals,* Message from the President of the United States, June 29, 1971 (Washington, D.C.: Government Printing Office, 1971), p. 1.

lem that leads to an evaluation of all and distribution to all on the basis of their value as producers and consumers rather than on the basis of their humanity, citizenship, or need. Because the radical feels this deeply, the struggle for economic justice for others is inseparable from the struggle of all people, including the radical, to be treated as people and not as commodities. The solution for others is the solution for all. The radical vision eliminates the possibility of a personal refuge for some, or of piecemeal solutions, and places the radical's personal solutions in the context of basic change for all. While these same linkages exist between the reformer's efforts and problems in the reformer's own life, the reformer tends not to see them or else experiences them implicitly, not explicitly. Consequently, reform efforts often seem to be conducted in an alienated and isolated fashion.[11]

Social work in particular identifies social reform with social service provision. However, the reality that social services do not deal with the major problems of the society cannot be avoided by social workers. As a consequence, social work's understanding of its role in relationship to social change cannot but lead to pessimism and fatalism. This necessarily demoralizes social workers and contributes to their political passivity. Carol Meyer has written, for example, "It is difficult to imagine how professionals, even an array of them, could achieve the power to effect basic social change through their separate technical expertise." [12] When people feel that their work will not have major kinds of meaning, the outcome may be a highly ritualistic practice. They become committed to means and to processes in the absence of a serious analysis of goals, since every examination and discussion of goals tells them that all their effort is basically futile

Data on the actual work experiences and reactions of social service workers confirm this impression. Early in their professional lives, social workers begin to experience frustration and disillusionment with the field, especially regarding the possibility of providing meaningful service to people. The reaction, as documented in a variety of empirical studies, is discouragement and cynicism and a turn to more personal pursuits in the form of seeking promotion and higher salaries.[13]

[11] Jonathan Kozol has suggested that we are systematically trained in our schools to be committed to the ongoing pursuit of strategies of change that are preordained to fail and to reinforce feelings of futility and impotence. See "How Schools Train Children for Political Impotence," *Social Policy*, 3 (July–August 1972), pp. 16–21.
[12] Carol H. Meyer, *Social Work Practice: A Response to the Urban Crisis* (New York: Free Press, 1970), p. 19.
[13] A summary of nine empirical studies documenting this reaction is found in Social and Rehabilitative Services, Department of Health, Education and Welfare, *Overview Study of the Dynamics of Worker Job Mobility*, National Study of Social Welfare, Rehabilitation Workers, Work, and Organizational Contexts, Research Report No. 1 (Washington, D.C.: Government Printing Office, 1971), Table 1, p. 30.

Reformism and Ideology

The underlying limitation of reformism is that it fails to understand that social problems are rooted in the social structures of society and, consequently, confuses dealing with the symptoms of problems with dealing with the problems themselves. Because reformism accepts the basic values and structures of the society, it has no way to work back from manifestations of problems to the causes of problems. Furthermore, it shares liberalism's belief that desirable social outcomes can emerge from the competitive interplay of the disparate units of society. This belief in the beneficial effects of competition and the negotiated settlements of interest groups is a fundamental part of the ideology of reformism. Because it is not a critical ideology, it is not adequate to the tasks before us.

It is infrequently the case that piecemeal approaches, even at particularly propitious times, can lead to changes in the whole. Sometimes certain social issues are so critical or some reforms are located at such a vital political juncture that the struggle on their behalf inherently forces the larger system to change. For example, it has been argued that the women's movement, by its very nature, will force revolutionary changes to occur simply by pressing for the liberal goals of equal treatment of women and men.[14] By the same logic, this position can be argued for many other groups and many other causes. However, we suggest that a radical program is necessary if we are ever to achieve fundamental social changes. There are a number of reasons why this is so.

What are our problems?   Our awareness of our needs as people has been subjected to a process of desensitization so that we tend to see the solutions to our problems as resting in acquiring more of the things that are commonly valued in the society. We have suggested that our society rests on a limited and distorted sense of priorities. To the extent that this is so, struggles for success that take place within a conventional framework will be struggles to achieve limited or distorted outcomes.

One of the essential roles of a radical ideology is to help us to stay in touch with our deepest needs as people and our best visions of a decent society. Our society has a tremendous capacity to coopt us and to deflect our attention from basic issues. Time and again, very funda-

---

14 For example, Jean Baker Miller has written, in suggesting strategy for the women's movement, that "a fight for full employment, including high quality daycare provisions, would seem to lead to basic changes in the economic institutions of society. It would seem to lead inevitably to an expansion of the public sector, e.g., housing, education, health, transportation. It would appear that women could not seriously pursue such a goal without confronting these basic changes." "On Women: New Political Directions for Women," *Social Policy*, 2 (July–August 1971), p. 45.

mental demands have been scaled down and made "reasonable" by conservative forces. Socially sanctioned reform efforts have functioned to dilute our understanding of the kinds of solutions and life possibilities that might be achieved. In a society as wealthy as ours, some resources can always be diverted to a sufficiently noisy and troublesome segment of the population. Responses of this sort have mitigated pressure for more fundamental change, not so much by "buying off" parts of the population as by encouraging people in a process by which their understanding of their own needs undergoes transformation. This is not to argue that people should not fight for "more" or that people do not have a right to more. They do. But change efforts must be based on a recognition that the fullest realization of demands for dignity, justice, and equality will not be met through the arrangements under which we presently live.

There are an enormous number of examples one can draw on to illustrate the process of deflection of the struggle for change. One of the most obvious is the transformation of all of our needs for a basically more satisfying life into the commonly held belief that earning more money and buying more things will produce happiness and security. Although money and the things it can buy are not unimportant, and their absence can be painful, money does not lead to the outcomes promised in the conventional propaganda. Yet it is very easy to allow earning money and buying things to become one's personal goal and the goal sought for others through reform efforts. However successful we might be, this kind of approach assures the continued dominance of market processes and the destructive institutions that are rooted in it.

Similarly, an important component of the women's movement and the black movement concerns the desire for dignity and justice in their broadest dimensions. However, part of the women's movement is very involved in the important but more limited task of fighting for equal pay for equal work, and part of the black movement has been attracted to the promises of black capitalism. In each case, the awareness of the nature of the oppression has not transcended the liberal notion of equal opportunity—an important but limited standard for a just society.

Another example of the process of deflection is psychological in nature. We may be aware that we are cut off from meaningful involvement with other people, but may interpret this as our personal neurotic hang-up. Individual therapy or encounter groups may help a lonely person feel more in contact, but they cannot change or lead to efforts to deal with the social, political, and economic arrangements that encourage our isolation from one another.

In every area of our lives in which we experience problems and feel pain, there is a socially sanctioned definition of what that pain is and what the solution to it should be. These definitions derive from and support particular kinds of values and arrangements in the society. A repressive society does not have to convince people that they are experiencing no problems. It does need to encourage them to believe that the solutions to these problems involve taking certain actions that are sustaining to the system. Reform activity is rooted in definitions of these problems that derive from existing institutions and values and produces solutions, or attempts at solutions, that support existing institutions and values. An alternative ideology is necessary as a basis for alternative definitions of need and of solution and, hence, is a challenge to the society as it presently exists.

Small changes and big changes.   The second specific reason why reformism is an inadequate approach to social change is that it lacks an analysis that could suggest the linkages between any specific change efforts and changes in the whole. A critical question for all of us is how the achievement of a more decent society can be pursued in the context of day-to-day life. Socially sanctioned reform efforts do not confront the underlying destructive structures and arrangements of society and so are not useful in providing guidelines that will help us utilize our daily work in a way that facilitates more profound changes. Reformism tends to isolate change efforts from one another, to play them off against one another, and to fail to work from the specific case to the general issue.

It is reasonable to assume that the fundamental social values of the society play out in some form in each of the major social institutions and processes. Destructive patterns in one sphere reflect the larger reality, and they are a part of it. By the same token, work in one sector can become a vehicle for raising a larger and more profound challenge to the whole if the underlying issues and the interconnections of events are understood. To do so requires a perspective that attempts to understand the whole fabric and especially the relationship between the parts. In essence, a radical ideology is required.

The cases of any number of reform efforts that have failed to develop and operate on the basis of such an ideology helps make this clear. For example, the enormous amount of protest energies mobilized to stop the war in Vietnam had the potential to raise the question of the negative consequences of the United States' involvement in the lives, economies, and governments of large numbers of people throughout the world. Had the concern raised by the war taken this direction, it could have opened opportunities for new political alliances, political education, and lasting forms of organization for social change. Inasmuch as the concern took the more limited form of antiwar activity, it did not raise these important larger questions and, in fact, got channeled into relatively unprofound electoral politics. In this arena, and in this light, all manner of people could support the antiwar effort, and the more fundamental problems to which the war was related became obscured.[15]

The narrowly constrained enthusiasm generated by electoral politics also illustrates the problem of reform strategy isolated from broader ideology. Each campaign brings its star and its manipulated enthusiasms. We work and we convince ourselves that the election of our candidate will be the beginning of a new day. Surely the election of some persons to office would make differences in some areas, and we should work for the election of these people. The problem comes when we substitute our effort to elect people for our effort to achieve social, political, and economic goals. Electoral politics ought to be one tool among many for pursuing large goals. Likewise, reformist programs ought to be vehicles for the furtherance of large goals. However, in the absence of other vehicles to pursue these goals, and in the absence of historical perspective on the consistency with which our enthusiasm and energy have been manipulated, we substitute "new-people strategies" for more systematic, profound, and enduring change efforts.[16]

Staying together in the struggle. The final reason why radical political consciousness is so essential is that in the absence of this consciousness, the gains that reformist groups seek may result in a loss of resources to other equally exploited groups and in the failure to consider dilemmas common to all. As long as the analysis and struggle are at the level of trying to obtain some resources for a particular group or in a particular area of need, a victory will most likely mean the redistribution of scarce goods to one group and away from some other equally needy group. To the extent that reformers support these struggles, they support the historical technique of the forces of the status quo that keep the disadvantaged in society fighting with one another.

For example, efforts by reformers and by clients to create changes in the welfare system have aggravated the tensions between interest groups in the society which, hopefully, will someday come together to make common cause against the larger patterns of economic maldistribution in the society. Liberals surely recognize that there is a problem of poverty in this country. In pluralist fashion, the National Welfare Rights Organization represents an important interest group with particular reason to seek changes in the prevailing patterns. Simultaneously, however,

[15] For a discussion of this important case, see John Judis, "The Triumph of Bourgeois Hegemony in the Face of Nothing That Challenges It," *Socialist Revolution,* 2 (November–December 1971), pp. 107–125.
[16] This problem and an important socialist statement of the use of reformist activity are presented in Rosa Luxemburg's *Reform or Revolution* (New York: Pathfinder Press, 1970, originally published in 1900).

there are other groups in the society seeking changes in the patterns of income distribution, for example, those representing middle-class and lower-middle-class taxpayers "in revolt." Each sees itself as a separate group with competing and valid claims for resources.

The antagonism of lower-middle-class workers to welfare clients is well known. In fact, it may not be misplaced, in the short run, since most programs for the poor have been disproportionately financed by lower-income working people and have been traded off against their programs. Inasmuch as middle-class liberals support the National Welfare Rights Organization, they do so at the risk of exacerbating these interest-group tensions, which means they must operate in an adversary situation. The welfare debate, as a consequence, ranges over amounts of money— $2,400 to $6,400 a year for a family of four, for example. The goal becomes to secure as much as possible, knowing it will be traded off against resources available for other needy groups.[17] The way in which this happens can be understood by examining some aspects of the pluralist form of democracy, which helps assure that such a mutually competitive and divisive process will take place.

Theodore Lowi [18] and Robert Paul Wolff [19] have convincingly argued that pluralism is not a sound basis on which to develop solutions to problems in the society above and beyond issues of distributive justice, or who gets how much of what. Pluralism's basis in the supposedly self-correcting and problem-solving techniques of interest-group competition allows for dealing with adversary-type problems but not for the redefinition and reassessment of social values. It does not foster public interventions in the name of justice. Wolff's summary of this critique is worth quoting in some detail. He writes,

> The net effect of government action is thus to weaken, rather than strengthen, the play of conflicting interests in society. The theory of pluralism . . . has a crippling effect upon government, for it warns against positive federal intervention in the name of independent principles of justice, equality or fairness. The theory says justice will emerge from the free interplay of opposed groups; the practice tends to destroy that interplay.[20]

Again,

> the theory of pluralism . . . has the effect . . . of discriminating not only against certain social groups or interests, but also against certain sorts of

---

[17] The destructive nature of American pluralism can be readily illustrated in a variety of policy areas. The job has been done admirably in regard to health care by Robert R. Alford, "The Political Economy of Health Care: Dynamics Without Change," *Politics and Society,* 2 (Winter 1972), pp. 127–164.

[18] Lowi, *The End of Liberalism.*

[19] Robert Paul Wolff, *The Poverty of Liberalism* (Boston: Beacon Press, 1968).

[20] *Ibid.,* p. 158.

proposals for the solutions of social problems. . . . The typical social problem according to pluralism is therefore some instance of distributive injustice. . . . But there are some social ills in America whose causes do not lie in a maldistribution of wealth and which cannot be cured by the techniques of pluralist politics.[21]

And finally,

Pluralism both as theory and as practice, simply does not acknowledge the possibility of wholesale reorganization of the society. By insisting on the group nature of society, it denies the existence of society-wide interests—save the purely procedural interests in preserving the system or group pressures —and the possibility of communal action in pursuit of the general good.[22]

Wolff is directing his criticism in large measure at the failure of liberal pluralism as a theoretical and practical scheme to help shape the overall dimensions of a planned and desirable society. He identifies the inability of pluralism to structure problem-solving mechanisms to deal with the most fundamental problems of the society. At the same time, others have presented convincing empirical studies in support of the contention that pluralism fails, even in its own terms, to deal with problems.[23] A common phenomenon is that the interest groups themselves come to represent the interests of an elite within that group and not the rank and file of that group. Each group operates internally on a competitive model in which the most powerful people rise to leadership positions and tend to dominate the group as much for their own interests as for the common good.

Inevitably, the agencies designed to regulate competition become captured by the most powerful of the competing actors and are no longer impartial arbiters. The regulatory agencies tend to represent the private sector rather than the public good. Inasmuch as they serve a regulatory function, they only regularize and stabilize the conditions of competition and the factors involved in production and sales. The goal becomes insuring predictable profits for business, as opposed to representing general social well-being.

From the liberal perspective, the problem of the role of the regulatory agencies is one of their capture by special interests. From a radical perspective, the underlying issue is not the misuse or misdirection of these agencies as much as their fundamental nature. Government does not serve as a transcending mechanism for achieving public well-being. These di-

---

[21] *Ibid.*, pp. 158–159.
[22] *Ibid.*, p. 160.
[23] For example, see the cases in Lowi, *The End of Liberalism;* Michael Lipsky, *Protest in City Politics* (Chicago: Rand McNally, 1970); and Henry Kariel, *The Decline of American Pluralism* (Stanford: Stanford University Press, 1961).

vergent analyses of the same observed phenomenon are important. The liberal analysis holds out the hope that the regulatory agencies might be made more responsive to the general well-being, for example, by the appointment to them of consumer representatives. The radical analysis suggests that the power of corporations to dictate the overall conditions of life must be challenged at its root and not at the level of regulatory agencies.[24] As would be expected, the liberal analysis contains its own interpretation of the failure of liberal institutions. Inasmuch as liberalism understands government as largely regulatory, it sees the failure of government as rooted in the improper balance of competitive forces. However, as capitalism itself is rooted in competition, so is the pluralist theory of government. As capitalism develops monopoly characteristics, so does government. The concept of the formation of equitable social and economic policies as rooted in competitive forces channels consideration of alternative outcomes in a way that fatally narrows the major choices the society could make.

The failure of reformism to develop a radical political analysis is, then, an essential element in its failure to reform. The reformist's preference for chipping away at problems in piecemeal fashion is unreasonable not as much because of its slowness and the modesty of its immediate goals as because of the fact that chipping away does not chip away. Reformism is an illusion. It may moderate, rearrange, or obfuscate deprivation and exploitation, but it does not deal with their well-springs in the basic dynamics of the society.

[24] See David Kettler, "Beyond Republicanism: The Socialist Critique of Political Idealism," in Marvin Surkin and Alan Wolfe (eds.), *An End to Political Science* (New York: Basic Books, 1970), pp. 34–81.

6

Social Work as Conservative Politics

INTRODUCTION

Social work theory and practice contain an overriding contradiction that minimizes the profession's ability to be of significant service. On the one hand, there can be little doubt that social work is sincere in its commitment to progressive ends, both in its concern for the welfare of individuals and in its desire to pursue larger social reforms. More often than not, it has taken a forward-looking point of view on social issues, and it has fairly consistently endorsed the right of individuals to maximum free choice and autonomy. On the other hand, as we have said, social work operates in a way that supports the most basic assumptions of the present society. In so doing, it strengthens this society's repressive characteristics in the long run—at the same time that it addresses itself to social problems in the short run. At the root of social work theory and practice are conservative, or system conserving, assumptions about individuals, the society, and the ways in which change occurs in the society. These assumptions accept what exists at present in the society as being, on the whole, both inevitable and proper. Further, they see the future of the society as being essentially like the present in its most important characteristics.

By supporting and reinforcing conservative values, social work reinforces institutions, processes, and ideologies that are destructive to human well-being. Social work practice is organized around values that represent a limited understanding of the potential of individuals and of the society. The practice that stems from these values reinforces these limitations and makes the realization of a liberated society more difficult to achieve.

This conservatism emerges from social work's too uncritical adoption of the values of the society of which it is a part. Social work as a profession is enmeshed in the society, and so it is not unreasonable that it would internalize generally accepted social values and beliefs. However, social work is also acutely aware of the regularity with which our society fails its citizens and has taken, or been given, the responsibility for dealing with some of these failings. Therefore, there is some reason to think that social work might develop a more fundamental critique of the social order. This has not happened. In trying to deal with the consequences of a destructive social system, social work has operated within the perspectives of that same system. Its failure to transcend that perspective is the reason that it has functioned in alliance with repressive forces and has not been able to be more than ameliorative.

It is not necessarily a conscious choice on the part of individual social workers or on the part of the profession to operate in the service of social conservation. Surely social work understands something of the difference between liberalism and conservatism and, by and large, has taken pride in aligning itself with the liberal camp. However, social work has not fully appreciated the contradictory impulses it contains, in part because it has failed to appreciate the limitations of the liberal position itself. It is insufficiently critical of the way in which liberalism sustains those same social institutions that must be transformed.

In this chapter and the next, the conservative politics inherent in social work theory and practice are discussed in four contexts. These are: social work's growing concern to become professionalized, social work's involvement with social policy formulation on the national level, community organization theory and practice, and social casework theory and practice. In general, each section tries to uncover and analyze the duality in social work—its social concern and its reinforcement of socially destructive values and institutions—in order to lay the base for thinking about a less contradictory, more fully committed social work theory and practice.

THE IDEOLOGY OF PROFESSIONALISM

The Debate over Professionalism

Professionalism per se is a focus of controversy in the social services. Critics argue that it has reactionary consequences and that the social services should be deprofessionalized.[1] Supporters argue that professionalism permits the professions to develop countervailing power in the society to offset sectarian political interests. In their view, it provides a base of legitimization from which to pursue positive social ends. To help analyze these positions, we will explore some aspects and consequences of the ideology inherent in professionalism, as that ideology emerges in the social professions.

From a political perspective, one of the most critical arguments in defense of professionalism is that the development of an independent set of norms and of specialized helping skills enables the profession to be more autonomous. Consequently, it is argued, professions are better able to represent humanitarian values in the face of narrow vested interests or repressive forces. The debate about community control, for example, contains within it an inherent challenge to professional autonomy. Bertram Beck, in questioning the desirability of community control, argues that the essence of professionalism centers on three principles, each of which is contradicted by the community control idea. The first is that the right to practice is based on individual merit, with the profession serving as the primary arbiter of that merit. The second is the notion of self-criticism, or the idea that the profession is responsible to itself and responds to its own criticisms before it responds to external criticisms. The third principle is moral impartiality, or a willingness to describe reality as perceived. This suggests that the profession has an internal code to which it adheres as a prior value, over and above externally imposed values.[2] Similarly, John Baird, writing in the *Journal of Education for Social Work,* cites social work's need for a professionalized base to act as a source of countervailing power to presumably less humanistic government and agency hierarchies and as a source of legitimacy for taking progressive public stands on social issues.[3]

However, these notions of the positive aspects of professionalism cannot be considered apart from the political environment in which professions exist. As a movement, a set of values and perspectives, and a form of organization of human effort, professions will inevitably come to reflect in their values, behaviors, and consequences some of the characteristics of the larger environment, even as they attempt, through professionalism, to exert countervailing force to these values. To the extent to which the

---

[1] For example, see the National Federation of Student Social Workers' (NFSSW) policy statement, adopted by the NFSSW National Conference, Chicago, March, 1970. See also Robert Reiff, "The Danger of the Techni-Pro: Democratizing the Human Service Professions," *Social Policy,* 2 (May–June 1971), pp. 62–64.

[2] Bertram M. Beck, "Community Control: A Distraction, Not an Answer," *Social Work,* 14 (October 1969), p. 17.

[3] John C. Baird, "Issues in the Selection of Growth Goals for Social Work," *Journal of Education for Social Work,* 8 (Winter 1972), p. 16.

greater entrenchment of professions enables them to function autono-
mously, and to the extent to which that autonomous functioning duplicates and supports vested interests and repressive social arrangements,
professions will serve as a further power base for privilege, working
against the best interests of the masses of people. Our understanding of
professionalism leads us to be critical of it, precisely because we find
built into the concepts and dynamics of professionalism the conservative
and limiting values and practices against which professionalism ought to
struggle. The fact that professionalism is rooted in our larger social values
and has not been sufficiently critical of them has led professions away from
their concern for social progress and service to others. The positive characteristics of professionalism, to which its defenders point, do in fact represent worthy ideals. However, they do not reflect the reality of professionalism as it finds expression in the United States today. Professionalism
has become one of the barriers to the pursuit of a more just society.

To understand how this occurs, the major dimensions of professional
ideology and their consequences must be explored. These dimensions are:
functional specificity, emotional neutrality, service to others, and impartiality.[4] In each case, we will find that a positive social impulse has been
turned in fundamentally antisocial directions as a consequence of the fact
that professionalism has developed in the context of an unfulfilling social
order.

Functional Specificity

Professions develop specific areas of competence within which their
members practice and limit the rights and obligations of the professional
relationship to those areas. The need to do so is rooted in the notion that
professions are distinguished by their command of a developed technology, that the client should be protected from the professional's involvement in his or her life in areas that go beyond that technology, and that
the professional should be protected from broad, undifferentiated demands
from the client. This quality of the professional relationship is developed
by accentuating the technological aspects of the helping situation and by
limiting the relationship to the tasks at hand. A relationship with potential

---

[4] This framework is based on Harold L. Wilensky and Charles N. Lebeaux, *Industrial Society and Social Welfare* (New York: Russell Sage Foundation, 1958),
pp. 299–303. The work of Wilensky and Lebeaux was chosen as a framework
because it discusses professionalism from the perspective of the social services and
because its analysis of the welfare state is widely known and widely accepted in
the helping professions. In turn, its analysis of professionalism is based on the
work of Talcott Parsons, as developed in *The Social System* (Glencoe, Ill.: Free
Press, 1951), pp. 433–439; and in *Essays in Sociological Theory: Pure and Applied*
(Glencoe, Ill.: Free Press, 1949), Chapter 8.

for intimacy is thus depersonalized for the sake of furthering the larger purposes of the interaction. The caseworker, for example, interviews a client on the basis of a professionalized interviewing technique and thereby circumvents difficulties that might arise if the worker's questioning were seen in the context of prying or of overpersonalization.[5]

This led to at least one problem that is already fairly widely recognized within the professions. Functional specificity creates a tendency to engage a piece of the life of the client at the risk of ignoring other problems the person might have and at the risk of seeing the person only in terms of the problem he or she has. In response to this tendency, professionals have become concerned with trying to be alert to the whole person while they deal with a particular piece of the person's situation and with trying to see the client as a person with a problem rather than only as a problem. Professions have also given attention to developing more integrated service networks and more elaborate referral systems, as well as to developing generalist practitioners to cope with this problem.

Of more concern, however, and less well recognized, is the way in which this aspect of professionalism reinforces a particular approach to problem solving which is inherent in the society as a whole, and which serves to inhibit the achievement of the very goals professionals ought to be seeking. Namely, as social problems become the concern of professionals, the professionals become involved in a problem-solving domain where problems and their solutions are seen as technical rather than as structural and political. The positive implications of limiting the focus of the professional's concern and of accentuating the technological capacities at the professional's command also limit the ways in which problems are interpreted and their solutions formulated. Solutions to problems that are seen in their more delimited aspects and are interpreted in technological terms will tend to be isolated from solutions pursued in the arena of structural social change and mass political movements in the society at large. The reason for this is that the broader changes necessary to fundamentally reorder a society must ultimately stem from massive redistribution of power and widespread changes in human consciousness. Professionalism points away from these approaches by the nature of its approach to problem solving.

As professions treat problems as concerns for the imposition of a helping technology, or for "social engineering," [6] they tend to come to see problems from the perspective of the solutions they have available. That is, as the professions become more specialized and come to depend for survival and growth on the public's acceptance of their specialized exper-

---

[5] Wilensky and Lebeaux, *Industrial Society and Social Welfare*, p. 299.
[6] *Ibid.*, p. 286.

tise, there is a natural growth in their own belief in the widespread applicability of their particular hardware. This leads to an analysis that starts with the solution rather than with the problem. In its most extreme form, this belief can be stood on its head, as it was in one attempt to explicate "the contribution of social work to the solution of social problems." This analysis suggested that a social problem be defined, from a social work point of view, as "any problem . . . capable of being helped by social work." [7] In this case, not only is social work technology seen as the answer to social problems, but no social problems are even to be acknowledged unless social work technology can respond to them.

In general, social work tends to view a wide range of social problems as potentially responsive to an increased array and intensity of social services. This analysis locates a wide range of problems and their solutions in an arena with which social work is trying to become particularly identified and in which it claims some special expertise. It defines problems as responsive to this particular kind of intervention strategy—which happens to be the very strategy that social work has at its disposal. Whatever the benefits of decent social services, it should be obvious that they are not, and cannot be, an adequate response to fundamental problems of exploitation and dehumanization in the society. Yet this is too often the suggestion that is implicit in social work's advocacy of a "services strategy."

One consequence of the struggle of the social service professions to achieve professional status is that each profession has limited the area in which it operates. This has permitted the social service professions to give more attention to developing specific expertise and to becoming identified with particular areas of competence. However, it has further accentuated the problem of substituting technology for broadly based political action. Political action that does not have clear boundaries and where sophisticated technology is not necessarily applicable cannot easily survive the quest for professionalization. [8] This is not to suggest that the quest for professional status is the only reason that social work is not engaged more widely in broad political efforts, but it is one of the reasons. The professional mandate of functional specificity is supportive of political quiescence. In a period when political quiescence is acquiescence to destructive social and economic patterns, professionalism leads to a passivity with destructive outcomes.

A final consequence of the quest for professionalization through greater functional specificity is each profession's need to identify those aspects of

[7] Nathan E. Cohen, "A Social Work Approach," in Cohen (ed.), *Social Work and Social Problems* (New York: National Association of Social Workers, 1964), p. 364.
[8] See Herbert Bisno, "How Social Will Social Work Be?" *Social Work*, 1 (April 1956), p. 18.

its practice that are unique.[9] If social work is to have a specific role, then it must define that role in relationship to psychiatry, psychology, recreation, city planning, and the other professions or semiprofessions that touch its boundaries. The need to delineate a distinct role in order to achieve the status of a profession has contributed to interprofessional rivalry by encouraging each profession to find and promote its unique contribution rather than simply contributing, in a unique way or not, to social well-being. A critical social analysis suggests that cooperative mass efforts are required to achieve a more satisfying society. Consequently, any social tendencies with divisive impact will perpetuate the continuance of the organizational forms with which we now live.

Emotional Neutrality

This mandate of professionalism specifies that the worker practice objectivity by becoming aware of, and controlling, the degree of his or her emotional involvement with the client. While this may be difficult to accomplish, especially for the beginner, its achievement has been said to represent the development of "the essence of 'professional self.'" [10]

This aspect of professionalism may be especially important for the development of a profession like social work, in which the helping technology tends to be contained in the interpersonal exchange, as opposed to medicine, for example, where pharmaceuticals are involved, or law where technical procedures involved in access to the court may be important. The primary tool of the social worker is his or her own person. If the worker is not emotionally self-disciplined, then the possibility increases that the interpersonal exchange could not be differentiated from the interchange of any two people and, consequently, the expertise of the professional could not be publicly identifiable. It follows, as one recent text on interviewing in social work has pointed out, that the social work literature "generally counsels against the worker's emotional response in the interview, instead suggesting objectivity, detachment, and affective neutrality." [11]

One of the consequences of this aspect of professionalism is that it asks professionals to deny, or at least to repress, a part of their own emotional experience. It asks them to discipline their spontaneous responses as persons in favor of conditioned responses as professionals.

[9] This struggle is discussed in Lydia Rapoport, "In Defense of Social Work: An Examination of Stress in the Profession," *Social Service Review*, 34 (March 1960), p. 68. See also Carol H. Meyer, *Social Work Practice: A Response to the Urban Crisis* (New York: Free Press, 1970), pp. 25–34.

[10] Wilensky and Lebeaux, *Industrial Society and Social Welfare*, p. 301.

[11] Alfred Kadushin, *The Social Work Interview* (New York: Columbia University Press, 1972), p. 53.

Whatever the positive functions of such self-discipline, and undoubtedly there are some, this pattern replicates and supports a similar pattern in the society at large, namely, an ethic of self-discipline about expressing, and ultimately even knowing, one's own feelings.

In general, it seems to be the case that people are encouraged to isolate and even to suppress their emotions as they fulfill various life roles as students, workers, family members, and so on. Students, for example, are encouraged to think analytically, but not to connect the material before them to the major emotional dynamics in their lives. Inherent in the typical classroom is a suppression of affect and a reward system that encourages intellectualized learning. Similarly, the survival needs of many workers dictate that they not feel, in any profound way, the emotional poverty of their work situations. However, if people were to get more in touch with their own feelings, expressing them and sharing them with one another, they might discover a deeply shared commonality in their lives. This discovery could lead to cooperative efforts to deal with common problems that could have radical impact on the society. To encourage people to deny and compartmentalize their emotions, therefore, serves to maintain a public myth about the acceptability of the social order, since it encourages the belief that the pain people experience is idiosyncratic. The professional who controls his or her emotional reactions to the client reinforces this myth in his or her own life and in the life of the client.

One further consequence of worker objectivity may be to permit the worker to keep enough distance from enormous problems to allow him or her to continue practicing without experiencing despair in the face of a stream of serious and depressing problems presented by clients. Simultaneously, this serves to isolate the professional from the fullest awareness of the amount of pain that exists in the society and the relative powerlessness of the professional to deal with it. And yet, unless more people come face to face with a realization of the despair produced by this society and the full extent of our inability to alleviate that despair in the old ways, we will not be able to develop realistic plans for change. Emotional neutrality, then, is a conservatizing influence because it tends to keep us from being fully aware of the profundity of the tasks before us.

Service to Others

The essence of this aspect of professionalism involves the ideal of service or the professional's devotion to the client's interests.[12] This service takes the form of the professional's making some resource available

---

[12] Wilensky and Lebeaux, *Industrial Society and Social Welfare*, p. 302.

to the client—time, energy, and technical skill. At least three undesirable consequences stem from this norm.

Service to others is rooted in the idea that the professional has an expertise not available to the client. This may in fact be the case. A consequence of the unequal distribution of expertise, however, is that professional expertise applied in service to others tends to produce inequality in the totality of the helping relationship. In fact, Beck has argued that without inequality "there would be no social worker-client relationship." [13] In what ways does expertise in service to others lead to inequality, and why is this undesirable?

One interpretation of inequality in the professional relationship is difference in technical ability. Surely, not all people have, can have, or should have the same knowledge and skill in this society or in any society. As one aspect of professionalism, specialization in itself can have positive consequences by allowing people to more fully develop a particular capacity to help others. (Professional groups tend to hoard expertise, creating an artificial condition of scarcity, but that is another problem of specialization.) Unfortunately, the greater knowledge and skill of the professional in a particular area of expertise tends to lead to a generalized inequality and nonmutuality in the helping relationship. Rather than simply making the professional's expertise a tool available to the client as a resource in problem solving, the professional also tends to have a disproportionate influence in defining the tasks and goals to which the expertise is applied. This may not be inevitable in a helping relationship, but may be a consequence of a more pervasive tendency in our society to generalize from specific differences between people serving different roles into hierarchies that lock people into relatively rigid places in the social system. This general problem of inequality is surely aggravated in cases where the professionals are middle-class persons and the clients are working class.

Among the consequences of generalized inequality in the helping relationship is the dependency it creates in the client (with its corresponding reduction of client energy available for problem solving), the greater likelihood that the professional's point of view will be imposed on the client, and a reinforcement of a larger social ethic that suggests that, to get what one needs in life, one must accept a measure of subservience in hierarchical systems.

A second problem deriving from the notion of service to others is that it suggests that the client's problems can be alleviated by the intervention of an outsider. It suggests that the solution to the problem rests in something the client needs help to get. This is both true and not true. What

[13] Beck, "Community Control," p. 18.

the client can get is a service. However, as was suggested when the technological base of professionalism was considered, the profession's goal of serving others moves both the professional and the client away from the consideration of broad cooperative efforts at creating fundamental change. It places the solution of social problems in the context of the private bargaining situation in which the client tries to personally secure those resources that can make life easier through some kind of purchasing arrangement or, at least, through a private negotiation. As such, it focuses away from the nature of the society at large or from necessary changes in the client's environment that go beyond what any one person can provide for another.

Third, the notion of service to others tends to create a focus on what is unique about the client's problems rather than on what is common about the client's and professional's situations. It focuses on what the client needs or on what clients in general need and leads to a separation of worker and client both conceptually and programmatically.[14] Despite the fact that liberal theorists and practitioners have attempted to align themselves with their clients and to be nonjudgmental, the very fact that a client is the focus of intervention is a very powerful message to the client about where responsibility is seen to lie. The diagnosis is made of the client, not the social structure. This has been described as clinicalism, or "social work's unique contribution to the ideology of the white man's burden."[15] It is characterized by the presumption of damage to the client, which must be repaired by expert intervention with the client. The underlying assignment of blame is not modified by an intervention strategy that focuses on groups or communities as opposed to individuals, or by an emphasis on self-help or community development as opposed to therapy. In either case, the client is led to understand that the problem and the solution to the problem rests with him or her.

It may be the case that some people labeled clients have unique problems and that special categories of analysis and special strategies of intervention need to be developed to help with these problems. However, this focus simultaneously encourages professionals and clients to look at that part of the client's experience that is unique to the client and where the client may have a special feeling of having failed. It focuses away from, or fails to identify, what may be the far more critical problems that we all have in common.[16]

[14] See Carolyn Dillon, "The Professional Name Game," *Social Casework,* 50 (June 1969), pp. 337–340.
[15] Henry Miller, "Social Work in the Black Ghetto: The New Colonialism," *Social Work,* 14 (July 1969), p. 70.
[16] Harry Stack Sullivan identified the same dynamic operating in psychiatry. A recent discussion of his work highlighted his concern that "physicians and nurses were trained primarily to do things to the patient rather than be things to the

Once again, this professional mandate supports a tendency to compartmentalize ourselves and our problems. While we all have special problems, we will not be able to take concerted action on broad and common social problems if we fail to identify the ways in which we are similarly influenced by the society. The notion of service to others, while enlightened on the one hand, is destructive on the other hand in its failure to see the need for all of us to join together to deal with our shared dilemmas.

Impartiality

This professional norm specifies the desirability of serving people impartially, that is, without regard to their race, religion, politics, or personal traits.[17] In a larger sense, its concern is that a professional not serve any sectarian political interest groups or be captured by any ideology. Rather, professions should stand above and beyond these differences, on the basis of a generally enlightened perspective, and be equally available to all people.

No issue is taken here with the notion that race, creed, sex, and so on, should be irrelevant as a basis for allocating services. These should be irrelevant criteria. However, this mandate, while desirable, carries with it a limited notion of fairness. This limitation stems from this society's professed belief in the liberal notion that the standard of equality is equality of opportunity, that is, that people have, or should have, an equal right to compete for resources. Civil rights laws of all sorts, of which the professional mandate for impartiality is a reflection, have sought to ensure such equality.

However, to define equality in terms of equality of opportunity is to overlook several important factors. One of these is that people start with important differences in the bases on which they seek to use services or any other resources. To guarantee equality of opportunity without assuring equality in the places from which people start to compete is to assure that equal opportunity will mean unequal outcomes.

Furthermore, to define political justice and a progressive professional stance in terms of equal opportunity ignores the political biases built into services once people get to them. Our analysis thus far suggests that the professional services contain a conservative politics. Equal access to them

---

patient, [and] thus were often led to consider the patient as somehow having more differences than likenesses to themselves. Such an attitude was unjustified in any medical specialty, he felt, but particularly in psychiatry." David Elkind, " 'Good Me' or 'Bad Me'—The Sullivan Approach to Personality," *New York Times Magazine* (September 24, 1972), p. 18.

17 Wilensky and Lebeaux, *Industrial Society and Social Welfare*, p. 301.

means equal access to a conservative and conservatizing process. To mask this reality with rhetoric about impartiality can be politically misleading.

The Social Work Code of Ethics

The social work Code of Ethics concretizes the tenets of professionalism for the social work profession.[18] An analysis of the Code highlights the ways in which a conservative perspective permeates social work through social work's understanding of professionalism.

As would be expected, the Code explicitly identifies social work practice as based on and requiring technical expertise. "It requires mastery of a body of knowledge and skill gained through professional education and experience." The end sought is the performance of a service "dedicated to the welfare of mankind." By definition, the means of achieving "the welfare of mankind," which would have to be thought of as a revolutionary outcome, is the "provision of service." A broad social process of the most profound magnitude is thus located by the professional code in an arena where technical solutions are called for which require technical training to accomplish.

Similarly, the mandates of professionalism urge the professional worker to separate his or her personal situation from professional practice and to take a pledge of self-denial by giving "precedence to . . . professional responsibility over . . . personal interests." While this proscription has the goal, in part, of mandating against the use of social work for personal aggrandizement, it also has the effect of placing the problems of the social worker apart from those of clients. The worker who identifies in his or her own life a manifestation of the same problem appearing in a client's life, who recognizes that neither of them will solve the problem in the absence of their joint efforts to change the society, and who takes action on that basis would be engaging in behavior that might be labeled as unprofessional.

Likewise, the social worker must pledge to "practice social work within the recognized knowledge and competence of the profession [and to] distinguish clearly between [his or her] statements and actions as an individual and as a representative of an organization." In its conservative implications, this plank of the Code serves to isolate and contain the worker within a limited vision of the role of the social worker. The worker must operate within the boundaries of the professional knowledge

[18] "The Code of Ethics," Adopted by the Delegate Assembly of the National Association of Social Workers, October 13, 1960, amended April 11, 1967. Reprinted in the *Encyclopedia of Social Work,* "Profession of Social Work: Code of Ethics" (New York: National Association of Social Workers, 1971), pp. 958–959.

base, which can only reinforce the isolation of one profession from another, inhibit innovation, and help assure that the work of each individual professional will be controlled by the mandates of the common wisdom. Additionally, the worker must fragment his or her life into one segment lived as an individual and one lived as an organizational representative. This reinforces internal schism and encourages the professional to deny personal responsibility for agency policy. Furthermore, the social worker is pledged to in-group loyalty over transcending standards of social justice ("treat with respect the findings, views and actions of colleagues and use appropriate channels to express judgement on these matters"), to elitism ("the principle that professional practice requires professional education"), and to a conservative version of social progress which is rooted in a dedication to interest-group competition ("I regard as my primary obligation the welfare of the individual or group served").

In summary, professionalism, as it has emerged in the context of our society, is not a progressive force. It has conservative implications for social change and destructive potential for the professional worker as a person. While the ideals of professionalism are theoretically worthy as they concern helping people achieve a more satisfying life, the specifics of professionalism in practice run counter to the notion of facilitating social well-being. What this suggests is that the consideration and analysis of professionalism—as is the case for the consideration of any aspect of the social services—cannot occur in isolation from an awareness of the larger political and social consequences. If it does, the risk is great that our understanding of what is going on around us will be seriously limited and even distorted.

SOCIAL REFORM—SOCIAL WORK STYLE

Movement Without Change

Social work has a long-standing concern with social reform through the vehicle of social policy formulation at the national level. This involvement was stimulated by a number of factors. One of the most important of these was the recognition that the one-to-one casework approach could be supplemented, if not rendered unnecessary in some cases, by appropriate national legislation which would get to the causal factors underlying the crises of individuals.

While social work's involvement with social legislation and its identification with reformist forces have been more or less strong at various times since the Progressive Era, such involvement has always been a part of the profession. Of course, general periods of political retreat in this country—for example, the two world wars and the 1950s—were also periods of greater political quiescence in social work. Social work and social workers were involved in political life during these times, but, as would be expected, they were involved in a way that was influenced by the overall political climate.

Even when social work has been more active, the dominant thrust of its reform efforts has carried conservative implications. To understand the inherent conservatism of these efforts, it is insufficient simply to argue that social work has not been concerned with reform at all. As indicated, it has been concerned. One could argue, as some do, that social work could and should do more. It is necessary to look more deeply into the nature of the efforts that have been made because, even where there has been activity, conservative politics have infused social work's theory and practice.

Both the agendas for reform and the manner in which reform is attempted contain and play out these politics. Change itself may not necessarily be progressive; it may be progressive only in the more limited sense that it makes a fundamentally unhealthy environment somewhat more acceptable. This kind of reformism may obscure the underlying issues and may even help to maintain destructive patterns. In fact, we will see that social work's agendas for reform have tended to be the kind that, even when achieved, have provided support for conservative forces in the society.

Similarly, the change strategies that social work has employed in pursuing its social policy concerns have contained a conservative politics. The problem is not simply whether social work has been effective in achieving any particular reforms by a given strategy; the problem is also the political message contained in that strategy. Social work's strategies have been of a sort that have built on the contacts and expertise of the few people at the highest level of the profession's hierarchy, who negotiate with the powers that be. Whatever the particular outcomes of the negotiation process, the process itself has not encouraged the notion or the reality of mass organization as a requisite for fundamental social change. It has suggested a change process that disengages the masses of people. It reinforces the notion of social change as a technological process in which experts and the powerful few are the guiding forces.

Similarly, this model of reform fails to use one piece of political work to build political consciousness, commitment, and mass organization for the next effort. Each effort, therefore, starts anew with the same overall weighting of advantage against the pursuit of justice, since prior campaigns were not used as vehicles to achieve both particular demands and mass mobilization. In this section, these dynamics will be traced over a number of historical periods.

The History

Social work's involvement in the charity organization of the late 1800s contributed to the formation of an agenda and style for later efforts at policy development. It is useful, therefore, to look at some of the early experiences, although they were not specifically oriented to social policy development at the national level.

The Charity Organization Society (COS) represented an early landmark in the development of an organized approach to almsgiving. It was a vehicle for the wealthy to express the variety of concerns they felt about the poor. As such, it embodied the general philosophy of the upper classes toward the social order as a whole and their relationship to the lower classes in particular. COS workers, forerunners of modern social workers, implemented the Society's policies. Their work and the points of view they developed became one of the streams of thought and tradition influencing the profession. Though the efforts of these early workers were largely directed toward individuals, the political philosophy and the strategies they represented have carried over into the arena of social policy development. However, in order to identify these influences in the present, it is first necessary to clarify the perspectives that the COS represented.

A number of historians have analyzed the vision and the role of the COS on matters of social and class relationships. Their work highlights the extent to which organized charity, from its earliest manifestations, operated with an eye toward maintaining existing class relationships. The dynamic of social concern within a framework of social conservation is critical in the COS, as it is critical in social work's reform efforts in general. Lubove has pointed out that

> No charity organization principles ranked higher in importance than the coordination of the community's welfare services and the stimulation of volunteer friendly visiting, or personal contact between rich and poor as a substitute for alms. . . . Working under the supervision of the central office, the district committee or conference hoped to establish itself as a focal point for "neighborly" association between classes.[19]

In other words, organized philanthropy, from the outset, substituted softer services (friendly visiting or counseling) for harder services (cash) and attempted to mitigate and obscure, without fundamentally influencing, the reality of social differences rooted in real class differences. The historian Marvin Gettleman, elaborating this point, argued that the "simultaneous recognition and evasion of the problem of social classes [was] the domi-

[19] Roy Lubove, *The Professional Altruist* (New York: Atheneum, 1969), p. 1.

nant characteristic of the formative years of the American profession and institution of social work." [20]

Charity workers tended to deny or were simply not consciously aware that they represented privileged interests in their work. They preferred to view their efforts as neighborly helping. Their analysis of their role was neither broad nor deep. It was not broad in that it did not place friendly visiting in a larger context which could comprehend the total situation of the poor in the society and the interests of wealthy sponsors in supporting charity efforts, and it was not deep in that it did not penetrate the roots of the practice of friendly visiting. It looked at the surface of the relationship between workers and clients. Workers may well have felt and expressed genuine concern for the poor without understanding the coercive nature of their practice and the fear, which lay at the root of the practice, that the poor might mobilize politically.

Gettleman has explored the intimate relationship between the COS and the business world and capitalist values. A major aim of the COS was to reforge the social ties that bound the society together, with the intention of bringing the poor back into their rightful place in the whole community. The COS, directed by the leading business people of the day, operated on the basis of a publicly stated ideology of protecting the rich from the poor. Furthermore, it operated with an explicit understanding that the charity movement was an "answer" to socialist and communist doctrines and was in fact a response to even more modest demands for reform. Intentionally or not, charity acted to perpetuate the existing class structure by pressuring the poor into accepting and remaining at "appropriate" positions in the labor force and adopting conforming values and life styles. While it is true that at the turn of the century the COS focused increasingly on the social conditions that hindered advancement of the poor, rather than on the "alleged individual causes of poverty," Gettleman has suggested that

> Even in their more collectivist stage, charity workers (and other reformers in the Progressive Era) specified a life style for the poor which involved what Jane Addams called "impossible bourgeois standards." While recognizing in practice the gulf between social classes, . . . the Charity Organization Society movement affirmed its bourgeois vision of a classless society dominated by the norms of middle-class gentility.[21]

There are a number of ways, then, in which the COS set the stage for a conservative version of social reform, as later practiced by social work. It suggested that change, while possible, is best understood to occur

[20] Marvin E. Gettleman, "Charity and Social Classes in the United States, 1874–1900," *American Journal of Economics and Sociology,* 22 (April–June 1963), p. 313.
[21] *Ibid.,* p. 422.

through the personal efforts of the individual to achieve private gains in his or her own circumstances and not through the modification of the social order. It also suggested that powerless and underprivileged people could count on those with the most power and privilege to make social arrangements for the well-being of all. Autonomous movements among the disenfranchised were considered simply disruptive.

The Progressive reformers from the next period of social work's involvement in policy development provide further illustration of the theme of social concern and reform within a system-preserving perspective. Jane Addams, a leading member of this group, embraced a broad range of concerns in her lifetime and engaged in a committed struggle for change on a variety of fronts. While she never actively endorsed socialist principles, she had socialist leanings and showed marked sympathy for socialists and socialist causes. As such, she recognized the existence of class conflict as a reality of capitalist society and was critical of the earlier COS approaches for their denial of this fact of social life. However, she did not feel that class conflict was an inevitable part of the change process and developed her own strategies of social change around her belief in the possibilities of cooperation among contending groups.[22] The political activities of the settlement house progressives, consequently, centered on lobbying, "selecting candidates, drawing up party pronouncements, advising officials and serving on public boards." [23] They were able to engage in these activities with some effectiveness for several reasons. On the basis of their own comfortable and even privileged backgrounds, they could establish connections with political and business leadership. Furthermore, the goals they pursued did not represent a challenge to the overall distribution of resources or to class relationships. They neither built mass organizations nor created independent leadership which might have represented a threat to established sources of power. Nor did they challenge capitalism itself. They chose to work to mitigate the effects of capitalist institutions, as well as they could, through child labor and public health laws, and so on. Although desirable in themselves, these reforms simultaneously helped to rationalize and stabilize the emerging industrial order of the day.

Clarke Chambers has described the same dynamics at work in the period between the Progressive Era and the New Deal.[24] The National Consumer's League, for example, "placed its faith in the intelligence and good will of the American people and in their desire to right social

[22] Merle Curti, "Jane Addams on Human Nature," *Journal of the History of Ideas,* 22 (April–June 1961), p. 248.

[23] Richard Wade, "Foreword," in Allen F. Davis, *Spearheads for Reform* (New York: Oxford University Press, 1967), p. viii.

[24] Clarke A. Chambers, *Seedtime of Reform* (Ann Arbor: University of Michigan Press, 1967).

wrongs," and "deliberately had worked through research and study, publicity and propaganda, to educate the public to the sources and consequences of social evil." [25] In fact, the leaders of the period often characterized themselves as "social engineers." [26]

The New Deal period contains somewhat more contradictory impulses. On the one hand, rank-and-file caucuses of social workers emerged during this period with a militant point of view about their own role, both as professional workers and as a part of the working class. The members of these caucuses were often active in grass-roots organizing efforts among clients and were vigorous allies of the Communist Party–organized Unemployed Councils and the Socialist Party's Workers' Alliance, organizations that were in some ways militant forerunners of the National Welfare Rights Organization which emerged in the late 1960s.[27]

The importance of these groups and this point of view should not be underestimated because of their broad influence at the time, which is generally unacknowledged in the profession's history of itself, and because of the radical tradition they helped to establish in social work. At the same time, they did not represent a dominant point of view and were no more successful in their radical efforts than was the radical movement as a whole in the 1930s.

On the other hand, the mainstream of social work thought tended to conform, in this period, to the profession's earlier models for reform. The fact that the New Deal programs represented a shift away from social work's control of the welfare territory in the private agency arena created opposition to New Deal programs in an important part of the profession.[28] In general, however, most social workers were disengaged from the struggles of this period, leaving the fighting to the few well-known social welfare elite who had gained important positions in the political hierarchies close to Roosevelt.[29]

[25] *Ibid.*, p. 4.

[26] *Ibid.*, p. 87.

[27] Some material on the rank-and-file caucuses is found in Bertha Reynold's autobiography, *An Uncharted Journey* (New York: Citadel Press, 1963), especially Chapter 10, "Vitality," pp. 153–169; and in the militant social welfare journal of the times, *Social Work Today*. For a discussion of the Unemployed Councils and Worker's Alliance, see Alice Brophy and George Hallowitz, *Pressure Groups and the Relief Administration in New York City*, Professional Project for the New York School of Social Work, New York, April 8, 1937.

[28] See Blanche D. Coll, *Perspectives in Public Welfare: A History* (Washington, D.C.: Government Printing Office, 1969), especially, "The Movement for Social Insurance," pp. 74–87; and Roy Lubove, *The Struggle for Social Security, 1900–1935* (Cambridge, Mass.: Harvard University Press, 1968), especially Chapter 2 "Social Drift and Social Planning," pp. 25–44.

[29] See Bertram M. Beck, "Shaping America's Social Welfare Policy," in Alfred J. Kahn, *Issues in American Social Work* (New York: Columbia University Press, 1959), p. 200.

Conservative thinking was not only reflected in the style of disengagement, discrete lobbying, and reliance on the activities of a select leadership, but also in the particular kinds of reforms that most social workers tended to support. Of course, in the years of the Depression, there was a range of points of view within social work, as within the society at large, about the kinds of changes that ought to be undertaken. On the more radical side were calls for using the crisis of the times as a springboard into a major new social order.[30] More generally, the goals were pump priming and more short-term ameliorative efforts to restore the status quo ante.

As Nathan Cohen has indicated, "The New Deal's philosophy was not that of the Marxists or Socialists, but that of the 'liberal capitalist economists.' "[31] The positions taken by social workers indicated their acceptance of this perspective. In each case, social work rejected the more radical alternatives and stuck to endorsements of the kinds of programs that became the background of our present arrangement of social policy in the United States.

A review of the mainstream of social work's stances in the early 1930s, as presented in *The Compass* (journal of the American Association of Social Workers, a forerunner of the National Association of Social Workers), makes this clear. For example, a 1934 AASW conference on "Government Objectives for Social Work" supported government actions to that time by "paying tribute to Congress and to the federal administration for recognizing its obligation to meet the needs of people in this emergency. . . . In carrying out this program, we believe the best traditions of social work have been utilized."[32] Social workers, as Harry Lurie said in 1932, have tended to accept the status quo of political and economic

---

[30] For example, see Jerome Davis, "The Consumers' and the Producers' Cooperative Movement and the Social Workers," *Proceedings, National Conference of Social Work*, Detroit (Chicago: University of Chicago Press, 1934), pp. 408–417; Karl Borders, "Social Workers and a New Social Order," *Proceedings, National Conference of Social Work*, Detroit (Chicago: University of Chicago Press, 1934), pp. 590–596; Rev. Abba Hillel Silver, "The Crisis in Social Work," *Proceedings, National Conference of Social Work*, Philadelphia (Chicago: University of Chicago Press, 1932), pp. 53–64; Bertha Reynolds, "Social Workers and Civil Rights," *Social Work Today*, 7 (June–July 1940), pp. 9–11; Mary Van Kleek, "Common Goals of Labor and Social Work," *Social Work Today*, 2 (October 1934), pp. 4–8; Mary Van Kleek, "Social Work in the Economic Crisis," *Proceedings, National Conference of Social Work*, Montreal (Chicago: University of Chicago Press, 1935), pp. 64–77.

[31] Nathan E. Cohen, *Social Work in the American Tradition* (New York: Dryden Press, 1958), p. 169.

[32] "The Conference on Governmental Objectives for Social Work," *The Compass*, 15 (March 1934), p. 7.

processes as fundamentally satisfactory.[33] It is true that when Roosevelt moved to cut back on the Civil Works Program in 1934, social workers reacted negatively.[34] Nonetheless, social workers in that period were not able to transcend the general assumptions of the perspectives presented by government about the problems of the Depression and so acted, when they did act, in support of the more conventional point of view.

The Present

The same pattern continued through the 1940s and into the present period. Social work leadership has continued to be closeted in bureaucratic cubbyholes, lobbying quietly on behalf of its version of progressive legislation and operating in a "depersonalized role as an interpreter of issues." [35] This behind-doors activity surfaces on occasion in the form of more or less admirable statements of policy goals by the better-known social welfare professionals. Typically, however, these statements are distinguished by the absence of significant analysis indicating a place for inputs by the people to be affected by those changes and by the lack of strategies for achieving the goals announced. By implication, the change strategy is the publication of the policy statement itself, or the quiet bureaucratic infighting done by the social welfare establishment to achieve these goals.[36] The policy issues are not analyzed in terms of the contending parties involved or the political pressures that would have to be generated to achieve change, but in terms of desiderata, the realization of which the average person can do little to facilitate.

For example, in July 1972, the central offices of the National Association of Social Workers issued a document entitled "Statement and Fact Sheet

---

[33] Cited in Wilbur I. Newstetter, "Second Thoughts on the Washington Conference," *The Compass*, 15 (April 1934), p. 9.

[34] For example, see "Recommendations of the Committee on Current Relief Programs," *The Compass*, 15 (May 1934), p. 7.

[35] Carol H. Meyer, *Social Work Practice: A Response to the Urban Crisis* (New York: Free Press, 1970), p. 22.

[36] This pattern, as it plays out in the public welfare arena, has been documented by Gilbert Steiner, in *Social Insecurity: The Politics of Welfare* (Chicago: Rand McNally, 1960), especially Chapter 6, "Influence, Information and Innovation," pp. 141–175. For the curiously apolitical way in which the antipoverty programs of the 1960s emerged, see Peter Marris and Martin Rein, *Dilemmas of Social Reform* (New York: Atherton, 1967); Sar A. Levitan, *The Great Society's Poor Law* (Baltimore: Johns Hopkins, 1969); and, James L. Sundquist, "Origins of the War on Poverty," in James L. Sundquist (ed.), *On Fighting Poverty* (New York: Basic Books, 1969), pp. 6–33. For the case of Medicare, see Theodore R. Marmor, *Doctors, Politics and Health Insurance for the Aged: The Enactment of Medicare*, Institute for Research on Poverty, Discussion Paper No. 18 (Madison, Wis.: University of Wisconsin, 1968).

on Public Welfare." [37] Both the criteria for reform and the suggested strategies contained in the document were consistent with the past history of social work's policy involvement. As a general position, the Association indicated its support for "a national income policy with a guaranteed annual income," surely a desirable general goal. In developing the specifics, however, no national income policy was in fact detailed, at least inasmuch as that suggests an overall national pattern of income distribution. Rather, a floor for the most poor was suggested, consistent in that respect with thirty years of social work struggle for higher benefit minimums in public programs. The floor suggested was $3,960 for a family of four, with a timetable (unspecified) for bringing the floor up to the Bureau of Labor Statistics' lower level of living for a family of four, then at $7,100 a year. This statement of policy represents a more generous position than would be supported in many circles, but is well within the range of policy alternatives that could easily be accommodated without altering the structure and dynamics of the system at large. At the same time, the action strategy suggested was the Association's plea for "all citizens to write their federal, state and local representatives and call for their support of true welfare reform based on the criteria listed above." Suffice it to say, the strategy of letter writing neither builds mass movements nor carries much likelihood of bringing about a significant reordering of relationships in the society.

The problem of attaining adequate retirement income through public programs provides further illustration of this pattern. Social Security experts are constantly exploring new possibilities for benefit increases based on life expectancy tables, the ratio of the number of present retirees to present wage earners, anticipated rises in the Social Security base tax amount, and so on. On these bases, adjustments are made, and Congress frequently legislates Social Security benefit increases, generally with the approval of all, and timed to politically benefit the incumbent party.

The problem of retirement income has been largely contained, in terms of public understanding and the political process, in debates over financially responsible manipulations of the Social Security system. The result has been some improvement in the economic situation of the elderly, but they continue to exist among the most generally deprived groups in our society. Simultaneously, attention has been shifted away from alternative approaches to income security for the aged. A basis for a more significant approach, for example, might question the relationship of adequate income during aging to the earlier relationship to the labor market. How-

---

[37] National Association of Social Workers, "Statement and Fact Sheet on Public Welfare" (New York: National Association of Social Workers, July 1972) mimeographed.

ever, if the labor market–income support relationship becomes attenuated for the aged, other groups might also demand support on the basis of their need rather than on the basis of their ability or luck in relation to the labor market.

This approach to social policy development has been increasingly confronted within the more progressive segment of social work. For example, Cloward and Piven developed an analysis of the welfare situation that was specifically linked to a mass-based theory of intervention,[38] in contrast to the COS's friendly visiting approach, the bureaucratic manipulation of welfare regulations, or the presentation of a well-meaning position paper. In a now well-known formulation, Cloward and Piven identified the fact that large numbers of potentially eligible welfare clients were not on the welfare rolls. They hypothesized that an effort to enroll them could lead to an overload of the welfare system that might cause its collapse and replacement by a new system. This analysis was rooted not in idealized desiderata or in a concern for system stability, but in the observation of a failed promise and a potential stress point in the system. The pursuit of this analysis would necessarily involve mass education and organization and a concerted challenge to a major welfare bureaucracy.

Similarly, a variety of analyses related to the needs of black people have been generated which consistently attempt to link analysis and intervention strategy. Perhaps in the present period this became most clear for social work at the several National Conferences of Social Work at the turn of this decade, which were marked by disruption and challenge to the established order of the Conference and to the established leadership of social work. As one summary of the 1970 Conference gently put it, in commenting on the floor response to a major address by Wilbur Cohen, former Secretary of the Department of Health, Education and Welfare and a social worker active in reform since the 1930s, "those who chose to respond directly to Dr. Cohen's address focused their response on the need for action, pointing up the lack of such an approach in Dr. Cohen's speech." [39] As a representative of one of the minority groups raising challenge suggested more sharply, "Dr. Cohen's faith in change through the ballot box, through the courts, through the development of adequate services, through jobs, through financial assistance, and through health insurance coverage, ignores our experience." [40] The kind of analysis and commitment represented in these comments does not reflect a major

[38] Richard Cloward and Frances Fox Piven, "A Strategy to End Poverty," *Nation* (May 2, 1966), pp. 510–517.
[39] T. George Silcott, "Social Welfare Priorities—A Minority View," *National Conference of Social Work*, 1970 (New York: Columbia University Press, 1970), p. 142.
[40] *Ibid.*, p. 143.

stream in social work thinking. However, it indicates that not all social workers are willing to accept political conformity and politically neutralized agendas for change.

SUMMARY

Over the years since it first attained a public identity, social work has been concerned about large questions of social reform at the level of national social policy development. Undoubtedly, it has not shown sufficient concern, and that is an important issue. We have suggested here, however, that greater attention to reform, as social work has understood and pursued it, would not be likely to make a very fundamental contribution to our overall well-being.

The pursuit of reform in itself is not necessarily progressive. The kinds of changes in social policies that have tended to occur in this country have been of the sort that gave with one hand and took with the other. They provided some benefits to people in need, and they alleviated some real deprivation. At the same time, they have worked within and strengthened social structures and institutions that perpetrate the worst kinds of conditions of deprivation. Social work, in its concerns for reform, has not grappled with this contradiction.

Similarly, social work has developed strategies for reform that have been politically neutralized and neutralizing. Its strategies have reflected its agendas; that is, they have operated within the society's present structure, with insufficient concern for a fundamental reordering of things. As a consequence, the strategies have not worked toward the politicization and mobilization of new constituencies and have perpetrated the illusion of the possibilities of progress arranged and negotiated within the confines of liberal politics.

It is not enough, then, to look only at the fact that social work has had concern for social reform as we try to evaluate the political meaning of this professioin. It is necessary to look more closely at both the what and how of that concern to get a clear perspective on the political purposes which have been served. When we do so, it becomes more clear that social work has represented a conservatized version of social reform such that success, when it has come, has not advanced the pursuit of a more fundamentally just society.

7

Community Organization
and Social Casework:
The Containment of Change

INTRODUCTION

This chapter continues the discussion developed in Chapter 6 by focusing on the conservative politics inherent in the theory and practice of community organization and social casework. We also examine some of the ways in which the social work profession channels and contains practical dialogue within the liberal-conservative framework to the exclusion of the development and dissemination of a radical perspective on theory and practice.

The practice of community organization has been, in part, explicitly identified with the effort to engage in the processes of creating social change. When social work has been criticized for conservatism, both from its own progressive wing and from outside groups, it could and did point to community organization as the place where reform efforts were said to be lodged. However, we demonstrate in this section that community organization, like social policy development, has operated in service of social adjustment not social change. It has accepted the fundamental assumptions of the society without serious challenge and so has served conservative political and ideological functions.

To fully understand community organization's conservative implications, it is necessary to explore some facets of the notion of planned social change. Community organization has rested on implicit and explicit assumptions about the ways in which social processes can be influenced by the self-conscious activities of individuals and groups. The assumptions on which community organization has operated are not unique to it, but are drawn from theories and beliefs about planned change prevalent in the society at large—and particularly from those that nucleate around the social services. These theories and beliefs must be examined if the inherent politics of community organization are to be clarified.

Planned Change

The notion that people could and should intervene in a deliberate way in the social order to bring about alterations in that order is not new. At the turn of this century there were major ideological debates about the appropriateness of such intervention. But by the height of the Progressive Era and even more firmly with the influence of Keynesian economics and the New Deal, the issue of the general appropriateness of such intervention was no longer at stake.[1] Planned change itself, however, can be and mean many things. Despite an assumption that sometimes seems to pervade community organization, planned change is not necessarily progressive. In fact, the dominant mode of planned change in this society has often served to retard the kinds of major changes that need to take place, as a consequence of the kinds of agendas it has pursued and the ways in which it has pursued them.

One of the major characteristics of planned change as it has occurred in the context of the welfare state programs in the United States has been isolation of change processes from the arena of social and economic conflict and the location of these processes in the existing institutionalized structures and dynamics of society. In *Beyond the Welfare State,* Gunnar Myrdal offers a clear interpretation of the way in which the coming of the welfare state obviates the necessity of social conflict as a mechanism for producing social well-being. Myrdal suggests that

> One interesting aspect of this gradual perfection of the modern democratic Welfare State is that many divisions of opinion, once of burning importance, now tend to fade away, or to change character and thereby to become less important. . . .

[1] For a review of some of these issues, see Warren G. Bennis, Kenneth D. Benne, and Robert Chin (eds.), *The Planning of Change* (New York: Holt, Rinehart and Winston, 1961), "Introduction," pp. 1–17.

The examples I have given . . . point to the increasing political harmony that has come to exist much more generally between all the citizens in the advanced Welfare State. The internal political debate in those countries is becoming increasingly technical in character, ever more concerned with detailed arrangements, and less involved with broad issues, since these are slowly disappearing.[2]

This view was expressed by Myrdal in the late 1950s, a period that has been characterized by Daniel Bell as heralding the end of ideology as a critical factor in social development.[3] The large problems and the great debates were understood to be phenomena of the past, and the further development and improvement of the society were seen to rest in the application of appropriate technology. While the social upheavals in the 1960s demonstrated that this analysis was not as accurate as it once seemed, nonetheless the welfare state continues to represent an effort to define problems as amenable to technological solution and as outside the boundaries of disruptive conflict. Within this view of change processes lies a more specific notion of planned change which directly affects the social services.

Community Organization and Planned Change

Whatever the specific tasks of change that community organization has undertaken, the underlying models of change have some common dimensions. The profession tends to identify the time-limited, technologically informed, professional intervention of a person specifically designated as a helper or change agent as potentially significant in alleviating some social or psychological problem in the interests of social progress. The professional is seen as containing in his or her own person a knowledge of human behavior and of social dynamics that is itself a primary tool for creating change. For example, a recent community organization text has suggested that "the major resource the practitioner brings to his task is his ability to engage himself analytically." [4] Similarly, the "professional function" is seen as "the direction or stimulation of community intervention by an individual with responsibility to guide social processes." [5] The social service professional, when acting as the welfare state's agent of change, performs essentially as other professionals, for

[2] Gunnar Myrdal, *Beyond the Welfare State* (New York: Bantam Books, 1967), pp. 62 and 66.
[3] Daniel Bell, *The End of Ideology* (New York: Free Press, 1960).
[4] Fred M. Cox, John L. Erlich, Jack Rothman, and John E. Tropman (eds.), *Strategies of Community Organization* (Itasca, Ill.: Peacock, 1970), p. *viii*.
[5] *Ibid.*, p. 4.

example, lawyers and doctors, do; that is, they diagnose a problem and take corrective actions to bring about changes.

On the one hand, this has an entirely reasonable sound to it, given the general assumptions about change on which it rests; that is, the concerns are not for system-reordering changes but for more ameliorative changes. As the matter was stated in one widely read formulation of roles in community organization practice,

> Community organization may be said in the broad sense always to include social change or social reform, typically middle range in character. . . . Change of a more extreme or revolutionary character undoubtedly would not be brought about within the context of social welfare practice but rather would occur in the broader political arena.[6]

On the other hand, while it is hard to disagree with the idea that social work will not be the spearhead for revolutionary change, this formulation takes another step. It pulls social work back from attempting to make even a contribution to broad change by accepting the notion that social work will contribute only to limited changes. On this basis, technological interventions by the worker make sense in that they fit the change agendas. These models of the professional role place the worker in a very central position in the change process. Models of change that see change as a fundamental reordering of the system would not place such emphasis on the role any one person would play, but would look for the roles many could play in facilitating change processes.

Another way in which social work conservatizes community organization is by equating change with the provision of social services. Community organization rests on a view of change in which change is interpreted as the creation or improvement of a service network. In fact, the social services have become the vehicle for a good deal of that version of social reform that receives official government sanction. In a recent analysis of the social services, the need for services is defined in just these terms.

> In any interaction between an individual and a part of the social system, the adjustment of each may not be sufficient to achieve behavior which is acceptable to self, others, and the community, without help through one or more of the social services.[7]

[6] Jack Rothman, "An Analysis of Goals and Roles in Community Organization Practice," Social Work, 9 (April 1964), p. 25.
[7] Dorothy Daly, Martin Loeb, and Frederick Whitehouse, "The Social Services and Related Manpower," a paper commissioned by the Social and Rehabilitative Services, Department of Health, Education and Welfare (Washington, D.C.: Government Printing Office, 1971), p. 7.

In this conception, the social services are the vehicle for the modification either of individuals or the social system at large, when one or the other is engaged in unacceptable behavior. The social services, then, carry the burden of change. In fact, in the same analysis, people who provide social services are defined as "change agents." They make "interventions" to "alleviate the present problems and to help develop the capacity of the person to deal more effectively with future problems." [8]

From this perspective social change becomes defined and understood as those activities carried out by and through the social services. As Colin Greer, executive editor of the journal *Social Policy* put it,

> We are seriously diverted from analyzing how we are really doing and what we might be doing to solve our social problems by our persistent and erroneous desire to regard the expansion of the human service professions as synonymous with the social progress our social rhetoric talks about. It isn't.[9]

Greer identifies the theme of service as being at "the core of an emerging national ideology." [10] Identifying social services with social reform leads to an equation that trivializes social reform at the same time that it creates a mystique about the role the services perform. It is within these broad perspectives that the specifics of community organization practice must be examined.

The Practice of Community Organization

Community organization was not initially concerned with organizing for social change, but rather grew out of the Community Council and United Fund movements. Its focus was on organizing social agencies in relationship to one another to help them avoid competition and to facilitate their fund-raising efforts. Eventually it adopted a planning perspective that, at one time, was encapsulated in the idea that community organization was primarily concerned with encouraging an improved balance of community needs and community resources. In fact, community organization has been defined as "the process of bringing about and maintaining a progressively more effective adjustment between social welfare resources and social welfare needs within a geographical area or functional field.[11] From this perspective, community organization was a

[8] *Ibid.,* p. 3.
[9] Colin Greer, "Human Service on the Road to Social Progress," *New York Times* (July 20, 1972), p. 33.
[10] *Ibid.*
[11] C. F. McNeil, "Community Organization for Social Welfare," *Social Work Year Book* (New York: American Association of Social Workers, 1951), p. 123.

help to the network of social service agencies which had become increasingly bureaucratized.[12] Community organization moved into grass-roots activity over time, although we should be cautious about interpreting this movement as signifying any growing engagement with the basic dynamics of change.

In fact, the stage of grass-roots work may have represented an even more conservative influence than the agency coordination of social planning stages because it worked with, absorbed, and contained, some change energies in communities which otherwise might have been available for more fundamental efforts. For example, in the mid-1950s, Violet Sieder defined community organization as a direct service when its focus was on social integration. The community organization worker, she wrote,

> is assigned to help people resolve inter-group tension situations involving such difficult matters as racial, nationality, or class conflict. In such situations we find the worker moving in to help a subcommunity as it struggles to meet a crisis and serving to isolate or minimize the difficulty as a protection to the larger community.[13]

The passage speaks for itself in its focus on conflict containment as opposed to the use of conflict in the service of change.

Rein has suggested that the conservative nature of community organization practice stems from its focus on community action as a means to encourage social conformity.[14] He highlights several major community organization efforts from various historical periods to illustrate this point. In the 1930s, the Chicago Area Project used a social action approach at the community level to reduce crime and delinquency by discouraging the deviant behavior of youth. In the 1940s, New York University sponsored a project to promote personality development through social action in East Harlem. In the 1950s, New York City's Youth Board Gang Project again utilized community organization as a technology to reduce juvenile delinquency. Similarly, community organization in the Model Cities programs was seen as "a major mental health service, an end in itself."[15] In these ways, Rein suggests, community organization has

---

[12] For a brief review of this history, see "Social Planning and Community Organization," *Encyclopedia of Social Work*, Vol. II (New York: National Association of Social Workers, 1971), pp. 1324–1351.

[13] Violet M. Sieder, "What Is Community Organization Practice in Social Work?" *Social Work Forum*, St. Louis (New York: Columbia University Press, 1956), pp. 170–171.

[14] Martin Rein, "Social Work in Search of a Radical Profession," *Social Work*, 15 (April 1970), pp. 13–28.

[15] Mathew P. Dumont, "A Model Community Mental Health Program for a Model Cities Area" (Washington, D.C.: Center for Community Planning, Department of Health, Education and Welfare, August, 1967), p. 3, mimeo. Cited in *Ibid.*, p. 24.

functioned as a technique for using "social action and self-help as strategies for promoting individual conformity." [16]

The War on Poverty represented at once the peak of social work's grass-roots community organization efforts and their demise in the current period. It was, perhaps, the last time that people's needs to organize for social change could be flirted with and contained within the structure of welfare state policies. The War on Poverty can be understood as an attempt to channel the civil rights struggles and the nascent social upheavals of the early 1960s into the social engineering context of welfare state planning. It failed to contain those pressures, however. They broke out and were in part responsible for a split that will not be easily reconciled between grass-roots organizing, on the one hand, and professional social work and the welfare state on the other.

Social workers played many roles in the War on Poverty, and undoubtedly there were radical social workers who pursued radical agendas while working for the Office of Economic Opportunity. However, the dominant concept in the organizing component, "maximum feasible participation," represented a conservative version of a more profound notion of participatory democracy in several ways.

This mandate identified community action as a program that

> mobilizes and utilizes resources, . . . which provides services, assistance and other activities of sufficient scope and size to give promise of progress toward elimination of poverty or a cause or causes of poverty through developing employment opportunities, improving human performance, motivation, and productivity, or bettering the conditions under which people live, learn and work, [and] which is developed, conducted, and administered with the maximum feasible participation of residents of the area and members of the groups served.[17]

What seems to have been the role assigned to grass-roots community organization in this legislation was to provide the kind of group supports and activities that would facilitate individual mobility of poor people through the system. As Marris and Rein have demonstrated, the agencies that implemented the programs of the War on Poverty did not, with the one exception of Harlem's Haryou, make a class analysis of the problems with which they were concerned. Alternatively, they tended to "advocate self-assertion primarily for its psychological value." [18] This analysis led to change strategies of "persuasion, encouragement, enlightenment

16 *Ibid.*, p. 23.
17 Section 202, Title II, Economic Opportunity Act. Cited in John C. Donovan, *The Politics of Poverty* (New York: Pegasus, 1967), p. 39.
18 Peter Marris and Martin Rein, *The Dilemmas of Social Reform* (New York: Atherton, 1967), p. 49.

and discrete pressure."[19] Their efforts were not directed to problems of social change or resource redistribution through real change in social organization. The War on Poverty became a community-based attempt to do what individualized casework had previously failed to do—mobilize persons for greater personal effort within the given structures of the society. In this view, citizen participation may best be understood as sociotherapy in which, as Rein and Miller put it, "the major task is to reduce poverty by reducing alienation, deviance, and the personal sense of powerlessness which is caused chiefly by isolation and the personal sense of apathy."[20]

Grass-roots organization, then, can be a conservative force. In the way that it has developed within social work, its focus has been toward conservation and social therapy, helping people obtain "some *sense* of belonging and control" and a "*sense* of neighborhood in the large metropolitan area."[21] Its view of the conflicting interests in the society is contained within the liberal pluralist view in which, whoever is the winner, the structures of the society remain unchanged. It is characterized by its noticeable absence of analysis of the social system and the divisions within the system and of the presentation of meaningful alternatives.

The most recent involvement of community organization with social planning is hardly more promising. Frances Fox Piven's remarks to the planning profession serve equally well in regard to social work involvement with planning. Social planning, interpreted as a further effort by the welfare state to rationalize social reform, is likely "to become the doctrine to justify professional agency imperialism."[22] Robert Goodman has analyzed in some depth the extent to which social planners, by virtue of the larger context in which they work, serve a repressive role despite, and even because of, their efforts at social reform.[23] The choices open to planners largely serve the interests of what Goodman has labeled the urban-industrial complex. Social planners, Goodman argues, have been part of a cycle of public monies' bankrolling private profits, of social reforms that failed to help and further exploited the poor, and of a pattern of urban development that reinforced a rigid and inequitable class structure. He is very clear that the assumptions of the planning profession and of reformism within that profession will need to be

[19] *Ibid.*, p. 89.
[20] Martin Rein and S. M. Miller, "Citizen Participation and Poverty," *Connecticut Law Review*, 1 (2), 1968, p. 225.
[21] Murray G. Ross, *Community Organization: Theory and Principles* (New York: Harper, 1955). (Italics added.)
[22] Frances Fox Piven, "Comprehensive Social Planning: Curriculum Reform or Professional Imperialism," *Journal of the American Institute of Planners*, 36 (July 1970), p. 227.
[23] Robert Goodman, *After the Planners* (New York: Simon and Schuster, 1971).

transcended if justice is to be served. At that point, social planning will bear very little resemblance to its present forms.

In this section, we have discussed some of the bases of community organization practice, especially its understanding of the meaning and nature of planned social change and the larger political-social uses to which organizing work has been addressed. It has become clear that this area of practice cannot be understood without understanding the assumptions about the social order and change in that order on which it is based. When these assumptions are explored, it becomes clear that community organization practice—supposedly representing social work's more forward-looking dimension—has been based on and has served conservative political ends.

PERSON-IN-SITUATION: CASEWORK AS POLITICS

The Casework Dilemma

Social casework faces a painful dilemma. On the one hand, it promises to engage meaningfully with the fundamental problems of human beings in a way that implies a radical intent. As Briar and Miller suggest,

> No other profession has taken the individual person so seriously, nor has made the promotion of each person's particular aspirations and potentialities its primary function, nor has set as its cardinal principle the notion that each person deserves respect and dignity no matter how offensive he may seem.[24]

On the other hand, social casework theory contains a vision of human beings in the context of their social situation that leads to a limiting conservative orientation in practice. This orientation finds its way into casework in significant part through casework's understanding of what it calls "person-in-situation." [25] Casework's perspective on the relationship of individual well-being to the nature of the social order as a whole is explored in this section.

Casework's stance is not an inevitable outcome of one-to-one counseling or of a helping relationship itself. Rather, it is a reflection of the

[24] Scott Briar and Henry Miller, *Problems and Issues in Social Casework* (New York: Columbia University Press, 1971), p. *v.*

[25] A second important locus of conservative thought in casework, not developed in this section, derives from the personality theories adopted by conventional casework practice. These theories posit sharp limits to human potential as an inevitable part of the human situation. When personality theory so analyzes the human psyche, it rests both on a misinterpretation of the nature of human growth and development and on an uncritical adoption of the larger values of the social order within which it is formulated. One useful analysis in this regard is Philip Lichtenberg, *Psychoanalysis: Radical and Conservative* (New York: Springer, 1969).

fact that casework has not been sufficiently self-conscious and critical about the philosophies and politics of the society in which it functions. As a consequence, it has adopted the political coloration of its environment, has become more like the society of which it is a part, and so has been turned against the purposes of liberation which it promised to pursue. Briar's call in 1968 for openness to "radically different conceptions of the social situation," has remained a call unanswered by the profession.[26]

It is surely no new experience for social casework to receive criticism for containing conservative tendencies.[27] Most commonly, that criticism has taken the form of explicating the ways in which casework transmits conservative values to clients and in which it encourages conforming behavior in clients as a condition of their receiving services. As Briar acknowledged in a review of social casework which appeared in the 1971 *Encyclopedia of Social Work,* caseworkers continue to be identified by some as "agents to protect and thereby sustain the status quo." [28] Similarly, concluding an assessment of social casework in Britain, Timms suggested that

> Social workers characteristically find themselves "standing for" the elements of solidarity in a society, but it is important for them to appreciate that the social services are often the meeting point of two or more groups whose interests may be, partially at any rate, in conflict.[29]

When the issue of the conservative tendencies in casework is expressed in this way, that is, as a problem of casework's facilitating conservative or repressive programs, exploring the issue becomes an empirical matter. The problem could then be explored by examining specific aspects of casework practice, especially the kinds of programs with which caseworkers are engaged and the specific outcomes they pursue. We could then test the validity of Hollis's statement, for example, that

> It is [a great] mistake to regard casework as primarily an agent of social control. Our effort is distinctly not to bend the client to the social system,

[26] Scott Briar, "The Casework Predicament," *Social Work,* 13 (January 1968), p. 9.
[27] This is in addition to a wide range of other criticisms casework receives on a fairly regular basis, including its tendency to disengage from those most in need, its inefficacy with those whom it does serve, its unresponsiveness to new theory and practice modes, and its unwillingness and/or inability to engage in broader processes of social change. These are briefly reviewed in Briar, "The Casework Predicament," pp. 5–11.
[28] Scott Briar, "Social Casework and Social Group Work: Historical and Social Science Foundations," *Encyclopedia of Social Work* (New York: National Association of Social Workers, 1971), p. 1238.
[29] Noel Timms, *Social Casework: Principles and Practice* (London: Routledge and Kegan Paul, 1964), p. 239.

but rather to increase his ability to deal with the complexities of modern organizations, enhancing rather than diminishing his autonomy.[30]

In defense of casework, one could argue that, in cases where practice was conservative, this conservatism was not essential to casework, but represented an unfortunate misuse of casework in particular instances. The debate about casework as a more liberating or more repressive force is then converted to a quantitative question, open to reassessment if and when more new parts of practice are uncovered.

A different point of view on the sources of conservatism in social casework is presented here. The essence of the present argument is that social casework is essentially conservative because it takes as a given and, consequently, lends support to the basic values and structures of the social order, by failing to examine the influence of the social order on the individual in a systematic way This produces diagnoses that do not go to the roots of the social issues influencing the individual and plans of action that operate within a limited range of alternatives. This is not to say that casework is unaware that people are influenced by their environment. However, casework's awareness represents a transformed and inadequate formulation of the reality. The casework version permits some accommodation of casework practice to the unmistakable fact that people exist in society without forcing casework into an uncomfortable position of challenge to the society. As a first order of business, the casework conception of person-in-situation must be explicated and then contrasted to its more profound alternative.

Psychological and Social-Psychological Views of Reality

Casework has alternated several times between more psychological and more social-psychological perspectives on the human condition.[31] During periods when psychological perspectives dominated, liberal voices challenged the attendant isolationism and political conservatism. At present, a more progressive wing in social casework has rekindled concern for the individual in his or her situation. This involves psychosocial diagnosis and an effort to encompass some awareness of the effects of poverty, racism, sexism, and other social-economic-political factors into an appreciation of the client's situation. It seems to be the case that an awareness of the way that social, economic, and political factors impinge on clients is not always followed by activities that make that awareness

---

[30] Florence Hollis, Casework: A Psychosocial Therapy, 2nd ed. (New York: Random House, 1972), p. 350.

[31] A brief review of this history is found in Carol H. Meyer, Social Work Practice: A Response to the Urban Crisis (New York: Free Press, 1970), especially Chapter 2, "Social Casework—Along the Route of History," pp. 35–53.

an integrated part of the casework process. Nonetheless, there is some development. We suggest that even this school, however, operates within an essentially conservative theoretical perspective and practice orientation.

Paul Baran has suggested a concept that is central to understanding the way in which casework's version of person-in-situation represents a conservative philosophy and leads to a conservative practice. He calls this viewpoint, as it finds expression in the various therapies and helping interventions, "socio-psychologism." [32] Socio-psychologism is a departure from and an enlargement of the earlier psychological world view. The socio-psychological view recognizes that "the individual is not entirely a man for himself but is influenced by society, is somehow affected by the social setting within which he grows up." [33] However, a critical shortcoming of the position is that its understanding of "society" is " 'environment': family, occupational stratum, inter-racial relations, residential community, and the like." [34] Socio-psychologism is, Baran indicates, a politically conservatized version of the Marxist view that

> The character of man is the product of the social order in which he is born, in which he grows up, and the air of which he inhales throughout his life; it is its result and indeed one of its most significant aspects. Yet it is of the utmost importance to understand that what is meant by "social order" in Marxian theory is at most only a distant cousin of the notion of "society" as employed in socio-psychologism. The latter, it will be recalled, refers to "environment," to "interpersonal relations," and to similar aspects of what constitutes the surface of social existence. The former, on the other hand, encompasses the attained stage of the development of productive forces, the mode and relations of production, the form of social domination prevailing at any given time, all together constituting the basic structure of the existing social organization.[35]

Baran is attempting to develop an understanding of people in a way that sees them in terms of their relationship to the basic structures of a society, rather than to its various surface manifestations. That people are influenced by their environment is an indisputable fact, and one that is incorporated into casework theories of nearly all varieties. However, the fact of seeing people in a social situation, as Baran suggests, is itself a perspective within which there is room for significant differences of interpretation.

The different perspectives on what is incorporated into and under-

[32] Paul A. Baran, "Marxism and Psychoanalysis," in Baran, *The Longer View* (New York: Monthly Review Press, 1969), p. 93.
[33] *Ibid.*
[34] *Ibid.*
[35] *Ibid.*, p. 98.

stood by the notion of the social context of individual welfare results in different perspectives on the way in which a given problem is analyzed or, in casework's terms, diagnosed. If the life situation of each client is not understood in terms of the fundamental nature of the society as a whole—as well as in terms of the particulars of the client's situation within the whole—then the diagnosis of the problem will go up to and not beyond understanding the client as he or she deviates from the commonly accepted norms. If a diagnosis does not incorporate a concern for the way in which the whole society may be pathological and produce pathology in individuals as a normal condition of functioning, then the condition of pathology that is shared by all will be, paradoxically, the standard of behavior and existence toward which treatment is directed.

The same limitation in perspective was described by C. Wright Mills in *The Sociological Imagination*. Mills wrote,

> Men do not usually define the troubles they endure in terms of historical change and institutional contradiction. The well-being they enjoy, they do not usually impute to the big ups and downs of the societies in which they live. Seldom aware of the intricate connection between the patterns of their own lives and the course of world history, ordinary men do not usually know what this connection means for the kinds of men they are becoming and for the kinds of history making in which they might take part.[36]

In these terms, Mills defines our entrapment in what Baran has labeled the socio-psychological world view.

A further consequence of a superficial analysis of the forces influencing people is the failure to appreciate the extent to which the problems experienced by individuals are not only rooted in basic social processes, but are functional for social maintenance. When their functional social purposes are uncovered, the intransigence and pervasiveness of many problems are more easily explained. For example, the suppression of affect, which can be limiting to the flowering of friendships and love relationships, may be an important survival mechanism for a person involved in repetitious, unchallenging work. Much work is organized in a way that encourages emotional disengagement, and we accept this stoically enough. But, when the response pattern that is engendered at the work place is manifested in family life, we become exercised about the ensuing disintegration of family ilfe. Similarly, the creation of dominant-subordinate relationships, limiting as a basis for friendships or marriage, is a reflection of a pattern encouraged by the typical hierarchies where people work. Such relationships are seen as necessary to maintain motivation and to organize work efficiently. In general, if

[36] C. Wright Mills, *The Sociological Imagination* (New York: Oxford University Press, 1959), pp. 3–4.

it is the case that this society is organized on the basis of values that do not have human maximization as a central concern, then we can understand why some behaviors seen as less healthy responses in certain arenas are both valued and promulgated elsewhere in the system.

The differences between the more encompassing view and the analyses and understandings of people in relationship to their society which are contained in the socio-psychological view have important consequences for the kinds of solutions which are then sought in the helping situation. These differences concern the profundity of the changes that are seen as necessary to overcome a particular problem and the inclusiveness or breadth of the changes.

As regards the question of depth, the socio-psychological view is rooted in liberal philosophy, with its intimate relationship to individualism and to social reformism as a strategy of change. From this perspective, the problems that individuals experience can be addressed either by personal efforts to obtain, for example, psychotherapy, more education, a different job, or by social reforms such as higher welfare benefits or improved public housing. These kinds of proscriptions flow logically from an analysis that sees the problems of individuals as either unique to them or reflective of some relatively minor dislocations in an otherwise sound society.

Baran's view suggests that the problems individuals experience are neither idiosyncratic nor reflective of minor dislocations, but are indices of the extent to which the society as a whole is organized on principles destructive to human well-being. As a consequence, social changes of the most profound sort are necessary to solve the everyday problems that people experience. To continue with an earlier example, whole, healthy, and joyous individuals who relate to others in the most mutually fulfilling ways are unlikely to emerge in large numbers from a society where people's wholeness is so denied by the everyday circumstances of life. To deal with the problem of limited, unfulfilling, and exploitative interpersonal relationships will require dealing with an economic system that encourages us to view one another as commodities, that measures personal success in terms of the dominance over others (career ladders, wealth, and so on), and that asks us to park our social concerns outside the doorsteps of the factories, offices, and agencies where we work. These are problems that require radical social change to overcome.

The depth of the changes required from this perspective is matched by the breadth. Baran's view suggests that the solutions to the problems of individuals will ultimately have to be the solutions to the problems of all people. As Baran writes, "the limits to the cure of man's soul are set by the illness of the society in which he lives." [37] Similarly, Lichtenberg

---

[37] Baran, The Longer View, p. 111.

has suggested that "What is necessary for the complete healing of any psychotic individual is a change in the organizing principles within the whole community such that all citizens are entitled to live to the maximum of their human capacities." [38] The socio-psychological view does not lead to a search for solutions in this depth. And yet, people will not be free of tinges of paranoia until the reality of a society in which each person's success is achieved at the expense of others is changed. People will not be free to experience and express love to its fullest until the society is so organized that experiencing and expressing love is not dysfunctional for one's life chances. When the human condition is understood in this perspective, it seems obvious that the hope of private solutions for some in the absence of changes for all is illusory.

Thus far, two theories of the relationship of the individual to the society have been identified. The first, socio-psychologism, represents an essentially conservative perspective on the social order in that it leaves the fundamental nature of the social order unexamined, therefore taking it as a given. The second theory represents a radical perspective in that it searches for the root or structural causes of the problems of the individual. In the following section, some aspects of social casework theory will be explored with an eye toward uncovering the model of person-in-situation in which casework most heavily relies and the consequences of this model for practice theory.

Casework Theory and Person-in-Situation

There are a number of theories of practice in social casework. There is considerable uniformity among them, however, in their understanding of person-in-situation. In general, these theories rest on what has been identified as socio-psychologism. However, the uniformity is not based on a highly developed theoretical understanding as much as on a relatively unexamined and uncritical adoption of that perspective. Bernece Simon, summarizing a symposium on seven approaches to casework practice (the psychosocial, functional, problem-solving, behavioral modification, family therapy, crisis intervention, and socialization), identified the level of development of thought in this area by suggesting that

> The problem was expressed in terms of the effect of environment on personality and personality change and the question of whether environmental forces are internalized by the individual and become part of the personality. There was agreement among most that environment has a crucial impact on personality. The nature of this impact was not specified. . . . The level of

[38] Philip Lichtenberg, "And the Cure of Psychosis Is for All of Us," in Lichtenberg, *Essays from Personality to Social Thought,* Bryn Mawr College, School of Social Work and Social Research, 1973, mimeographed, p. 83.

generality at which this discussion proceeded, combined with the sparseness of consideration of environmental aspects of treatment in the exposition of theory, attests to the concept of man-in-environment as a most compelling area for study, examination, research and theorizing in casework, if not in all social work.[39]

The absence of theoretical clarity about the relationship of the person to the social situation does not mean that there is no view of these relationships inherent in the literature on casework practice. It does mean that there is not a high degree of self-consciousness about the position that is adopted. Consequently, casework theorists adopt a perspective and develop a political base for casework theory without making clear to themselves and their readers that there is political content in their theory. To illustrate the extent to which casework is informed by the socio-psychological perspective and to demonstrate the conservative implications this has, we now look at the writing of a number of casework theorists, representing a spectrum of schools of thought in casework.

Helen Harris Perlman has suggested that one of the major focuses of diagnosis in the casework process is the "finding and assessment of what factors and forces deter or thwart his [the client's] motivation or his capacity or his opportunity." [40] She suggests that

> Those factors or forces may lie in his past life experience and its impress on him, or they may lie in the present situation; they may emanate from the significant other persons in the client's life, past or present, or in the immediate relationship between him and the caseworker; they may reside in his physical, emotional and intellectual makeup, in their deficits or sickness or strengths; they may lie in the actual lack or failure of social means and resources by which the problem either is created or is amenable to change.[41]

In this listing of forces that "deter or thwart," Perlman's reliance on the socio-psychological view emerges. In searching for ways to understand the problems facing a client and especially for the roots of these problems, all of the possible factors identified are seen as rooted in the personal history of the individual ("past life experience," and so on), unique to that client or situation (found in "his physical, emotional and intellectual makeup"), or of a transient nature. Her consideration of social and economic factors is couched in the language of the aberrant (the "lack or failure of social means and resources") rather than in the language of basic

---

[39] Bernece K. Simon, "Social Casework Theory: An Overview," in Robert W. Roberts and Robert H. Nee (eds.), *Theories of Social Casework* (Chicago: University of Chicago Press, 1970), pp. 389–390.

[40] Helen Harris Perlman, "The Problem-Solving Model in Social Casework," Roberts and Nee, *Theories of Social Casework*, p. 165.

[41] *Ibid.*, p. 166.

social criticism (that is, the consequence of present forms of social and economic organization). This kind of analysis creates the image of a client as influenced largely by the more surface manifestations of the social order which need not be or cannot be examined in its more fundamental aspects.

At the same time that Perlman, like casework theorists in general, means to take the individual quite seriously and to identify the individual as the most central unit of concern, she actually diminishes the individual by conceptually isolating him or her from the major forces that create and define the human condition. As was suggested in contrasting socio-psychologism with the radical perspective, the socio-psychological view has a limited understanding of both the nature of the forces influencing the human condition and the extent of the impact of these forces. Perlman's work shows the consequences of this limited understanding.

In an earlier but typical formulation, Perlman wrote that

> The reality is that we cannot pit man against his society or lead him to isolation from it, because he is a societal creature. He knows himself only in his likeness to, and difference from, other members of his society, and his own conception of adjustment, like ours, is based on what is considered "normal" or held to be "good" by at least one of the special groupings of which he is a member.[42]

She suggests that "social workers stand in humble recognition that most human beings find and fulfill themselves as they find themselves in consonance with their society."[43]

What is Perlman saying here? She begins with the undeniable observation that people are social, that is, that they define themselves in relationship to their environment. However, she moves quickly to the conclusion that the environment is a given within which people must function and within which casework practice must operate. Because Perlman does not view the relationship of individuals to the social order as one of mutual interaction and accountability, but rather takes the social order as a given, she is left to deal with the resulting problems of the individual in the free space that is left—the individual's adjustment to what is. A theory of casework that is not critical of the way in which the social order works in and through the individual does not have a firm basis for helping the individual deal with problems by pursuing strategies of social change.

Florence Hollis's understanding of casework, which enjoys some degree of acceptance in the field, focuses on the person-in-situation as a "threefold configuration consisting of the person, the situation, and the inter-

---

[42] Helen Harris Perlman, "Social Components of Casework Practice," in Perlman, *Perspectives on Social Casework* (Philadelphia: Temple University Press, 1971), p. 39 (originally published in 1953).
[43] *Ibid.*, p. 43.

action between them." [44] However, in Hollis's theory, the environment tends to be seen not in terms of the fullest social and political context, but as a more circumscribed social-psychological background. This becomes clear as she identifies the three possible sources of problems in interpersonal adjustment. These are (1) infantile needs and drives left over from childhood; (2) a current life situation that exerts excessive pressures; and, (3) faulty ego and superego functioning.[45] As with Perlman, problems are seen as rooted in the special dilemmas of an individual psyche or as a result of some special "excessive pressures" not characteristic of the society. Similarly, in considering the caseworker's obligation to intervene in the social setting influencing the client, Hollis suggests that "a radical change in environment will sometimes bring about a genuine personality change as, for example, when a particularly fortunate choice of marriage partner leads to a long period of satisfying living." [46] If the choice of marriage partner is described as a radical change in environment, what words are left to describe social revolution?

Briar and Miller similarly have suggested that diagnoses must "always attend to the social matrix of behavior; they must always, in short, be psychosocial." [47] In practice, they mean that

> Casework diagnosis includes the following levels of analysis: 1) the individual, including both interpersonal factors and his location in a social network, 2) interpersonal systems, or the interaction units (dyads, triads, etc.) implicated in the case situation, 3) the family unit as a social system, and 4) the family unit's interchanges with its social network.[48]

Once again, the social component of the psychosocial analysis speaks in terms of social networks rather than the social order and of the impact of the family rather than the economic and political order as a social factor. In like fashion, Reid and Epstein identify target problems for what they have called "task-centered casework" as being (1) interpersonal conflicts, (2) dissatisfactions with social relations, (3) relations with formal organizations, (4) role performance, (5) social transition, (6) reactive emotional stress, and (7) inadequate resources.[49] These formulations are among the more progressive in social casework in that they reflect an attempt to bring a social perspective to bear on the casework process. In their effort to do so, however, they clearly define socio-psychologism, with all the limits of that understanding.

[44] Hollis, *Casework*, p. 10.
[45] *Ibid.*, p. 24.
[46] *Ibid.*, p. 27.
[47] Briar and Miller, *Problems and Issues in Social Casework*, p. 159.
[48] *Ibid.*
[49] William Reid and Laura Epstein, *Task-Centered Casework* (New York: Columbia University Press, 1972), p. 20.

In socio-psychologism, fundamental social structures and processes are either seen as acceptable or are not seen as particularly relevant for the individual. It is not surprising, then, that the goals of the casework process, as they are frequently formulated in the casework literature, accept or ignore fundamental changes in the social order as a possible or desirable outcome.

In the 1930s, for example, Gordon Hamilton suggested that the goal of casework is found "not so much in the mastery of physical resources, as in the management of human relations so that people . . . may work and rest and play and be at peace with themselves and one another." [50] Similarly, she has described the purpose of casework as encouraging "adaptation to reality." [51] More recently, but in a way that reflects the continuity of this perspective, Hollis has written of the power of new casework techniques to more quickly "bring relief" to the client,[52] suggesting some equation of social casework with commercial analgesics, and adds that

> In a world where mistrust is rampant, values in flux, and bureaucracies ever more powerful and remote, the individual . . . must use his capacity for love to build islands of refuge and strength in his family, with friends, and with neighbors, so that he and his children may be nourished and may come to value, respect, and trust themselves and one another.[53]

At the root of this prescription is some notion of the separation of the political-social side of people from the personal, as though it were possible to build walls that protect one from the force of society.

In a similar vein, Perlman has suggested that

> Changes in the social environment consist of readjustment of living conditions, supplementation of inadequate resources, removal of persons from certain conditions of living, substitutions of one for another kind of physical or psychological situation, and so on. . . . Placement of a child or of an aged person in an institution, the provision of recreational opportunities to an adolescent, the arrangements for a man's surgery, the readjustment of a child's school program, the staying of an eviction notice—each of these is an example of the caseworker's efforts to effect some "environmental modification" for his client.[54]

[50] Gordon Hamilton, "Basic Concepts upon Which Case-Work Practice Is Formulated," *National Conference of Social Work*, Indianapolis (Chicago: University of Chicago Press, 1937), p. 149.
[51] Gordon Hamilton, *Theory and Practice of Social Case Work* (New York: Columbia University Press, 1951), p. 237.
[52] Hollis, *Casework*, p. 3.
[53] *Ibid.*, p. 349.
[54] Perlman, "Social Components of Casework Practice," p. 48.

In like manner, Reul identifies some of the deepest sources of emotional poverty or deprivation in the United States through approving citation of Leeper and Madison, who argue that emotional deprivation "may be what lies back of many of our difficulties of modern life."[55] The solutions to these rather profound difficulties, however, are seen to be more community services and resources, such as individual counseling, health services, financial assistance, housing, recreation, and so on.[56] The disparity between the analysis and the proffered solutions seems enormous.

We have shown that social casework fails to move from a consideration of some specifics of human psychology and the social situation to a perspective on the totality of the human condition. Rather, social casework operates on the basis of a limited social-psychological view that does not look sufficiently deeply into the social roots of people's dilemmas. Consequently, it cannot develop strategies to deal with the more profound causal factors behind these dilemmas. We have suggested that this is inevitably a conservative position that limits what casework can hope to accomplish, as it reinforces the present social order.

This kind of criticism does not mean that casework practice should be abandoned. It does suggest, however, that casework reconsider the standard interpretations of clients' problems, the strategies that are developed, and even the understanding of who should be a caseworker, who should be a client, and what the appropriate setting and the basic casework process should be. All of these reassessments, however, will need to be based on a rethinking of casework's conception of person-in-situation. Baran's view of people as social beings in the fullest sense may provide the basis for that rethinking.

THE CONTAINMENT OF RADICAL IDEOLOGY

In the previous sections, some of the ways in which a conservative political perspective infuses the social work profession were identified. In each instance, it was suggested that the roots of that conservatism were an uncritical acceptance within social work of the major values and institutions of the society at large. While social work has tended to represent a liberal position within the society and, in this respect, has had a progressive thrust, even this progressivism has occurred within the frame-

---

[55] Myrtol R. Reul, "Deprivation amid Abundance: Implications for Social Work Practice," National Association of Social Workers, *Changing Services for Changing Clients* (New York: Columbia University Press, 1969), p. 59, citing Robert Leeper and Peter Madison, *Towards Understanding Human Personalities* (New York: Appleton-Century-Crofts, 1959), p. 247.
[56] Reul, "Deprivation amid Abundance," p. 76.

work of the dominant social order. It has, therefore, served to reinforce that social order. The cost has been social work's own vitality and its ability to be of the utmost service in meeting human needs.

In this final section, we explore some of the ways in which the dominance of conservative politics is reinforced in the profession. We posit no conspiracy at work, but suggest that these dynamics develop as we all play out our beliefs about what we see as the best choices for ourselves and the profession. These dynamics have had the effect of keeping a radical alternative from being more widely known and discussed. In understanding the processes that occur, we can hopefully enlarge the possibilities that a radical position will develop in the profession and prove attractive to growing numbers of social service workers.

The Profession's View of Radicalism

One of the ways in which the profession attempts to contain the emergence of a radical perspective is by ignoring in its official response to dissent and in its internal dialogue the possibility of a radical interpretation of social reality and of radical alternatives for itself. The major professional social work journals, as was argued recently in an article which appeared in one of them, do not represent "militant" perspectives.[57] ("Militant" was used in this context, as it so often is, to refer to a radical analysis as well as to a militant style.) As will be familiar to students of behavioral psychology, an effective way of extinguishing unwanted thoughts or behaviors in others is to ignore them. To some extent, the unwillingness of the official journals to acknowledge the existence, let alone the legitimacy, of a radical perspective forces many to keep their skepticism about the conventional wisdom under wraps. Each person sits on his or her doubts in the belief that his or her feelings are unique. The Emperor's Clothes phenomenon operates. People feel personally responsible for failing to be able to appreciate and utilize the solutions contained within the normal range of professional techniques.

It is necessary to acknowledge the contribution of the political left to this situation. The left in the United States has been guilty of not always finding ways to speak to large numbers of people in terms they could understand and could use to explain the dilemmas they experienced. It has tended to be isolated and esoteric. Similarly, within social work, a clear left position has not been articulated sufficiently well. There is, however, a powerful left tradition in the United States. Specifically, within social work, there are people with a commitment to radical system change and to social work's involvement in it. While the radical position has not

[57] Harry Specht, "The Deprofessionalization of Social Work," *Social Work*, 17 (March 1972), p. 5.

been highly articulated or developed in the profession, it has existed and has had a great deal to say about the needs and role of social work. However, when the existence of a radical perspective in the profession is acknowledged, it is generally not given extended treatment, or is crudely dismissed.

An example of the handling of the leftist position is the comment of one writer on social work who recently identified the radical approach as "the abandonment of responsibility [which] results in the kind of glorification of deviant, criminal and retreatist behavior that has become increasingly evident in the practice of some social workers." [58] Another identified Marxian thought, one of the most important ideological and intellectual forces of modern times, as the "tired scenario of the Left's class analysis" [59] and urged an end to radical action based on " 'honest dialogues,' confrontations, appeals to public morality and 'consciousness-raising.' " [60]

Equally problematic, the concepts of radical change and the radical social worker have been watered down and confused by sympathetic left-liberal observers and commentators who have classified a broad range of analyses and strategies as radical. In the absence of a systematic radical perspective, a variety of militant and reformist approaches have been labeled as radical, with no special gains for the cause of fundamental change.

For example, in an article entitled "The Social Worker as Radical," a professor of social work argued that we must marry radical content to liberal change-seeking processes to achieve change aimed at a diffuse bill of social ills. [61] The strategies suggested included offering critiques of the services of our agencies, being more honest with our clients, becoming more politically sophisticated, and addressing larger publics. The problems with this approach are twofold. First, liberal strategies do not have to be tried to see if they will work. They have been found wanting long ago. This history of failure is not dealt with in this article. Second, the radical strategy defined as the less acceptable alternative is poorly developed and is presented as an unattractive, isolated extremist view. A rational and realistic alternative to liberalism is not identified.

Strategy aside, the radical position itself is defined in this same article as a broad concern with social ills which are to be attacked at their roots. This is not a position on which there can be disagreement, only confusion and multiple interpretation. What are the root causes, and what is the

[58] *Ibid.*, p. 8.
[59] Harold Weissman, "The Middle Road to Distributive Justice," *Social Work,* 17 (March 1972), p. 93.
[60] *Ibid.*
[61] Joseph C. Ryant, "The Social Worker as Radical," *Iowa Journal of Social Work,* 3 (Summer 1970), pp. 84–86.

nature of the social ills requiring change? In the absence of greater specificity, this prescription becomes a free-association test, subject to cooptation by every variety of reformer.

Similarly, in another article, "The Social Worker as Radical: Roles of Advocacy," the radical's commitment is understood to be seeking to benefit the poor.[62] The strategy is advocacy on behalf of individuals and groups. Despite the militance of the approach and the undoubted risk to the worker in job security and advancement, advocacy perpetuates the "worker as savior" myth, regardless of its underlying good will. It rests on the assumption that the sources of accumulated power and wealth will be responsive to requests or demands from the social worker in a way that will lead to fundamental change. It is a view of radicalism that is based on the liberal concern for the deprivation of others, rather than the oppression of all, and on a continued belief in the potential of the existing system to be responsive, if only the correct approach can be found.

Some of the major debates in social work have similarly channeled professionals' awareness of radical possibilities. Alternative positions in these debates have, in fact, represented a real choice on some dimensions, but have excluded the consideration of other important positions. Debate itself can hinder consideration of meaningful alternatives when the choices offered within the debate are narrow. If these debates capture the forum and organize and channel the terms of discourse, then a framework will not be developed to formulate and debate other alternatives.

The underlying dimensions on which there has been agreement within these debates are the acceptance of the basic structure and organizational principles of the society and of social work's role in relationship to them. At the same time, these debates have represented a conservative-liberal split and have represented some real differences in the profession. One consequence has been that social work has not debated the radical alternatives and has discouraged such a consideration by channeling potentially radical dissent into support of the liberal position.

The two debates that we consider here are: Should social work be identified as cause or function? and Is social work most appropriately organized under private or public auspices? While these debates are not as active at present as they sometimes have been, the issues they represent are still alive in the profession. Examining the debates will help shed light on the theories of society and of change contained in social work practice. In examining each debate, we look for the real differences they represent

---

[62] Paul Terrell, "The Social Worker as Radical: Roles of Advocacy," *New Perspectives: The Berkeley Journal of Social Welfare*, 1 (Spring 1967) pp. 83–88. Reprinted in Paul E. Weinberger (ed.), *Perspectives on Social Welfare* (New York: Macmillan, 1969), pp. 355–362.

and contrast these differences to the commonalities they share on the underlying issues of social conservation or social change.

The Cause–Function Debate

The cause-function debate was first articulated in those terms in Porter Lee's well-known formulation of 1929, "Social Work: Cause and Function." [63] Lee identified the profession's conflict between the dual concerns of social reform and individualized service to clients. The question he posed was whether social work should or could deal with social problems at a societal level where many problems have their genesis or at the level of the individuals who experienced these problems. Reformers, that is, those carrying the banner of social work as cause, argued then, as now, that the individual-treatment approach intervenes too late in the chain of causal events to have much effect on problems and, in any case, can deal only with a small percentage of the casualties of the system. In addition, involvement at the level of individual treatment drains energy and attention from the need for system reform. Caseworkers have argued, on the other hand, that there must be a place for those with individual problems to turn while larger reforms are undertaken. People will always have problems regardless of reforms made in the society. Social work represents, in this view, the fulfillment of an important social function at the retail, rather than the wholesale, level. Furthermore, caseworkers have suggested that casework is the arena to which social work brings special expertise. Social work's overinvolvement in reform carries political risk to the profession and the possibility of social work's becoming absorbed into other professions and into broader social movements, thereby losing its special identity.

The debate has not flagged over the years, although some of the terms used and perceptions of the debate have changed.[64] For example, at a point roughly halfway between Porter Lee's address and the present, Arthur Altmeyer wrote that

> We are all too prone to look back with a sigh to the great days of social reform and the great deeds of social workers of a bygone day. We are accused, and indeed accuse ourselves, of having had our attention directed away from the environmental causes of human misery and unhappiness in our preoccupation with applying our new-found knowledge and skills to

[63] Porter R. Lee, "Social Work: Cause and Function," *Proceedings of the National Conference of Social Work,* 1929 (Chicago: University of Chicago Press, 1930).
[64] A review of this debate is found in Clarke A. Chambers, "An Historical Perspective on Political Action vs. Individualized Treatment," *Current Issues in Social Work Seen in Historical Perspective,* Council on Social Work Education (New York: Council on Social Work Education, 1962), pp. 51–64.

analyzing and solving the personal causes of individual maladjustment and family problems.[65]

And in the 1970s, Alvin Schorr wrote in the professional journal *Social Work*, that "casework has been on the defensive now for some time. It has taken some of the blame that has been accorded to social work for failing to prevent the great distress that we suffer in this country." On the other hand, he points out, "its fiercest commitment is to the importance of individuals, and it reaches those it reaches. This is not a small achievement, as scorn for helping individuals is itself a depersonalizing idea loose in our land."[66]

This is not a vacuous debate. Social work has wrestled with and agonized over these alternatives. The positions represent real differences in that they do focus, alternatively, on individual change and/or adjustment versus community action or attention to social policy. Furthermore, it is generally assumed in this debate that the casework aspects of the profession are more conservative and the community organization aspects are more progressive. In fact, as we suggested earlier, casework has generally focused on individual adjustment at the expense of any explicit attempt to alter structural relationships in the society, and community organization has dealt with larger entities, working at the least with groups of people, theoretically with some attention to the need for social change.

However, there is serious limitation imposed on an analysis when the alternatives are presented in this way. Namely, the profession has taken a real dichotomy between working with individuals and working with communities or at the level of national social policy and suggested that this is simultaneously a dichotomy on a more conservative versus a less conservative or even radical dimension. This is an unwarranted jump in logic. There may be a real difference in the levels of intervention in social work practice. To equate this difference with more or less progressive activity, as the cause-function debate has done, illogically intertwines the poles of what are two separate dimensions of practice. The cause-function debate has suggested one polarity, consisting of two elements—level of intervention and degree of political progressivism. There are two polarities here.

Neither casework nor community organization is inherently conservative or progressive in itself, as we demonstrated in earlier sections. In practice, both have served to reinforce the existing values and structures of the society. To understand the alternatives available as delineated by the cause-function debate obscures for the profession and for individual

---

[65] Arthur J. Altmeyer, "The Dynamics of Social Work," *Social Welfare Forum*, San Francisco, 1955 (New York: Columbia University Press, 1955), p. 99.
[66] Alvin Schorr, Editorial, "The Real Thing," *Social Work*, 16 (July 1971), p. 2.

professionals the range of political positions available. It has made it all the more difficult for progressives to identify theory and practice consonant with their desire to be socially useful.

As we have previously suggested, community organization practice, which has supposedly carried the reform or cause burden of the profession, has in fact been as or more conservative than social casework in its theory and practice. The focus on communities and on dealing with the relationship between groups in the community, or the focus on social amelioration at the policy level can, and generally has, taken a form that could best be described as social therapy. Far from being oriented toward the establishment of social as opposed to economic values, these changes ultimately have served the needs of economic development and of social control. There is an alternative, but this has not generally been represented in social work. Rather than be seen as social therapy or as directed toward the achievement of social harmony, community work could be focused on the development of political awareness and on the capability to struggle for radical changes. The end-point of community work, however, has not been specified in the arguments for social work as cause. In fact, the practice has not focused on facilitating fundamental social change.

Social casework, on the other hand, while functioning conservatively in practice, also has radical potential. Psychological liberation is a part of social casework's concern, although it is deeply submerged in the conservative framework of casework practice. The concept of individuals struggling to maximize themselves as people, to make the most of their potential as human beings in and through a changed society, has radical psychological and political implications if freed of its specific current and historical political trappings. Casework as function in the social work debate, then, is conservative not for any inherent reasons, but because of the way in which helping has been defined and practiced. The dichotomy created by the cause-function debate, while recognizing some points of real difference, has helped to obscure the conservative perspective contained in both sides of the argument.

It is interesting to note that in a recent empirical study of 821 practicing social workers, a clinical-social division did not emerge.[67] The majority of workers studied felt that they exhibited elements of both in their practice. Furthermore, a high rating on clinical orientation did not necessarily reflect a low rating on social orientation. One conclusion drawn by the researchers was that workers are forced to integrate both perspectives into their thinking and practice by the nature of their tasks. This

[67] Merlin A. Taber and Anthony J. Vattano, "Clinical and Social Orientations in Social Work," *Social Service Review*, 44 (March 1970), pp. 34–43.

finding offers some evidence that gives us much cheer in trying to develop radical practice. Social welfare workers, being people as well as professionals, can and do break through the boundaries of established ideologies; they can and do see things in a way that runs counter to and resists categories of thought and action established by the official dogmas. This provides the soil in which nonconventional alternatives can thrive.

The Public–Private Debate

The same kind of analysis made of the cause-function debate can be made of the question of whether social work functions best under private or public auspices. A question that contains some real differences is represented as containing a greater political diversity than it actually has, thereby obscuring the existence and development of more profound alternatives.

Particularly during the Depression, many social workers were much disturbed by the possibility of social work's absorption into public bureaucracies. For this reason, one sector of the social work profession resisted some elements of the New Deal programs. The private sector in social work continues to couch its propaganda, as it did in the 1930s, in terms of the need for social work to maintain its independence from public bureaucracies, to offer variety and flexibility of services, and to stay close to local communities. However, the private sector in general has been seen as the more conservative sector and the public sector as more progressive. Liberal social workers have pushed for greater involvement of social work in the public sector. For example, Roy Lubove's well-known book, *The Struggle for Social Security*, interpreted the increasing assumption of public responsibility for social work functions as a victory for progressive forces.[68] Indeed, the private sector has been on the receiving end of a wide variety of criticism since the Depression years.

[68] Roy Lubove, *The Struggle for Social Security* (Cambridge, Mass.: Harvard University Press, 1968). It is interesting that Lubove has since reassessed the political premises that brought him to these conclusions. In a seminar at Bryn Mawr College School of Social Work and Social Research, Bryn Mawr, Pennsylvania, on March 3, 1972, he indicated that, since completion of the book, he had come to feel that the assumption of public responsibility in itself was no necessary good and in fact has come to represent a rather undemocratic control by government of more areas of people's lives. Unfortunately (from the perspective of the present study), rather than seek alternatives in a radical direction, he has chosen to explore further the nineteenth-century conservative view, as represented in the United States, for example, by the economist Milton Friedman, once Barry Goldwater's economic adviser. This view involves deescalating government, generally within the framework of a capitalist market perspective, in an attempt to make the capitalist market function. Hence, for Lubove, the voucher system for social welfare services has become attractive as an alternative to government-provided services.

Social reform, by and large, has called for government intervention as though reform and the enlargement of government activity were synonymous demands.

Again, this is a real but limited dichotomy. In fact, it may be true that the private sector has tended to operate in a more conservative fashion than the public. It has increasingly focused on the middle classes rather than on the working classes, and it has stressed remedial psychosocial rather than social action approaches.[69] The public sector has been the locus of community action, a War on Poverty, and large-scale efforts to raise standards of living.

These differences, however, obscure the extent to which the public and private sectors have merged and are little distinguishable on some dimensions. They share underlying philosophies and political perspectives in much the same way that casework and community organization have done, and they are so interwoven structurally that their differences are less important than their commonalities. Furthermore, criticizing the private sector as conservative or lauding government action as progressive ignores the ultimate locus of basic change in any society, namely, large numbers of ordinary people who join together. The private sector, because it represents potential, if not actual, voluntary grass-roots organization, might well be the first place where we would look for grass-roots action designed to bring about basic social changes.

The extent of the differences between these two sectors has been much exaggerated. In fact, it would be difficult to find any private sector of activity that is not heavily dependent on public monies from one source or another.[70] Furthermore, this trend is accelerating, even with recent cuts in federal financing for social services, as traditional private sources of money become harder to tap, and private agencies turn with more urgency to public funds. Increasingly, for example, state departments of welfare are divesting themselves of their social service functions for welfare clients and arranging to provide these services, as minimal as they may be, through contract with private agencies. It is hard to say whether this represents an absorption of the public by the private sector, or vice versa.

The reality is that these are two arms of the same octopus. Not only is the funding increasingly public but the people and ideas dominating the structure are the same. It would be uncommon, for example, to find a state welfare system in which the leading persons, both the social work

---

[69] Richard Cloward and Irwin Epstein, "Private Social Welfare's Disengagement from the Poor: The Case of Family Adjustment Agencies," in George Brager and Francis Purcell (eds.), *Community Action Against Poverty* (New Haven: College and University Press, 1967), pp. 40–63.

[70] See Gordon Manser, "Implications of Purchase of Service for Voluntary Agencies," *Social Casework*, 53 (June 1972), pp. 335–340.

professionals and the business people who tend to get appointed to the political posts, were not also active in the local United Fund or Community Chest. Even social welfare has its patterns of interlocking directorates and power elites.[71]

Both public and private spheres are controlled by other than the clients they serve. Ultimately, the most important point of commonality of these spheres is that they do not represent the best interests of the majority of people. It is clear that private social agencies and United Funds represent the largest business concerns of their communities. Their boards of directors are fairly consistently dominated by the local business and financial leaders. Furthermore, the public welfare sector also responds to the imperatives of big business. In both cases, therefore, similar economic and political needs are fulfilled. There may be some differences between public and private sponsorship for social work, but the outcomes for clients are not substantially different.

To focus, therefore, on the public versus private sector as a critical dimension for understanding social work's development is to contain our understanding of social work within a debate that does not deal with the critical issue of the impact of these differences on the lives of the recipients of social work service. It does not necessarily follow that public assumption of responsibility leads to social progress. The alternatives represent alternative modes of control of social work and of its clients, but the master and the vision are the same in either case.

[71] The literature documenting this pattern is large, but tends to be focused on particular communities. One of the best local studies is "Centers of Power in St. Louis: Interlocking Directorates and the United Fund," a RAP Pamphlet, October, 1970, mimeographed. For analysis in other periods, see Arthur Stone and Martin Kahn, "Relief: A General Motors Product," *Social Work Today*, 3 (October 1935), pp. 11–13; Robert W. Kelso, "Banker's Control of Community Chests," *The Survey*, 68 (May 1932), pp. 17 ff; F. Emerson Andrews, "New Trends in Corporate Giving," *Social Welfare Forum*, Chicago (New York: Columbia University Press, 1952), pp. 251–259. See also Carol Deming, *A Study of the United Community Fund of Chester and Vicinity, 1969*, Chester, Pennsylvania, mimeographed; and, Robert Green et al., *A Study of the Boards of 23 Selected Welfare Agencies in the Richmond Metropolitan Area*, completed in partial fulfillment for the degree of MSW at Virginia Commonwealth University, School of Social Work, January, 1970.

8

Affirmative Visions

INTRODUCTION

To this point, our task has been to analyze the failure of the social services to achieve the kinds of outcomes to which they are ostensibly committed. The underlying cause of this failure, it was argued, is the structural and ideological integration of the services with a social order in which human fulfillment is relegated to a secondary position. Unless and until these destructive commitments are understood and the ties they represent are broken, the social services will continue to fail their clients, frustrate service providers, and sustain lesser possibilities for our society.

Critical analysis of the social services and of the society at large is important in the effort to develop an alternative approach to practice. Such analysis helps us to understand what it is that we are struggling against. By itself, however, critical analysis is not a sufficient basis for developing radical commitment and activity. We need more. Particularly, we need some positive visions of what we are working toward, some hopes that these visions might someday be achieved, and some strategies and tactics that will help us work better in everyday situations and that will simultaneously point to long-run accomplishments. The remaining chapters of this book are devoted to developing these parts of the overall perspective. The present chapter specifically deals with one dimension of this task, namely, the development of some notions of the kinds of long-range goals we might achieve. These are presented not as a blueprint for the future, but as a stimulus to our visionary hopes, which are all too often buried in the despair of the present.

VISIONS OF A HUMANIZED SOCIETY

We live in a time in which utopian models for our society are not widely discussed. We are so rooted in what we think of as pragmatism and realism that the essential work of creative social fantasy has been nearly abandoned. Our analyses and our plans for the future build on the notion that the development of society has reached its pinnacle and finale in the twentieth-century welfare state of the United States.[1] Yet, it is important that we develop images of attractive alternatives for our society. As Erich Fromm suggested in an introduction to *Looking Backward* (the widely read utopian novel of the late nineteenth and early twentieth centuries), utopia is no more than "a society in which man has reached such perfection that he is able to build a social system based on justice, reason and solidarity."[2] Without visions of what such a social system might look like, we may fall prey to distorted notions of "justice, reason and solidarity" and lose our way in the morass of daily activity.

Unfortunately, those alternatives most generally available as models too often seem no more desirable than what now exists. Socialism tends to conjure up images of bureaucratic, dictatorial, and gray societies. For many, the Soviet Union would come to mind as the embodiment of socialist ideas. China is emerging in the 1970s as a society with attractive qualities, but to many seems remote from the circumstances of Western industrialized society. This is also the case with Cuba and with some of the emerging African socialist societies. The Scandinavian countries with their advanced forms of welfare statism seem to experience many of the same dilemmas as the United States.[3] We will not attempt to evaluate

[1] For example, see Robin Blackburn, "A Brief Guide to Bourgeois Ideology," in Alexander Cockburn and Robin Blackburn (eds.), *Student Power* (Baltimore: Penguin Books, 1969), reprinted in Richard C. Edwards et al., *The Capitalist System* (Englewood Cliffs, N.J.: Prentice-Hall, 1972), pp. 36–46.

[2] Erich Fromm, "Foreword," in Edward Bellamy, *Looking Backward* (New York: Signet, 1960), p. *vii.*

[3] For example, see Jacques Hersh, " 'Welfare State' and Social Conflict," *Monthly Review*, 22 (March 1970), pp. 29–43; and Lars Erik Karlsson, "Industrial Democracy in Sweden," in Gerry Hunnius, G. David Garson, and John Case (eds.), *Workers' Control* (New York: Vintage Books, 1973), pp. 176–193.

these models here, though it is a worthwhile task to learn about other countries, the solutions they have sought for the basic questions of social organization, and the problems they experience. Were we to research these examples more fully, we would likely discover that we cannot easily find other countries that have moved from where the United States is today to something that is clearly better, and that could be models for us. We need to develop our own visions of the best hopes we have for ourselves based on our particular circumstances.

In the following sections, some structural alternatives for our society are suggested. They have a common goal—to conceptualize a society in which every person is afforded maximum opportunity to enrich his or her spiritual, psychological, physical, and intellectual well-being. A concern for the quality of life of each person is foremost. How quality of life is defined and how it may be achieved differ in this account from liberal views, as does the seriousness with which we insist that no person's welfare can be gained at another's expense. But each person's welfare is and must be the prime concern of a program for social reconstruction.

Social Rationality and Economic Life

If we are successful in creating a world more conducive to human well-being, it will surely mean finding ways to dominate, rather than be dominated by, economics. Neither the "unseen hand of the market" nor the massive corporation that government-business-military have become has the will or the way to make economic decisions in the light of their implications for human welfare. However, it is absolutely essential that social priorities dominate if human life is to prosper.

There is no way to describe our present system from a social perspective other than as irrational. Our material well-being does not give us freedom to pursue rich, rounded, and whole lives, but rather ties us to a cycle of production and consumption. We produce goods, make investment decisions, and determine the number and nature of jobs that will be available for people who need them on the basis of the criterion of profitability. The consequences are an overabundance of goods that do not add up to a fundamental sense of well-being for most people, an absence of goods that we need but that are not profitable to produce, jobs that are destructive to the people who hold them,[4] a national psychology organized around competition and consumption, ecological destruction, and exploitation of large parts of the rest of the world to enable us to maintain our standards of material achievement.[5] Human well-being is not, as

[4] See Hunnius, Garson, and Case, *Workers' Control.*
[5] On this point, see Gabriel Kolko's excellent *The Roots of American Foreign Policy* (Boston: Beacon Press, 1969).

it should be, the rationale for our actions. Rather, it is another of the factors that the huge corporation we all live in must consider, to the extent that it influences the overall production process.

In what ways would economic decisions be modified if they were made in the light of social and psychological consideration? In general terms, a commitment to this suggests that determinations about what would be produced, in what quantity, when and how, would be made according to their impact on our overall well-being. The decision to produce cars, for example, would not be made exclusively on the basis of their salability, but according to socially determined priorities about the relative emphasis to be given to private versus public transportation, problems of pollution, use of raw materials, the nature of the work experience for the people who produced the cars, and so on. A new factory would be located not solely according to the availability of inexpensive raw materials, labor, and transportation, but according to the developmental needs of the various regions of the country and in the light of concerns for population concentration and dispersal, ecology, and so on.

Thinking rationally about how to manage our economy also permits us to make decisions about patterns of distribution of wealth using various criteria. We would have a basis, in such a system, for equalizing the distribution of goods and resources both among the people in this country and among the populations of other countries (if, in this restructured society, we are still limited by nation states as a form of organization). Contrary to our present practices, we can operationalize an often-stated belief in the dignity of each human being with a real commitment to assuring each human being full economic rights, along with the political rights we ostensibly enjoy at present.

Equality needs to be understood as implying something beyond equal access to school, a job, or a home. The fact that people start with unequal social, economic, and psychological resources means that equal access to opportunity does not produce equal opportunity. Because of prior deprivations, for example, students are not equally prepared to make use of what public-provided education now exists. Because of educational deprivations, in turn, they are not equally prepared to understand their own political and social situations and to make equally effective use of political processes. The notion of equality of opportunity, to be effectively implemented, actually contains within it in latent form a necessary commitment to prior equality in the distribution of various available resources.

To help achieve greater equality and to promote greater individual freedom from economic constaint, we might institute a plan providing for the public provision of the basic necessities of life for all citizens, including such items as food, shelter, clothing, education, and basic services such as health care, day care, and transportation. This would free people to move from periods of paid work to periods of education, recreation, and experimentation of all sorts. Any society, the utopian society being no exception, will require responsible behavior of its citizens. But we can modify the definition of responsibility so that people will be freer to experiment with their lives. People ought to be free to choose not to take what we have traditionally considered to be paid work, to the extent to which that choice can be made consistent with the larger needs of the society.[6]

It may be the case that one consequence of such changes will be that we function with fewer material goods available to us. Whatever choices we make voluntarily, revolutionary movements throughout the world may force us to disengage from economic exploitation of other countries and, consequently, may force a lower standard of material well-being on us. We may well decide on our own, however, that the human cost of high material standards of living are not justified for other reasons. The high level of production that is required is costly to us in the disproportionate share of human energy devoted to it, the consumption of natural resources involved, and the extent to which organizing our lives around material goods puts us out of touch with a more natural and organic relationship with ourselves and our environment.

However, at the point at which we decide to live more simply, it will likely be with a sense of gain rather than loss. If we do not need to fear the lack of food, shelter, and clothing, if education and recreation are available to us, if we all have relatively equal shares of whatever goods are available, we will not have the need, as we do now, to pursue private accumulation against the attacks of a predatory environment. In a real sense, our personal resources will be those of the whole society, and the whole notion of a nest egg or of insurance will hopefully be a vague historical memory.[7] Furthermore, our psychological needs for material wealth may well wither away, as we have the opportunity to experience the more profound wealth found in rewarding human experience. Our desire to feel rich will be met in a rich and rounded way and not in the more limited ways we now pursue.

We have, then, several levels of goals in mind. At the first level, we

---

[6] Theobald and others have presented evidence to counter the argument that under such a system most people might stop working, or that the United States' economy would disintegrate. See Robert Theobald, *The Guaranteed Income* (Garden City, N.Y.: Doubleday, 1967). For evidence that challenges the assumption that economic equality would necessarily undermine motivation to work, see David Macarov, *Incentives to Work* (San Francisco: Jossey-Bass, 1970), especially Chapter 4, "Motivation to Work," pp. 61–108.

[7] Here, as elsewhere in this discussion, the reader can do no better than turn to the delightful and profound utopian novel of the late 1800s, William Morris's *News from Nowhere* (New York: Longmans, Green, 1905, first edition, 1891).

need to rationalize the economic system from a social perspective. Social values must be placed in a primary position in decision making about economic matters. This opens the door to producing goods for their utility rather than for their profitability, to a consideration of the variety of costs of production (social, ecological, economic, and so on), and to the possibilities of making social determinations about the distributions of the wealth of the society.

At the second and more profound developmental level, we can begin to move toward the fuller transcendence of the economic system. Here we not only make economic decisions on a social basis, but we reevaluate the meaning of economics in our lives. We may discover that the assumption that more is better, which most of human kind has lived with for some time, was not a natural desideratum of the good life, but a product of material scarcity, inequitable distribution of what was available, and an underdeveloped social ethic.

Under what kinds of arrangements are we likely to realize such outcomes? If we eliminate profitability, as we now understand it, as the basis for economic decisions, we must find another way to accumulate and invest capital to produce what we want. Only a system in which capital is accumulated and invested by the society in general in the name of the whole society can do this. This means doing away with the private ownership and control of the means of production. The people in general must own and control production, since it is they who are both the instruments of its maintenance and the beneficiaries of its products. Furthermore, if we are to produce for social use in a social manner, only a system in which everyone who is affected by the decisions made helps to make them will ensure responsiveness of the system to everyone's needs. Centralized state control and ownership of the means of production, as opposed to capitalist control and ownership, is a seriously inadequate form for achieving these ends. Our criteria point in the direction of the creation of a decentralized, democratic, socialist society.

In a capitalist system, profitability must be the criterion for decision making. Large private accumulations of capital are a consequence, but they are also a necessity in a system that can invest and grow only on the basis of such accumulations. But if the accumulations are made by the society as a whole and if the motives for reinvestment are social utility and human welfare rather than the protection and expansion of capital, then investment in production can be made under circumstances that would not be possible in the old system.

We are hopefully not far from the time when the folly of entrusting what is fundamentally the shared wealth of us all to the private decision making and use of the few will be widely apparent. That will still leave open, however, the critical question of the bases on which shared or social decision making will proceed. What will be the units of decision making, and who, precisely, will make determinations about investment and production, as well as other critical matters facing the society?

Social Organization

In thinking about forms of social organization for a society that would best promote human welfare, we inevitably face questions about the balance between centralized and decentralized decision making. If there are no structures for making encompassing decisions about overall matters, the society will not be able to be as rational as we would like it to be about larger questions, and this will surely have an adverse effect on localities. If most decisions are made centrally, however, we lose vital and desirable local autonomy and run the danger of dictatorship or oligarchy. Although no formula answer can be found and any arrangement may need to change over time, we can develop some guiding principles. Perhaps the primary commitment we should maintain is to the maximum degree of community autonomy. As a general principle, we ought to strive to build society and all larger decision-making structures on the basis of the strongest possible collective units at the local level.

At this point, we function on quite another basis. The units of activity are individuals who attempt to influence overall decisions either as individuals or as members of pressure groups. Pressure groups, as we now understand them, are only distantly related to the notion of collectivity. In a collectivity, people come together around a range of common concerns and build their lives with each other. In a pressure group, people band together temporarily and around limited concerns, not to build a common life, but to win some concessions over others through political pressure.

The problem in a society in which larger bodies make central, society-wide decisions is not with the fact that general decisions are made. Rather, it is with the fact that power and autonomy accumulate in fewer hands at the top at the expense of disaggregated individuals at the bottom. Therefore, we must build strength from the bottom. Ultimately, as Martin Buber has suggested, we must accomplish the substitution of a genuine society for the state.[8] The state is necessarily coercive, since it is outside the most direct, immediate experience of each of us. It is a political form. For this we must substitute the "social principle—the principle of inner cohesion, collaboration and mutual stimulation." [9] We must, says Buber, renew people and awake the "inner statehood" that resides in each of us.[10]

---

[8] Martin Buber, *Paths in Utopia* (Boston: Beacon Press, 1958, first published, 1949).
[9] *Ibid.*, p. 80.
[10] *Ibid.*, p. 48.

Perhaps the key element in any such renewal is the development of a true collectivist spirit. A renewed society will be peopled by renewed individuals. Collectivism in this society will be both the vehicle and the expression of that renewal. As a first step in considering the larger questions of social organization and decision making, therefore, we must consider the meaning of collectivism and some of the issues it raises.

Unfortunately, collectivist ideas frequently elicit fears that the individual will be dominated and denied by the will of the majority. In one respect, these fears are not entirely misplaced. Our collective engagements, at present, tend to have coercive elements in them, since they take place in a framework of, and frequently in subservience to, a hierarchical and coercive superstructure. (In discussing the alternative of individualism, however, we suggested that people are not as free to pursue their own visions in our society as is commonly assumed. We also suggested the ways in which the pursuit of individual welfare tends to produce collective diswelfare and, therefore, does not eventually lead to individual welfare. It is important to keep these dilemmas in mind because we ought to juxtapose an evaluation of a collectivized society against the reality of individualism and not against a fictional image of it.)

Collectivism does not imply abandonment of self, passive acceptance of the will of the majority, or loss of privacy. Not does it mean uniform blandness or submission to "the group." [11] It does imply recognition of the reality that individual welfare is ultimately unachievable in the absence of collective welfare. Consequently, it points to the necessity for struggle with others to organize life so that the very best decisions for oneself become the very best decisions for all and the very best decisions for all become the very best decisions for oneself. This is not to deny that these two areas of decision making may conflict at times. The goal is to reduce that conflict as much as possible.

Collectivism as a social model suggests taking seriously the fact that people form a society, a social entity, when they live together. Collectivism means, therefore, subjecting decision making in those areas that, in fact, impact the whole to collective thought and to collective action in the light of collective needs and resources.

What may seem restrictive actually contains the potential to increase choice. People acting together actually create more social, psychological, and physical options for one another. Nor does collectivity mean that private choice is abandoned. It does mean, however, that choices that look private, but really involve others, are subject to collective decision making that takes that involvement into account. For example, the individual

---

[11] A useful discussion of this point is found in Erich Fromm, *Marx's Concept of Man* (New York: Ungar, 1961).

decision to buy a car affects everyone through its impact on traffic congestion and pollution, as the decision of two adults to have children affects all people, and not just that couple, through its effects on population density and the use of resources. Collectivization suggests that all those impacted by a choice by any one person ought to have a say in that choice, commensurate with the impact that choice will have on them. Similarly, decisions of the individual that influence others little or not at all should not be gratuitously subjected to collective decision making. Collectivism, then, recognizes and tries to account for the pattern of our influences on one another. It tries to organize social life around the realities of our mutual dependencies.

A society that was more collectivized would likely place much greater stress on varieties of communal living. Again, privacy is not necessarily foregone in such arrangements, nor are notions of men and women forming long-lasting primary relationships. Collective living does imply a sharing of a variety of aspects of family and home life which make sense to share. These might include physical resources (dwellings, incomes, home utilities, and so on), chores, and child care. Equally important is the sharing of emotional experience and the important sense of psychological support that comes through involvement in a meaningful collective experience.

While collective living may not ever be desirable for all persons under all circumstances, it might well be the case, in a humanized society, that it will be a preferable model for many people. What may be a natural impulse toward collectivity is thwarted by the ways in which we are encouraged to believe that our well-being is dependent on the extent to which we can purchase privacy and can claim exclusive ownership of goods. The collective impulse is also weakened by the forms of social organization with which we live that encourage mutually competitive behavior. The desirability of communal life will undoubtedly increase as our lives become more collectively intertwined in a cooperative, rather than a competitive, fashion.

Similarly, work places will be much humanized by decentralized collectivist management. They might be organized through the creation of small units of workers, whose work could be coordinated by decision-making councils, the members of which could be elected from the subunits. Work supervision would be a mutual and collective task. This kind of direct democracy could extend to all aspects of the work situation (hiring, firing, production decisions, and so on), consistent with a framework of larger priorities of the community. While there would undoubtedly need to be specialized tasks, people performing those roles would not be seen as necessarily higher in a hierarchy, but simply as carrying on other aspects of the collective work, and would be responsible to the collectivity.

A guiding principle must be to organize so that all decisions are made at the lowest possible level at which they can be made. If a job permits a worker options in its performance, then the worker should choose among those options rather than have that choice made by some other person. If decisions about the nature, quantity, and timing of production can be made by workers in factories, they should be made by them. This principle brings together the making of decisions about any activity with the people who actually are responsible for conducting that activity. Ideas for activity may originate at a variety of levels, and coordination may require the denial of the short-run interests of any one unit. Nonetheless, the principle of decision making from the bottom seems desirable because it takes seriously the idea that people ought to shape their environment as much as possible, as part of the general belief in self-determination.

Collectivizing work in this fashion has many advantages, for example, the increase in the quality and quantity of information available for decision making and the increased willingness of the participants to carry out decisions reached collectively. For the individual, the advantages of collectivism become apparent by contrasting collectivism with its alternative, which is the individual's pursuit of a career through some hierarchical ladder. The typical effort to make a successful career is limiting and destructive in some important ways. Careerism may require demonstrating uniqueness and originality, a difficult or impossible task for some. Often, it also means moving to supervisory work, which may differ in nature from the direct work for which a person is trained. This means leaving what may be a preferred area of work, and it implies that ground-level work is somehow undesirable, since it is what gets left once the individual achieves success.

In general, collectivizing work situations can potentially increase the total rewards of work for all workers and can spread these rewards through a lifetime of work rather than hold out the highest rewards as possibilities to be encountered toward the end of a career. For example, pay might be far more equal over a working career and more dependent on need than on time on the job or place in a hierarchy. Thus, younger workers with dependent families might earn somewhat more pay. The ability to influence decisions at work would exist throughout one's working life and not only once one had attained an "executive" position. Similarly, if work at the ground level is valued and not something to be abandoned as quickly as possible for better rewards elsewhere, then prestige as a work reward could come as the result of meaningful accomplishment at any task. Likewise, over time, a collective group of workers might build into their activity variety that is otherwise available only by moving through a career ladder. Changing a job would not depend on moving up a ladder of some sort, but could come as the result of a collective determination about the desirability of variation.

Developments in work places in China, which we are now hearing about, are very instructive in these matters. Increasingly, the Chinese seem able to organize even complex production in a democratic way that involves all workers in decision making. The rise in spirit and in levels of production has been widely noted. While complete rotation of leadership and workers has not been achieved, accountability is a mutual process and collective effort is consciously developed, even under conditions where high degrees of specialized skill are required of some, for example, in medical care.[12]

The development of strong, viable collectives, building at the local level of work and community and stimulating what Buber called our "inner statehood," allows us to conceptualize the creation of larger co-ordinating bodies that do not weaken a commitment to direct, radical democracy. For example, Alperovitz has suggested a model for public ownership and control in

> thousands of small communities, each working out its own priorities and methods, each generating broader economic criteria, and each placing political demands on the larger system out of this experience. The locality should be conceived of as a basis for (not an alternative to) a larger framework of regional and national coordinating institutions.[13]

It is possible, in other words, to conceptualize models of social organization that attempt to develop a creative balance of local collective initiative and democracy with the establishment of plans and priorities on a national level. This is especially appealing when we view each successive larger unit as consisting of representatives of the units below it, accountable to that unit, and recallable by it. Units of collectives can join to-

[12] Of special interest in the social services is Joshua Horn's *Away with All Pests: An English Surgeon in People's China, 1954–1969* (New York: Monthly Review Press, 1971). A chapter of that book is reprinted as "Hospitals in China," *Monthly Review*, 22 (April 1971), pp. 12–30. See also Ruth Sidel and Victor Sidel, "The Human Services in China," *Social Policy*, 2 (March–April 1972), pp. 25–34; and William Hinton, *Fanshen* (New York: Vintage Books, 1966), especially Chapter 27, "The Work Team," pp. 259–268.

[13] Gar Alperovitz, "Socialism as a Pluralist Commonwealth," in Edwards et al., *The Capitalist System*, p. 528. Alperovitz acknowledges the complementarity of this view, in important respects, with that developed by Percival Goodman and Paul Goodman in *Communitas* (Chicago: University of Chicago Press, 1947). Also see Arthur Waskow, "Notes from 1999," in *Working Papers for a New Society*, 1 (Spring 1973), pp. 62–74.

gether to form the next larger bodies of decision making, whether in the factory, town, community or region of the country.[14]

Furthermore, as local collectives become more effective and well-knit the number and magnitude of the decisions that have to be made at the larger level will be reduced. By following the principle of decision making at the lowest possible level in the system, the number of decisions that have to be made at the larger levels are reduced to issues of coordination and administration. Policy in such a situation comes from the bottom up, not the top down. In addition, such a society will, hopefully, do much to explore the possibilities for what have been called "self-organizing systems."[15] That is, we are very accustomed to operating in hierarchies, with fixed lines of communication and command and fixed roles—including decision-making roles. Alternatively, we need to think about organizing in such a way that each person and each unit can play an ever wider number of roles, in a changing association with one another, in which the particular forms of any given moment represent the best collective possibility for that moment, though not forever. In this view, society can be seen as a "complex network of changing relationships, including many structures of correlated activity and mutual aid, independent of authoritarian coercion."[16] Once again, the underlying belief is that people can be self-determining about social forms and can shape and reshape them to meet their current needs.

SUMMARY

This overview of the possibilities of a more rational society is meant only to be suggestive. Undoubtedly it will create in some minds many more questions than it answers. But that is just the point: we need discussion. We need to look again at the parts of our society that we have heretofore taken as givens and begin to see them for what they are— namely, artifacts of a particular historical time and social situation and not the inevitable, concluding forms of human history. We need to think about the quality of our lives as we experience them on a daily basis and to try to understand this quality in relationship to the social order in which we live. Subsequently, we need to think about how we might like

[14] For another conceptualization, see Theodore Roszak, *Where the Wasteland Ends* (Garden City, N.Y.: Doubleday, 1972), especially Chapter 12, "The Visionary Commonwealth," pp. 413–445.
[15] For example, see John D. McEwan, "The Cybernetics of Self-Organizing Systems," in C. George Benello and Dimitrios Roussopoulos (eds.), *The Case for Participatory Democracy* (New York: Grossman, 1971), pp. 179–194.
[16] *Ibid.*, p. 191.

to live and the kind of social order that would enable us to realize that way of life. At that point, we must start looking around for allies. The following chapter begins to suggest some of the places that those of us in the social services can look to find them.

9

Counterforces

INTRODUCTION

How likely is it that the United States might someday be structured on the basis of the principles suggested in the previous chapter? No one can answer that question. The classic Marxist prediction is that capitalism will not prove viable over time and will inevitably fall under the weight of its internal contradictions. Clearly, however, the capacity of our system to maintain itself, despite its irrationality and destructiveness, is great—in some measure as a result of the kinds of modifications of laissez-faire capitalism which the welfare state represents. On the other hand, it is also true that there are social forces at work that suggest that there can someday be very basic changes in the United States. If prediction of ultimate outcomes is not possible, prediction of the inevitability of conflict and struggle is possible. Our society will not be at peace with itself unless it changes in some fundamental ways because it continues to generate its own opposition as a consequence of its destructive nature.

It may be that the destiny of the United States will be determined only partially by its internal dynamics. Revolutionary movements throughout much of the world will undoubtedly influence the United

States in profound ways by denying it access to raw materials, cheap labor supplies, and consumer markets. If and when more countries in Asia, Africa, and South America decolonize themselves, one result may well be internal economic crisis in the United States that could unhinge one of the key supports that has enabled this country to maintain some semblance of domestic peace, namely, a high and rising standard of living.

Simultaneously, however, there are internal pressures in the United States with potential to create disequilibrium.[1] Large parts of the population are dissatisfied with their economic and social conditions. These dissatisfactions cannot be alleviated in a definitive way within the context of the present society. It is true, however, that they have been largely controlled to this point. There is presently little self-conscious and organized mass movement for change, although the more visible movements of the 1960s are not as defunct as the mass media suggest.[2] Nonetheless, people do not generally interpret their own dissatisfactions in such a way that they are led to seek radical alternatives. When some do, structures for the pursuit of radical alternatives are not generally available.

However, the pressures for basic change continue to exist, creating social and political instability and the potential for radical mass movements. It is useful to identify the sources and nature of these pressures, as a way to be more clear about ways and places to work for radical change. Here we focus on those pressures located in the welfare state. The welfare state and the social services give rise to new pressures and problems as they attempt to respond to those that already exist. In this section, we suggest some of the ways this occurs and explore the extent to which this pattern is inevitable, given the present structure of the welfare state.

UNINTENDED CONSEQUENCES OF THE WELFARE STATE

The welfare state is intended largely as a responsive mechanism. That is, it comes into play to supplement and support other institutions when other institutions fail to accomplish their tasks. However, the welfare state does not deal with the sources of the dilemmas that it responds to. As we have said throughout this book, it is a servant of the very forces that give rise to the problems in the first place. As a result, welfare state

---

[1] An excellent review article of the "profound forces working to undermine the social and economic equilibrium which has reigned in the United States for more than twenty-five years" is Ernest Mandel, "Where Is America Going?" *New Left Review,* 54 (March–April 1969), pp. 3–16.

[2] Some evidence for this statement is presented in the next chapter.

programs tend not to be effective in meeting people's fundamental needs though, as we have seen, they are more successful in their latent role of maintaining the status quo.

However, the failure of welfare state programs to meet people's needs has important by-products in the generation of new problems and new pressures. Welfare state programs are assigned responsibility for the resolution of a large and growing number of problems. As welfare state mechanisms become more extensive and elaborate, their status as a relatively minor supplement to the primary institutions of the society changes. The welfare state, instead of playing a marginal role as originally intended, begins to assume its own dynamics. As it does so, it creates imbalances in relationship to the primary institutions to which it was initially responsive. These imbalances create new social problems which in turn lead to the need for a second and third generation of welfare state programs, adding to the cycle of more complex responses and still additional problems.

Nathan Glazer has identified a number of ways in which the welfare state helps to create a variety of new problems and often aggravates the same problems it was designed to overcome.[3] The primary dynamic he sees at work is the encouragement, by welfare state programs, of a further weakening of society's traditional problem-solving structures as the welfare state attempts to deal with breakdowns in these mechanisms when they first appear. In his words,

> Every piece of social policy substitutes for some traditional arrangement, whether good or bad, a new arrangement in which public authorities take over, at least in part, the role of the family, of the ethnic or neighborhood group, or of the voluntary association. In so doing, social policy weakens the position of these traditional agents, and further encourages needy people to depend on the government rather than on the traditional structures, for help.[4]

Glazer's example of the welfare system illustrates this pattern. The AFDC program, as society's effort to "soften the harsh consequences of family breakup," may have made it "easier for fathers to abandon their families or mothers to disengage from their husbands."[5] It may be the case that welfare programs have contributed to family breakup by the possibility they create for parents to abandon their families, knowing that some alternative, if minimal, support is available to them.[6]

[3] Nathan Glazer, "The Limits of Social Policy," *Commentary*, 52 (September 1971), pp. 51–58.
[4] *Ibid.*, p. 54.
[5] *Ibid.*, p. 57.
[6] We should be aware, however, that the causal relationship between the availability of welfare and family breakup has not been conclusively demonstrated.

A similar pattern is observable in other areas of welfare state programming. In the housing field, it is increasingly acknowledged even by government planners that the United States' public housing effort has led to the destruction of significant amounts of old housing and failed to make good its promises to provide sufficient new housing.[7] The housing program has simply not resulted in substantially more housing for people. Likewise, government-funded drug-treatment programs have created a new generation of methadone addicts,[8] and government intervention in the medical industry has caused a spiraling of health costs that has had the perverse effect of making medical care more difficult for some parts of the population to obtain.[9] The welfare state, then, creates new social problems or exacerbates old problems, as it becomes more elaborate and pervasive. These problems, in turn, give rise to new political forces with potential for disruption.

The public welfare categorical assistance programs offer examples of welfare state programs developing new political dynamics and, subsequently, new political forces. At the inception of such programs in the 1930s, it was anticipated by welfare state planners that the categorical assistance programs would be short-lived. The social insurances, it was felt, would subsume the categorical programs which, in Gilbert Steiner's phrase, would then "wither away."[10] Inasmuch as the insurances are financed in considerable part by direct contributions of workers and operate in symbiotic relationship to the labor market, the anticipated withering away of the categorical assistances would have meant the withering away of all welfare activity in the income maintenance sector. This did not happen. The categorical assistance programs grew larger and more costly, both economically and politically, and became one of the roots of what is now considered to be the crisis in welfare.

An association between these two factors does not prove causality. We must also be cautious about such data because of the extent to which the conservative bias in conventional social science has led researchers to interpret various family patterns as "broken down" rather than as healthy, adaptive responses to particular conditions. An important analysis of the assumptions in the conventional analyses of these problems is developed by Charles A. Valantine, *Culture and Poverty* (Chicago: University of Chicago Press, 1968).

[7] In the case of the public housing and urban renewal programs, a net loss in the absolute amounts of available housing has resulted. See Martin Anderson's "The Federal Bulldozer," in James Q. Wilson (ed.), *Urban Renewal* (Cambridge, Mass.: MIT Press, 1967), p. 495.

[8] See Nicholas M. Regush, *The Drug Addiction Business* (New York: Dial, 1971).

[9] See data in Chapter 3.

[10] Gilbert Steiner, *Social Insecurity: The Politics of Welfare* (Chicago: Rand McNally, 1966), especially Chapter 2, "The Withering Away Fallacy," pp. 18–47. In another version, Gunnar Myrdal has predicted the gradual diminution of all state interventions in the face of an activated populace looking after its own interests. See *Beyond the Welfare State* (New York: Bantam Books, 1967), Chapter 6, "The State and the Individual," pp. 72–87.

That the welfare program has become intensely politicized is clear. Politicians use their positions on welfare as a way to identify themselves on the political spectrum, and important political struggles are waged in and around welfare. This has occurred, in large part, because of the association of welfare with race. Attacks on the welfare program have been perceived by those attacking and those being attacked as an attack on blacks,[11] and defensive actions by blacks in the welfare sphere have heightened black political consciousness and black organization in all spheres.

To summarize this process, the public assistance program emerged in response to the economic crisis of the Depression. What was originally a very small program became a major program, as the underlying economic dilemmas that gave rise to the Depression continued to cause unemployment and underemployment. The growing numbers on welfare, influenced by the larger politicization of the black population in the early 1960s, created a new organized political force. This force took action on its own behalf and in turn contributed to the politicization of new populations and further creative social tension in the country at large.[12]

The emergence of other rights groups concerned with a wide variety of welfare state programs is a further example of these developments. The concept of rights groups implies something beyond the traditional pressure group or interest group. Rights groups consist of people directly affected by some regulation or segment of the welfare state, who see their problems with the welfare state as intimately related to larger struggles for liberation and even for revolution. Thus, in what is known as the corrections field, groups of prisoners and ex-prisoners—such as the Fortune Society, the Barbwire Society, and the Prisoner's Rights Council —see in their struggles a microcosm of larger struggles of oppressed peoples. The Addicts Rights Organization has conducted its struggle for addicts in the context of an analysis of the relationship of drugs to class conflict. The same pattern is observed in the cases of the Mental Patients' Liberation Front (and, from the providers' side, the ideologically aligned radical therapy movement), the more militant segment of the tenant's movement (which links tenants' rights to community control not only of housing but of other significant institutions), and a variety of radical health consumer groups (and the providers' Medical Committee for Human Rights). These movements are spawned, in part, by the same fundamental forces that spawned other radical activities in the 1960s.

[11] For example, see Daniel P. Moynihan, "The Crises in Welfare," *The Public Interest* (Winter 1968), pp. 3–29; and Alvin Schorr, *Explorations in Social Policy* (New York: Basic Books, 1968), especially pp. 21–43.

[12] The pattern is developed as it appears at the municipal level by Frances Fox Piven, "The Urban Crisis: Who Got What, and Why," in Robert Paul Wolff (ed.), *1984 Revisited* (New York: Knopf, 1973), pp. 165–201.

However, they are also attributable to developments within the welfare state itself. They are its unanticipated consequences.

These movements develop for at least two special reasons. First, the fact that the welfare programs are highly selective in the kinds of programs provided and the populations served has the effect of creating new constituencies, brought or thrown together by administrative arrangements and provided with a base for organizing. Second, as the welfare state has grown, it has created new groups with increasing amounts of dependency on the welfare state and, hence, with an increasing stake in organizing in their own best self-interest. When the welfare state touched a small part of people's lives, it was not a focus for organizing. As it became increasingly central to larger numbers of people, it became a vehicle for bringing people together around programs that had a large impact on their well-being.

RISING EXPECTATIONS AND UNFULFILLED PROMISES

The welfare state, as we have suggested, fails to deal adequately with the problems people experience in their lives. In their responses to people, welfare state programs represent a bare minimum quantitatively and a serious distortion qualitatively. At the same time, welfare state programs raise people's expectations. Simply as a consequence of their existence, they suggest that the society is willing to take some responsibility for the welfare of its citizens. Furthermore, welfare state programs contain within themselves some promise of a real solution to problems. They speak of equality, of adequate minimums, and of the rights of people in a democracy. However, they fail to keep their promises. Because these promises continue to be made, despite the failure, they offer the visible and sharp contrast of what is to what might be. They keep alive in people's minds and in the social ethic some latent vision of a better society. As such, they offer a sharp contrast to the realities.

This contrast contributes to what has been identified as the revolution of rising expectations which has taken place in the United States since the end of World War II.[13] Inasmuch as major political unrest in the United States and elsewhere has tended to occur during periods of rapidly rising but unfulfilled expectations (if not necessarily of rising material circumstances),[14] the welfare state, as a provocateur, makes an important contribution to social instability.

[13] Glazer, "The Limits of Social Policy," is among the many who have identified this phenomenon. See also Herbert Gans, "The Equality Revolution," *New York Times Magazine* (November 3, 1968), pp. 36–37, 66–76.
[14] See Michael Harrington, *Socialism* (New York: Saturday Review Press, 1972), especially Chapter 6, "The American Exception," pp. 109–133.

The welfare state contributes to a sense of frustration in two ways. First, it attempts to respond to people's needs for minimal material life supports, for example, adequate shelter and income. For those for whom the welfare state minimum is the level at which life is actually lived, the welfare state must inevitably be perceived as a niggardly and degrading response to human needs. Surely this is a key message from those groups most dependent on welfare state minimums, for example, public welfare clients and the aged. Second, the welfare state, as it inadequately responds to material needs, fails to address questions about the quality of life. It suggests that people will experience an enrichment in their lives as welfare state programs expand. However, several decades of opinion polls have documented the fact that as a people, we report ourselves to be increasingly less happy in general, at the same time that we recognize that we are materially better off than we were previously.[15]

The malaise goes beyond a concern for physical well-being. If the welfare state begins to deal with issues such as environmental decay, public transportation, and the fear of crime, it will undoubtedly make some difference to our sense of well-being. However, past history of people's responses to an increased experience of physical well-being suggests that these changes alone will not get to the root of the discontent which so many report experiencing. What the welfare state fails to provide, contribute to, or even seriously address are issues related to sense of purpose in life, to the building of community, and so on. Rather, by suggesting that these are problems that the individual faces as an individual, the welfare state vigorously denies an overall social responsibility for addressing these issues.

Our analysis of the welfare state has suggested that, by its very nature, it is not capable of responding adequately to people's real needs, either quantitatively or qualitatively. In quantitative terms, there are some strong indications that the inability of the state to support social welfare services is becoming more pronounced. On the one hand, we have argued that social welfare expenditures provide both direct and indirect benefits to corporate interests. They are a way to stimulate and regularize sources of profit, and they are a way in which various costs of productivity (for instance, retirement benefits or disability insurance) can be taken off the shoulders of private industry and placed on the shoulders of the public at large. On the other hand, the ability of the state to pay for these costs is limited.

Part of this limitation comes from the rapidly rising costs of the social services in the face of their slowly rising productivity. That is, with increased unionization of public employees and the attendant political

---

[15] Nicholas Regush, *Welfare: The Social Issues in Philosophical Perspective* (Pittsburgh: University of Pittsburgh Press, 1972), p. 41.

pressures, public employees, including social service workers, have experienced major wage increases.[16] However, these wage increases do not reflect increased output per worker, as wage increases are more likely to do for workers in other sectors of the society, especially in those more influenced by advanced technologies. The provision of the same amount of services becomes progressively more expensive at the same time that the demand for those services is rising rapidly.[17]

The constraint is also located in the difficulty the state experiences in taxing to the extent required to pay for services. Working people, who have borne the major brunt of taxation, are applying political pressure against further taxation. Further, the more they are taxed, the greater they call on and further overburden the very public services which are underfinanced in the first place. Similarly, corporations resist taxation politically and can demonstrate, probably correctly, that heavy taxation undermines their profits, hence their ability to invest, grow, and keep the capitalist economy moving. Government's overreaching of its ability to pay for social programs has been exacerbated in recent years by the war in Vietnam and more broadly by its investment in the military. In general, this has produced a serious fiscal crisis for the state.

O'Conner has summarized this crisis in this way.

> At least 25 per cent and perhaps as much as one-third of the work force is directly or indirectly employed by the state. Further, tens of thousands of doctors, welfare workers and other self-employed professionals and technicians use facilities provided by the state and are dependent in whole or in part on government budgets. Finally, tens of millions of men and women are dependent on the state budget as clients and recipients of state services. On the other hand, the state continues to rely on taxes—even though traditional state functions have been greatly expanded and many new functions added. In other words, private capital, at times alone and at times allied with labor, has socialized many costs and expenses of production but has not socialized profits. In modern capitalism, state expenditures tend to outrun taxes; what people need from the state exceeds what they are willing to pay the state.[18]

It is this internal and inevitable contradiction of advanced capitalism that contributes in a significant way to the instability of the welfare state form of social organization.

---

[16] For example, during the 1960s, salaries of New York City public employees went up by 49 percent, as reported in the *Wall Street Journal* (December 30, 1970), and cited in James O'Conner, "Inflation, Fiscal Crisis, and the American Working Class," *Socialist Revolution*, 2 (March–April 1972), p. 30.

[17] Piven, "The Urban Crisis."

[18] James O'Connor, "Inflation, Fiscal Crisis, and the American Working Class," *Socialist Revolution*, 2 (March–April 1972), p. 33.

THE DISCONTENT OF SOCIAL SERVICE WORKERS

Developments in and around the welfare state cannot fail to have an impact on the workers who staff social service programs. For several reasons, the situation of these workers is becoming increasingly difficult. A variety of forces are operating on these workers, making their job situations less acceptable to them. They are in a position to create internal pressure in social service programs that cannot be fully resolved in the context of welfare state solutions.

In Chapter 4, some ways in which the welfare state controls social service workers were discussed, and the forces stimulating worker discontent were reviewed. Among these factors are the increased bureaucratization and routinization of work, the social worker's difficulty in making a positive difference in the lives of clients, the close supervision, and the downgrading of the value of the line worker's accomplishments. As we suggested, the routinization and control of social service workers is a function of the nature of the welfare state itself. As the welfare state comes to play an increasingly important role as an agent of social control in the lives of clients, its functions cannot be left to the independent views and values of workers. Workers must be organized and controlled in such a way that their performance ensures the proper functioning of the welfare state in relationship to the dominant institutions.

Furthermore, the pressures on welfare state workers take place within a context of changes in the composition and nature of the working class as a whole. Changes in the political stance of social service workers must be assessed within the context of an understanding of changes in the larger sector of the labor force of which they are a part. This sector has been identified as the new working class. A brief examination of new working class theory will be helpful in understanding what is happening and may happen to social service workers and in assessing the role social service workers might play in bringing about fundamental changes.

One of the critical debates about radical change in the United States, or anywhere for that matter, concerns that sector of the population most likely and able to be a revolutionary force. The Marxist tradition clearly locates that force in the working class. While the conservatism of labor in the United States has forced many to question Marx's prediction, some socialist theorists continue to see the working class as the sector most likely and able to bring about such change.[19] Other theorists, however, have identified the critical thrust for basic change as located in the

---

[19] For example, see Harrington, *Socialism*.

struggle of women against sexism,[20] in the youth and counterculture movement,[21] in the struggle of blacks against racism,[22] or in the revolutionary potential of that group once most scorned by Marx as revolutionnary agents, the lumpenproletariat.[23] Others have argued (more convincingly, it seems) that the kind of total change that is required can come about only through a multipronged approach in which a variety of forces pursue their special concerns and simultaneously come together around the common issues that all face. In this view, each movement mobilizes its constituency, at the same time that they identify and nurture points of mutual dependence and commonality.

If we accept, at least for the moment, that we must encourage multiple fronts for struggle, what analysis can we make of the potential role of social service workers and of the social services in general? What is the relationship of this sector to the larger struggle? Few social service workers now operate as autonomous professionals. The vast majority of social service workers are the salaried employees of large bureaucracies in the service sector. As a consequence, an evaluation of their role rests, in part, on an evaluation of the role of the larger population of service and white-collar workers of which they are a part.[24]

New working class theory suggests that white-collar workers have become a new proletariat with revolutionary potential. As Oppenheimer describes the essence of this line of reasoning,

> New working class theory states that white collar workers are displacing blue collar workers as the major working class grouping in the technologically advanced societies. As the rationalization of their work develops and as they become subject to the economic and social crises of advanced capitalism/imperialism, their political consciousness will develop along lines roughly analogous to their European blue collar predecessors: from trade unions to social democracy to revolutionism.[25]

[20] See Jean Baker Miller, "On Women: New Political Directions for Women," *Social Policy*, 2 (July–August 1971), pp. 32 ff., and Shulameth Firestone, *The Dialectics of Sex* (New York: Bantam Books, 1970).

[21] See Charles Reich, *The Greening of America* (New York: Random House, 1970); Theodore Roszak, *The Making of a Counter-Culture* (Garden City, N.Y.: Doubleday, 1968); and, Philip Slater, *The Pursuit of Loneliness* (Boston: Beacon Press, 1970).

[22] See James Boggs, *Racism and the Class Struggle* (New York: Monthly Review Press, 1970).

[23] See Eldridge Cleaver, "On Lumpen Ideology," *The Black Scholar*, 4 (November–December 1972), pp. 2–10; and C. J. Munford, "Social Structure and Black Revolution," *Ibid.*, pp. 11–23.

[24] Within this new working class, the size and growth of the larger numbers of workers who are in the service sector has been analyzed by Victor Fuchs in *The Service Economy* (New York: Columbia University Press, 1968).

[25] Martin Oppenheimer, "What Is the New Working Class?" *New Politics*, 10 (Fall 1972), p. 29.

Furthermore, new working class theory suggests that this population, in conjunction with other class groupings, can develop the capability to overthrow the present society in the name of socialist society.

Oppenheimer argues, however, that the size of the new working class is sometimes overstated by proponents of this viewpoint, through the inclusion of persons who are, in actuality, managers, officials, proprietors (in the U.S. government classification scheme), and small and not so small entrepreneurs. These persons cannot be included in this analysis because they are not subject to the kinds of forces that play on working people, for example, receiving wages, engaging in union struggles, and so on. When the issue is considered in numerical terms, the new working classes, Oppenheimer feels, would necessarily be forced to create linkages with blue-collar workers to develop the force needed for revolutionary change.

Numbers aside, new working class theory is subject to question on the critical issue of the relative importance of the new working class to production. The power of blue-collar workers in revolutionary theory and practice is that their active mobilization could bring about the paralysis of the vital production centers of the society. However, this may be true as well of white-collar technical workers, for example, engineers, managers, planners, computer operators, and so on.[26] In an indirect and longer-range sense, the roles of teachers in educating and socializing the labor force or of welfare workers around issues of social control are also important in the production process, although strikes by these populations have a less damaging impact on social stability. In the long run, however, they do have a vital relationship to critical economic institutions in the society and cannot be dismissed as a potentially insignificant partner in struggle.

Finally, new working class theory raises the question of the extent to which the objective movement toward worker status, or proletarianization, in fact leads to the growing radicalization of white-collar workers. The trends and evidence are contradictory,[27] although we cannot say that such radicalization has taken place to this point on any widespread basis. However, the crucial and growing problems which this country faces and the particular pressures white-collar workers are increasingly facing (for example, those of unemployment)[28] offer some possibility for the growth of political consciousness in this population.

Social service workers, then, as part of this larger population of

[26] Stanley Aronowitz, "Does the United States Have a New Working Class?" in George Fischer (ed.), *The Revival of American Socialism* (New York: Oxford University Press, 1971), pp. 188–216.
[27] Oppenheimer, "What Is the New Working Class?"
[28] For example, see "White Collar Blues: Salaried Workers Find Cherished Job Security Is a Thing of the Past," *Wall Street Journal* (June 23, 1971), p. 1.

workers, are aligned politically and sociologically with a group whose potential as a revolutionary force is presently unclear, although potentially promising.[29] There are some reasons to think that social service workers may develop radical consciousness more rapidly and more profoundly than will the general body of white-collar workers. In turn, this may lead them to have a greater influence than their numbers, or than some analysts of new working class theory suggest.

A number of factors are coming together to particularly influence the political consciousness of social service workers. As social service workers are brought together in large bureaucracies and in strained working conditions and increasingly are unable to find satisfaction in their work, the potential for their developing a group consciousness of themselves as working people is greatly increased. The growing unionization of these professions is testimony to this possibility.[30] While unionization and working-class consciousness do not automatically lead to engagement in radical activity and in fact have frequently led to their opposites, such consciousness is a necessary, if not sufficient, condition for enabling welfare state workers to begin to see the commonalities of their problems and of the potential solutions to their problems with the problems and solutions of other working people. Similarly, social service workers are experiencing an increasing financial squeeze on their professions, through cuts in federal government spending in social service programs. Government funding for the social services is being cut drastically.[31] This must eventually lead to a growing difficulty for social service workers to find jobs at the relatively high salaries they have previously experienced [32]

[29] A useful overview of new working class theory and its applicability to social service work is Adam Finnerty, "An Exploration of New Working Class Theory: Implications for Social Service Practice," unpublished, Bryn Mawr College, Bryn Mawr, Pa., 1969.

[30] See "Unions in Social Work," *Encyclopedia of Social Work* (New York: National Association of Social Workers, 1971), pp. 1507–1511, for the case of social work. In general, white-collar workers represented 16 percent in 1970 of all union members, though only 12 percent of all white-collar workers are unionized (versus 22.6 percent of the total labor force in 1970). These data are from Oppenheimer, "What Is the New Working Class?" p. 40.

[31] For a review of the funding problems in professional social work, see "These Trying Times: Siding with Virtue Is Not Enough," *NASW NEWS* (June–July 1972); and *The Social Work Education Reporter,* 19 (September–October 1971), and 20 (December–January 1972).

[32] For example, the median salary of the 1971 graduates of the June Addams Graduate School of Social Work, University of Illinois, was $10,500 as reported in the *Social Work Education Reporter,* 20 (April–May 1971), p. 15. Likewise, the median salary of the 1971 graduates of the School of Social Administration, Temple University, Philadelphia, was in the $10,000–$10,500 range, with a mean of $10,845, as reported in the "Final Report on Employment, Graduating Class of 1971, School of Social Administration, Temple University," October 25, 1971, unpublished.

and will raise the reality to the worker of his or her vulnerability and dispensability.

A variety of other forces are operating to politicize social service workers in a way that has not previously happened. These forces are operating to help make workers much more aware of the political nature of their work and of the considerable crisis about their work and lives. One of these forces is the growing strength and challenge represented by several special interest caucuses, which contain the potential for a broad challenge in the profession of social work. Among these are the black caucus, now formalized in the Alliance of Black Social Workers, the caucus of Asian People, and the American Indian Caucus.[33] In addition, recent years have witnessed the development of explicitly radical caucuses in social work, for example, the short-lived but important Social Welfare Worker's Movement of the late 1960s, the socialist collective that organized around the journal *Hotchpot*, the movement into professional training and work roles of college radicals, and the sometimes-militant social work students' organization, the National Federation of Student Social Workers.[34] Each of these reflects a growing politicization in the society at large as well as a response to problems within social work itself. These groups and the forces they represent may have an important impact on social work.

Part of the reason for this impact is that each particular group is organized around a very powerful set of interlocking perceptions. Black social workers organize because they feel the need, as black people, to organize against a racist society, because they see that social work, largely white-controlled, has not served the best interests of black people, and because they feel, as black social workers, the discrimination against them within the profession. Similarly, as the women's movement attracts more women, the impact on social work, still a predominantly female profession, may be profound. A widely read anthology on the women's movement included a "Letter to Our Sisters in Social Work." It contained this passage: "When will women social workers recognize our common bond with poor women, including unmarried mothers? We share with such women the common oppression of our sex. Every insult to a woman insults you."[35] Increasingly, women social workers are rec-

[33] For example, see Billy J. Tidwell, "The Black Community's Challenge to Social Work," *Journal of Education for Social Work*, 7 (Fall 1971), pp. 59–65; and Ford H. Kuramoto, "What Do Asians Want? An Examination of Issues in Social Work Education," *Journal of Education for Social Work*, 7 (Fall 1971), pp. 7–17.
[34] John L. Erlich, "The 'Turned-On' Generation: New Antiestablishment Action Roles," *Social Work*, 16 (October 1971), pp. 22–27; and Armand Lauffer, "A New Breed of Social Actionists Comes to Social Work: The Community Organization Student," *Journal of Education for Social Work*, 7 (Winter 1971), pp. 43–53.
[35] Robin Morgan (ed.), *Sisterhood Is Powerful* (New York: Vintage Books, 1970), p. 525.

ognizing this bond.[36] The resultant coming together of personal and professional roles and concerns is an example of the kind of integration that has been lacking in our society and in the social welfare professions as well. It forms a very powerful amalgam.

Social service workers may be especially subject to discontent and thus more open to alternative analyses and strategies, precisely because they are the kinds of people who choose to engage in work that promises to be of service to others. Several studies have documented the extent to which persons choosing social service careers are motivated by concerns for social change to a greater degree than are persons doing other kinds of work, including other professional work.[37] Furthermore, there is some evidence that increased professional identification does not lead inevitably to increased political conservatism, as is frequently assumed.[38] We have argued that much of social work theory and practice are organized to structure the thinking and practice of social work in a conservative direction. However, at least two factors intervene in this process. The first is that social workers are not only professional workers, but people as well. They are subjected not only to professional training, but to the varieties of life experiences that help them maintain a healthy degree of cognitive dissonance in relation to professional ideology.

Secondly, there is, within social work and the welfare state at large, some suggestion of a radical alternative to our present society. Within social work itself, there has existed a current of radical thought, though it has often been muted and isolated. Nonetheless, it has been a theme in social work and has left a residue in social work thinking. During the 1930s, for example, social work and social planners were influenced by the radicalization that was taking place in the society at large. The journal Social Work Today, published in those years, represented a rank-and-file point of view, as the journal put it, that understood the need for mass struggle in creating change. This contrasts rather sharply with the more traditional point of view represented by the establishment welfare journal of the day, The Survey.[39] In Social Work Today, and

[36]See Carolyn Washburne, "Feminism and Professionalism: Memoirs of an ex-Social Worker," Unpublished paper, Philadelphia, Pa., 1975.
[37] A number of these studies are reviewed in the National Study of Social Welfare and Rehabilitation Workers, Work, and Organizational Contexts, Research Report No. 1, Overview Study of the Dynamics of Worker Job Mobility, Social and Rehabilitative Services, Department of Health, Education and Welfare (Washington, D.C.: Government Printing Office, 1971), p. 39. See also Herbert Bisno, "How Social Will Social Work Be?" Social Work, 2 (April 1956), pp. 12–18.
[38] Irwin Epstein, "Professionalization, Professionalism and Social Worker Radicalism," Journal of Health and Social Behavior, 11 (January 1970), pp. 66–77.
[39] Unfortunately, Social Work Today has not been subjected to any organized historical/political analysis, to the best of my knowledge. The journal is available in many libraries, however, and still provides insight and refreshment. The Survey

occasionally in the *Proceedings of the National Conference of Social Welfare,* social workers called for political alliances with labor,[40] for socialist economic alternatives,[41] for communal forms of economic organization,[42] and for radical revisions of the society as a whole.[43] Marxist thought influenced some segments of social work and vitalized many collective groups of social workers with its hope for a radical revision of the society.[44]

It is well to remember, too, that psychoanalytic theory, while generally identified as a conservative force in social work, was identified with radical political thought and thinkers at the time of its introduction to the United States. Although it became transformed, the use of psychoanalytic thought as an underpinning for a true human liberation, along with the use of casework as a liberating tool, was understood by some. While casework has become a conservative discipline, caseworkers such as Bertha Reynolds well understood both its conservative impulses and its radical potential.[45] In her classic, "Re-Thinking Social Case Work," she wrote,

> The new scientific orientation of social case work was pushing relentlessly toward a democracy of approach to human beings which was quite at variance not only with the traditional assumptions of social case work but with the practices of society in general and of the financially supporting society in particular. How could there be any escape from severe conflict for case workers who had managed to maintain themselves fairly happily in the past by sharing the assumptions of the group which supported them? A review of the period from 1920 to 1929 shows that the conflict was growing but was felt at first only as a division among case workers themselves.
>
> Awareness of conflict with society came late to psychiatric social case

---

has been studied by Clarke Chambers in *Paul U. Kellogg and The Survey: Voices for Social Welfare and Social Justice* (Minneapolis: University of Minnesota Press, 1971).

[40] Mary Van Kleek, "Common Goals of Labor and Social Work," *Social Work Today,* 2 (October 1934), pp. 4–8.

[41] Mary Van Kleek, "Social Work in the Economic Crisis," *National Conference of Social Work,* Montreal (Chicago: University of Chicago Press, 1933), pp. 64–77.

[42] Jerome Davis, "The Consumers' and the Producers' Cooperative Movement and the Social Workers," *National Conference of Social Work,* Detroit (Chicago: University of Chicago Press, 1934), pp. 408–417.

[43] Karl Borders, "Social Workers and a New Social Order," *National Conference of Social Work,* Detroit (Chicago: University of Chicago Press, 1934), pp. 590–596.

[44] For some discussion of the role of Marxist thought in social work in the 1930s, see Bertha Reynolds, *An Uncharted Journey* (New York: Citadel Press, 1963), especially Chapters 10, "Vitality," and 11, "Rethinking," pp. 153–187.

[45] For example, see her "Re-Thinking Social Case Work," *Social Service Digest* (San Diego 1946).

workers. . . . Psychiatric case workers did not realize for some time the full implications of the theories they had drawn from dynamic psychiatry.[46]

While this analysis of the contradictions of social casework has, admittedly, not led where Reynolds would have liked it to, it stands nonetheless as a representation of the kind of radical thinking that was part of the formation of social work practice.

In the field of community organization, conservative perspectives are tempered by visions with a radical quality, especially in their suggestions of utopian socialist thought as defining goals of practice. Some of the fairly conservative community organization theory of the past twenty years reflects the vision of small units of cooperative, self-determining collectives of men and women as the end point of community organization practice.[47] Murray Ross, whose *Community Organization: Theory and Principles* helped define the field for a period in the late 1950s and early 1960s, wrote that community organization is

> a process by which a community identifies its needs or objectives, orders (or ranks) these needs or objectives, develops the confidence and will to work at these needs or objectives, finds the resources (internal and/or external) to deal with these needs or objectives, takes action in respect to them, and in so doing extends and develops cooperative and collaborative attitudes and practices in the community.[48]

In general, community organization practice in the United States was very much influenced by the work of European sociologists who saw urbanization and industrialization as critical problems undermining cohesiveness and community.[49] This practice, consequently, built on "the tradition of local autonomy and the values of self-help and self-sufficiency—long favored in this country—[which] contributed to the belief that the community should be organized and helped to resolve its own problems."[50] While community organization practice has failed to understand the need for struggle to achieve these ends, it nonetheless often transcends advanced welfare-statism in its visions of desirable social alternatives.

None of this is meant to suggest that, somehow, social work is secretly

[46] *Ibid.*, pp. 16–17.
[47] For example, see Murray G. Ross, *Community Organization: Theory and Principles* (New York: Harper, 1955); and William M. Biddle, *The Community Development Process* (New York: Holt, Rinehart and Winston, 1965). See also Pranab Chatterjee and Raymond A. Koleski, "The Concepts of Community and Community Organization: A Review," *Social Work*, 19 (July 1970), pp. 82–92.
[48] Ross, *Community Organization*, p. 39.
[49] Letty Santiago, "From Settlement House to Anti-Poverty Program," *Social Work*, 17 (July 1972), p. 73.
[50] *Ibid.*, p. 76.

radical in a way that is not generally appreciated. Rather, we suggest that social work, like liberal thought in general, has been influenced by radical thought and contains strands and suggestions of radical thought within itself. These strands are not generally acknowledged and understood. Nonetheless, they exist, and they influence the social welfare field, though often in latent ways. The radical dimension in social work thought adds to the ferment in the social welfare field and provides both historical continuity and fresh inputs into the process of change among social service workers.

SUMMARY

In this chapter, a number of forces at work within the welfare state complex were reviewed, each of which suggests that change and ferment, as well as stability and quiescence, are found in the welfare state. In each of the areas reviewed, we assessed some of the potential linkages between the ferment and discontent within the welfare state and the possibilities for change in other areas of the society. In the following chapters, these connections will be elaborated in the context of a discussion of strategies and practices for radical social change.

10

Strategy

INTRODUCTION

The severity of the problems facing our society is practically unmistakable, as is the extent to which these problems find their way into the various corners of all our lives. Unfortunately, there is no easy connection between seeing, feeling, and knowing about this social pathology and developing plans to combat it. In fact, as we see more clearly how distorted things are and how firmly connected that distortion is to the basic fabric of the society, we may become increasingly frustrated.

However, if we are able to find strategies and tactics for change, our analysis can help to mobilize and direct us, rather than immobilize us. These strategies and tactics must account for the seriousness of our situation and hold some promise of promoting fundamental change. At the same time, they must not be grandiose or unrealistic. Appropriate strategy can energize us, encouraging us to take action and risks, and not seem to require so much of us that we become overwhelmed and neutralized once again. Such strategy must enable us to link the events of our everyday lives to the larger ends we seek. It must be realistically attached to what is, so that we retain a base from which to work and do not become isolated, at the same time that it points toward and leads to something that is fundamentally different from what is. We need a conception of an overall process of social change and, simultaneously, specific handles for ourselves on that process. The task of this chapter is to suggest some possible strategy that meets these requirements.

LOCATING OURSELVES IN THE STRUGGLE

The strategies adopted by people in any particular sector of the society, or in any community, in pursuit of broad change objectives, ought to be informed by a general awareness of the current state of other movements for basic social change. This does not mean that those in a given sector must be bound or limited by developments in other sectors. It does mean that the struggle to create basic changes, as it is waged in any one arena, ought to be informed by struggles in other arenas. It ought to take support and guidance from other struggles, lend support and give guidance to other struggles, and work, to the extent possible, toward the eventual unification of those struggles.

Part of the guidance that segments of the movement need to give one another is to help one another develop realistic expectations about what is possible at any given time. It is important to recognize that, thus far in the 1970s, there are no coherent and organizationally powerful forces for basic social change in the United States. This must be acknowledged realistically. In the past ten years, what is loosely called the movement has gone through a variety of phases and periods of ups and downs.[1] At present, there is no clear sense of direction among activists and little unity among the various forces that once showed some promise of coalescing.

Despite the general political quiescence, however, there are some very encouraging developments. The backlog of experience of the past ten years has left a residue of insight, sophistication, and commitment to long-term struggle. While the level of overt political activity is relatively low, that does not imply that the visions that led to overt struggle in the

[1] Some useful reviews of this period are James Forman, *The Making of Black Revolutionaries* (New York: Macmillan, 1972); Andrew Kopkind, "The Sixties and the Movement," *Ramparts* (February 1973), pp. 29–38; Paul Potter, *A Name for Ourselves* (Boston: Little, Brown, 1971); James O'Brien, "A History of the New Left, 1960–68," originally in *Radical America* (May–June, September–October, and November–December, 1968), reprinted by the New England Free Press, Boston, n.d. See also Gabriel Kolko, "The Decline of American Radicalism in the 20th Century," originally in *Studies on the Left*, September–October 1966, reprinted by the Radical Education Project, Ann Arbor, Michigan (n.d.); and Michael Rossman, *The Wedding Within the War* (Garden City, N.Y.: Doubleday & Co., 1971).

past have been abandoned.[2] Furthermore, the absence of more visible activity does not mean that there is no activity of a less visible type. For example, the depth of feeling and commitment tapped by the women's movement suggests the possibility of enormously important society-wide struggle as the women's movement increasingly finds organizational handles for the sentiment it represents. Similarly, grass-roots work of many varieties, collective building, and other forms of consciousness raising are continuing quietly but persistently.

Of special interest to social service workers is the fact that social service issues have increasingly become a locus of political activity. Although the black movement, in the 1960s, began with concerns for equal educational opportunity and for civil rights and the white radical movement centered first on campus activity, then on independent community organizing, and then on antiwar work, both black and white activists have focused increasingly on social service issues. The War on Poverty was one stimulant for this involvement. Another was the general frustration with political activity in other sectors. Recent cuts in social service spending have brought even more attention to this sector. In the 1970s, social services have become an important focus for political work.

Staying tuned to the currents in the movement can be helpful in several ways, but most particularly in enabling us to develop strategies appropriate to the times. Strategies built on the necessity for broad participation and widespread struggle, to which we must ultimately come, are not realistic approaches in this period. Multitudes of people are simply not mobilized. Even in the social services, where there is ferment, a mass demonstration in Washington, D.C., in February 1973 to protest the anticipated budget cuts for social services could draw only 20,000 people, by optimistic count.[3] On the other hand, a variety of strategies are suggested on the basis of a realistic assessment of current trends.

A sound analysis of what is possible is also useful as an antidote to discouragement. Pegging expectations at the proper level—high enough to stimulate effort but not so high as to lead to failure and discouragement—is important in any undertaking. It is especially important in the struggle to radically transform the society. Inasmuch as we will receive little confirmation of the impact of our activity from the usual sources of validation, we will be especially prey to discouragement. The media, public announcements, and the conventional reward system will not generally acknowledge even the existence, let alone the progress, of

---

[2] For a useful review and analysis of the ongoing strength of the left, see Kilpatrick Sale, "The New Left: What Is Left?" *WIN*, 9 (June 21, 1973), pp. 4–11.

[3] "Capital Rally Protests Nixon Budget Cuts," *The Guardian* (February 28, 1973), p. 4.

movements working for their transformation. We will always be officially invisible. We will remain, in Harvey Wheeler's phrase, a second city— an establishment within the establishment, but unacknowledged by it— until the moment we prevail.[4] Consequently, we will need to develop our own criteria of success and look to them to validate our existence and our importance.

This is not meant to suggest that we should be or can be complacent, inactive, or fatalistic. A realistic assessment of where the movement is and of what each of our roles in it might be should lead not to inactivity, but to realistic planning. If we wait for the perfect moment for a pure activity, through which we can make a vital thrust for social change, we will neither prepare ourselves to use such a moment should it come, nor contribute to bringing such a moment about. We must work in the present time, at whatever level and in whatever way conditions dictate. And, in fact, there is much we can do.

A MODEL OF REVOLUTIONARY CHANGE: THE BOTTOM-UP/COLLECTIVE APPROACH

There is no unanimity among theorists of radical change about the way that such change might occur in the United States. There is not even agreement about what sectors of the population might reasonably be expected to mobilize to bring about such changes—even leaving aside the question of the general strategies they might pursue. Despite lack of unanimity, however, a number of elements of a model of revolutionary change have been emerging in the past decade with special relevance to the United States. Despite the preliminary nature of some of this analysis, it offers much hope for the development of a revolutionary strategy applicable to our particular circumstances.

The most exciting models of revolutionary theory, both in terms of the values they represent and their appropriateness to current circumstances, build on the commitment to small collectives, necessarily dispersed, at work on a variety of different projects in a variety of locations, and uniting at some future time for larger efforts.[5] This is what is meant by the bottom-up/collective approach. Such theory acknowledges the reality that a broad base for action or for the development of a radical national party does not presently exist. It does build on the fact that many pockets

[4] Harvey Wheeler, *The Politics of Revolution* (Berkeley: Glendessary Press, 1971), especially Chapter 1, "The Revolutionary Situation," pp. 9–41.
[5] For example, see Carl Oglesby and Richard Shaull, *Containment and Change* (New York: Macmillan, 1967), especially Chapter 9, "The Search for a New Style of Life," pp. 184–198.

or groupings of self-conscious radicals are at work on various issues with the potential ultimately to educate, influence, and mobilize large numbers of people with a radical agenda.

At the same time that this model recognizes a political reality, it also develops an understanding of revolution that is richer than those to which we have been generally accustomed. This model is attractive, in part, because it attempts to create in the present prerevolutionary society some aspects of the future postrevolutionary world. That is, it tries to connect means and ends. By developing units for revolutionary struggle on a collective basis in the present, radicals model, experiment with, learn about, and begin to develop some of the building blocks of a better society. This strategy leads to the creation of democratic groups, collectively organized, to carry on political work and to support our efforts to be fuller human beings in the process.

There is no question that radical change of a whole society requires the mobilization of large numbers of people whose struggles overlap to at least some degree. Similarly, there is no question that as we build collectives at the local level we must also be challenging large institutions that have an impact on us all, such as the military, corporations, unions, political parties, and government itself. But the bottom-up/collective strategy suggests that in so doing we ought not to build a mass party or mass basis for unified struggle that consists of only two elements, individuals and the party. That format recreates in the struggle, and likely after the struggle as well, oppressions similar to those in the present society. That format also fails to lay the groundwork for developing self-determining, self-governing, democratic collectives and communes. We must struggle at all levels, but our struggle must always be rooted in our own experience. We can and should join with others, but we must do so in a way that integrates the larger issues with our daily issues. Our efforts to create a national party or to transform national institutions must be the logical extension of local work, not a substitute for it.

The bottom-up/collective strategy also stems from a desire to conceptualize revolutionary change as leading to more than a reordering or even a humanizing of the economy or of state power. It recognizes that revolutionary change means change in each one of us as people and in the way we relate to one another as well as change in institutions and larger systems. Small collectives are a good vehicle for this level of work. This does not imply that changing people *is* the revolution. It does suggest that changing people can be revolutionary and, in fact, is an important part of the work that must be done. If the building blocks— individual people and small collectives—are not made more human, their creations will not be humanized.

However, working to change people is not a *precondition* to larger political action. Personal, small collective, and larger political-social struggle must go on simultaneously. We need each one to enable the others to move forward, though none can be completely successful until all are successful. The bottom-up/collective strategy is important in the emphasis it provides on the need to reorganize society both in its detail and in its overall dimensions and in seeing those efforts as intimately related.

THE "REVOLUTION"

Thinking about political struggle in these terms influences the way in which the "revolution" is understood. Richard Flacks has suggested that

> Fundamental social change in advanced industrial society is not initiated or mediated through the political system, nor is it likely to result from mass insurrections or rebellions. Instead, fundamental political change occurs only after a prolonged period of ferment and conflict within the principal cultural, social and economic institutions.[6]

This in no way implies a wishy-washy approach that does not take the realities of state power seriously. Rather, this approach recognizes that state-corporate power is exercised and is manifested in and through the values each of us holds personally and in the institutions with which we come in daily contact. It further recognizes that the capitalist spirit resides throughout the society, and, therefore, can be challenged throughout the society. It recognizes that there are no shortcuts, no simple levers, for radical change, and it recognizes that we must create the revolutionary situation and revolutionary change from within us and not simply wait to respond to external imperatives.

Martin Buber has described the meaning of revolution in a way that is consistent with these concerns. In *Paths in Utopia* he wrote that

> Revolution is not so much a creative as a delivering force whose function is to set free and authenticate—*i.e.*, it can only perfect, set free, and lend the stamp of authority to something that has already been foreshadowed in the womb of the pre-revolutionary society; . . . the hour of revolution is not an hour of begetting but an hour of birth—provided there was a begetting beforehand.[7]

[6] Richard Flacks, "Strategies for Radical Social Change," *Social Policy*, 1 (March–April 1971), p. 10.
[7] Martin Buber, *Paths in Utopia* (Boston: Beacon Press, 1958), p. 45.

Revolutionary activity, at present, is at the begetting stage. At the same time, we must not lose sight of the fact that we are part of a process that is going someplace and is not forever at the threshhold or at the distant gates of becoming.

In what might be called the indigenous, as opposed to the imported, brand of revolutionary thought in the United States, there is a rejection of the notion that revolution could or should occur through a violent overthrow of those in power. This applies equally to notions of a centralized struggle and takeover and decentralized guerrilla activity.[8] The imbalance of physical resources—the ability to engage in violence—is so uneven that such strategies are suicidal. In any case, as radicals conceptualize the necessity for profound change in cultural, social, and psychological forms, violent struggle is viewed as not especially useful to achieve the desired ends. Changes of these sorts do not come about simply through overthrow of a ruling class—whether or not the new ruling class is the proletariat. They come about through a process of struggle which occurs at many levels and which changes people, value systems, and institutional forms, as well as the nature of state power. While violence may potentially defeat enemies, it has little power to build and to humanize, which must be our aim.

DEVELOPMENTAL STAGES

One of the critical issues in the bottom-up/collective approach is the problem of uniting the various segments of struggle into common action at appropriate times. Decentralized struggle does not necessarily produce the kind of coherent ideology and movement that can change a country. The way in which such struggles might come together around common goals is not clear, and this has led some to suggest the necessity of multiple, simultaneous levels of struggle at both the local institutional and national political levels.[9] Others have argued that local struggles of all sorts lay the groundwork for revolutionary action on a larger basis, in ways that cannot be planned or predicted precisely. Bookchin suggests that the system will fall

[8] For example, see Murray Bookchin, "On Spontaneity and Organization," *Liberation*, 16 (March 1970), pp. 5–17; and Martin Oppenheimer, *The Urban Guerrilla* (Chicago: Quadrangle Books, 1969).

[9] For example, see Roy Bennett, "Strategies for Radical Social Change," *Social Policy*, 1 (November–December 1970), pp. 14–17. The New American Movement has been an effort to bring together local struggle and national unity. Introductory materials on NAM can be found in "The New American Movement," *Socialist Revolution*, 2 (January–February 1972), pp. 31–68, and 2 (May–June 1972), pp. 115–138. See also Michael P. Lerner, *The New Socialist Revolution* (New York: Dell, 1973).

only when its institutions have been so hollowed out by the new Enlightenment, and its power so undermined physically and morally, that an insur-
rectionary confrontation will be more symbolic than real. Exactly when or
how this "magic moment," so characteristic of revolution, will occur, is
unpredictable. But, for example, when a local strike, ordinarily ignored
under "normal" circumstances, can ignite a revolutionary general strike, then
we will know that the conditions have ripened.[10]

In general, there is some agreement that extensive local work is critical to the success of a larger effort. There is less agreement about
whether it is desirable to develop a national party for unified struggle
at the present time.[11] Eventually, there must be unity, which logically
would occur at that point in the struggle at which local groups realize
that the success of their particular effort requires larger changes. At that
point, national work or mass work will not substitute for local work, but
would be its logical extension. As the various liberation movements
mature in the United States, as is already clear in the women's movement, the black movement, the gay movement, the rank-and-file trade
union movement, the consumer movement, and others, the more developed political thinkers in those movements begin to understand and
educate others to the need for a broader democratic, socialist struggle
to achieve the fullest possibilities of the particular movement.

Susan Carroll, George Lakey, William Moyer, and Richard Taylor of
the Movement for a New Society (Quaker Action Group, Philadelphia)
have attempted to develop scenarios for unified struggle. They conceptualize multiple levels for struggle at the present time, largely occurring
outside existing institutions, including small action cells (nonviolent
revolutionary groups), radical caucuses, counterinstitutions, and training
centers. They conceptualize two possible scenarios for a transition to a
new society, building from a strong bottom-up orientation. The first of
these envisages a

revolutionary party, controlled and supported by a non-violent people's
movement, which wins elections and eventually gains a majority in Congress
and control of the presidency. Using education and legislation, it sets about
the transformation of the political and economic system, creating public
corporations, setting up cooperatives and worker controlled enterprises,
passing a maximum income and assets law, organizing a comprehensive
planning system, dismantling the military forces, setting up child-care facilities and social and medical services, working out equitable relationships with

[10] Bookchin, "On Spontaneity and Organization," p. 10.
[11] See discussion in these articles: Leo Frederick Burt, "Do We Need a National
Organization?" *Liberation*, 17 (August 1972), pp. 5–10; "Response," Staughton
Lynd, *op. cit.*, p. 10; Mabel Dodge Brigade, "On the Road to New Nations,"
Liberation, 17 (May 1973), pp. 31–42; Letter from Berkeley NAM Chapter, *Lib-
eration*, 17 (May 1973), pp. 2 and 43.

the Third World, transnationalizing some functions formerly filled by federal government, and so on. When it meets resistance from entrenched wealth, privilege and power, it cooperates with the people's movement, using non-violent protest, non-cooperation, and intervention to support its initiatives.[12]

A second possible approach is the nonelectoral people's movement route. Here:

The transition comes about after the establishment finds itself unable to make any more concessions. An active and well-organized people's movement has engaged in widespread demonstrations, mass boycotts, and strikes, all aimed at protesting existing inequities and demanding radical change to a new kind of economic and political order. At first, the government and corporate system is able to make concessions in the shape of reforms, but eventually every "outpost" of reform is taken and the "fortress" is reached—the establishment realizes that it cannot give further changes without radical reduction in its privileges and power.

Discredited and confronted on every hand by protesting groups, it tries to defend its privilege, but finds that even the formerly reliable police and military can no longer be counted on because of movement fraternization and non-violent tactics. Repression discredits the government still further. Eventually, the government and business establishments find themselves powerless to prevent radical caucuses and workers' cadres from taking over existing institutions and factories, or to stop local action groups from occupying and controlling the organizations of local and national life. These action groups, parallel institutions, radical caucuses, and other people's groups elect representatives to regional "Congresses of Free Americans," to which more and more citizens pay their taxes and which become, in effect, the functioning government. The old delegitimized structure of government and corporations collapses and is replaced by new structures which grow directly out of people's institutions. The regional Congresses institute much the same kind of eco-democratic socialist system described in the movement electoral party route, and then cooperate with revolutionary movements in other countries in creating transnational institutions.[13]

Surely it is premature to suggest which of these possible routes is the more likely, or what other routes may eventually emerge as more desirable and feasible. In any case, the general dimensions of this line of thought should now be clear. The immediate unit of struggle is the collective, working on the central issues of the society as they emerge in daily life in local context, and sometimes joining in national struggles against the massive corporations, unions, and so on. In any number of ways when the appropriate levels of readiness and sophistication are reached, local collectives coalesce around the common points of their struggles. The way in which national transformations will occur, in keep-

[12] Susan Carroll, George Lakey, William Moyer, and Richard Taylor, *Moving Toward a New Society,* manuscript forthcoming, pp. 134–135.
[13] *Ibid.,* pp. 135–136.

ing with the direction of local struggles, is unclear. But if the local struggles have created strong, unified, numerous, politically sophisticated, and democratically organized units, the battle will be more than half-won at that point.

THE NATURE OF LOCAL WORK

We turn now to the critical questions of the bases on which local collectives organize and the specific agendas on which they work. Of course, there is no simple or single possibility. People will, and do, organize on any number of bases for radical change. Even at this early stage, there are collectives organized on a geographic basis to struggle on community issues; rank-and-file organizations in unions and work places; radical caucuses in professions; and collectives that come together on the basis of color, sex, and age, or around particular issues, for example, the antiwar movement, the consumers' movement, the ecology movement, or welfare rights. All can be appropriate units for struggle.

Needless to say, not all groups working on community issues, on problems of sex discrimination, or within unions have a radical perspective. In every movement and in every problem area, people come together to deal with issues with a variety of political beliefs. The fact that a group of people are working on issues of sexual exploitation or on any other issue does not, by virtue of that fact, necessarily make them radical, liberal, or conservative. Their political orientation and consequently the long-range impact of their work are determined by how they understand themselves, how they understand the issues, and how they go about their work. We can distinguish those collective units with an approach consistent with the larger strategy and analysis outlined here on a number of dimensions.[14] These dimensions are important because they begin to uncover the qualities of organization and action that can move collective struggle beyond the more limited reformist approaches.

First, collectives organized toward radical ends must develop their analysis of the ways in which the basic structure of the society is the locus of the problems they experience and is in need of radical change. A piecemeal approach or an approach that does not locate any particular issue as it surfaces in a particular place within the context of the whole social order will not be successful. It will be diverted, it will attack the

[14] This discussion draws from an analysis developed by the People's Fund in Philadelphia. The People's Fund is an alternative fund which raises money to support community organizations working toward radical social change. The dimensions outlined here for radical work are based on the criteria used by the People's Fund in making determinations about which applicant groups will be accepted for funding.

wrong problems, and it will create new divisions among groups and people that must eventually unite. The effort to develop a systematic radical analysis of the society and of the relationship of a particular problem or social issue to the whole must be a critical part of the work of local collectives.

Second, as the analysis on which collectives proceed must be radical, so must their ultimate goals also be radical. Whatever the particular long-range visions a collective develops, it must work to develop some notions of both the immediate and more distant future that encompass what it understands as the best possibilities for humankind. Developing these notions helps to keep the purpose of struggle clearly in mind, informs the development of strategy and tactics, and encourages members of the collective and others to transcend the present in their conceptualizations of what is possible. At the least, visions and future goals would necessarily include a commitment to a society so organized that every member was afforded basic human rights.

Third, collectives ought to attempt to mirror in their structure and daily practice the qualities they seek in the postrevolutionary world, to the extent that such mirroring is possible in the old society. This implies that they structure their work in a democratic manner that encourages the broadest possible involvement of members and constituencies in decision making and program activity. The personal development of each member of the collective, the increased strength and unity of the collective, and a concern for mutual support, as well as external political struggle, must all be parts of the collective's agenda.

The final criterion for local work concerns the immediate tasks of the collective. The most clear-sighted analysis, the most enlightened visions of the future, and an admirable and enabling internal structure do not in themselves create an agenda for action on the specific issues around which the collective is organized.

It is not possible to define the particular tasks of such collectives. Collectives may work on any number of particular issues and may pursue these issues in a variety of ways. They may struggle for community control of existing institutions, develop radical caucuses in these institutions, or attempt to create new institutions, engage in community organizing on a more or less broad basis, engage in education and politicization of their constituencies, and so on.[15] As general guidelines, however, we can suggest some characteristics of activities that pursue a radical intent.

As a general concern, radical work must be two-pronged. It must be relevant to the immediate needs of the collective's constituency and help that constituency in working toward the resolution of immediate

---

[15] In the following chapter, these possibilities will be made more specific for those in the social services.

needs. In fact, it is necessary to meet immediate needs better than conventional organizations and responses can do. At the same time, it is necessary to work toward larger and more fundamental transformations. To work on local issues without an eye toward the larger issues is to fall prey to the dilemmas of reformism. To work on long-range larger issues without attention to immediate local concerns is to require self-denial, sacrifice, and dedication that can only lead to isolation of the radical effort.

The critical question for radical work is how these two thrusts can be related. Carroll, Lakey, Moyer, and Taylor elaborate one approach to this problem that is becoming more well known in radical circles. That is the idea of nonreformist reforms. It was first given broad exposure through the work of André Gorz, who argued in this way:

> A reformist reform is one which subordinates its objectives to the criteria of rationality and practicability of a given system and policy. Reformism rejects those objectives and demands—however deep the need for them— which are incompatible with the preservation of the system.
>
> On the other hand, a not necessarily reformist reform is one which is conceived not in terms of what is possible within the framework of a given system and administration, but in view of what should be made possible in terms of human needs and demands.
>
> In other words, a struggle for non-reformist reforms—for anti-capitalist reforms—is one which does not base its validity and its right to exist on capitalist needs, criteria and rationales. A non-reformist reform is determined not in terms of what can be, but what should be. And finally, it bases the possibility of attaining its objectives on the implementation of fundamental political and economic changes.[16]

Carroll, Lakey, Moyer, and Taylor have attempted to operationalize this notion. They suggest that a nonreformist reform has six characteristics. It helps to decentralize power and control and, simultaneously, to restrict centralized power and control; it develops, in the present, some aspects of the social forms and values which might be desired in a radically changed society; it brings about greater people's control of resources; it supplements the resources of people's movements; it erodes the power, privilege, and wealth of the establishment; and, it is located "where the action is"—that is, it builds on and facilitates political movements. To these six criteria we ought to add that a nonreformist reform also serves as a vehicle for political education and consciousness raising. On these dimensions, it is possible to identify those struggles that,

---

[16] André Gorz, *Strategy for Labor* (Boston: Beacon Press, 1967), pp. 7–8. The same notion has been well developed using the case of workers' control by Ernest Mandel, "The Debate on Workers' Control," in Gerry Hunnius et al. (eds.), *Workers' Control* (New York: Vintage Books, 1973), pp. 344–373.

even if won, would be unlikely to contribute to the building of a radical movement for change. An increase in a public welfare benefit level, for example, may give more resources to people, but may also increase the power of the state. It does not necessarily build a movement and, in fact, may be granted in order to weaken a movement. It does not necessarily raise consciousness, but may lead to a strengthening of the illusion of government as generous benefactor.

This is not to suggest that it is undesirable to struggle for benefit increases. We do suggest that, in itself, a benefit improvement cannot make a fundamental difference in the overall social situation. If the struggle for a benefit improvement is part of a larger organizing drive structured around the building of a radical movement, then it more nearly meets these requirements. It helps to satisfy an immediate need, but it organizes to raise the larger issues that are unresolvable within the old system.

Harrington has developed the same notion at the level of national planning.[17] He takes exception to Gorz's conception of structural reform inasmuch as Gorz views such reforms as building toward a climactic revolutionary moment. For Harrington, structural reforms, in twentieth-century United States, are the bread and butter of the development of a socialist nation. He has identified some of the kinds of reforms that would bring about structural reform in the United States (recognizing the danger that these reforms might be utilized to further rationalize rather than to transform capitalist institutions in the absence of a vital mass people's movement). Among these are the gradually increasing socialization of investment, the demand for social ownership, the development of cooperative and neighborhood forms of ownership, and tax reform.[18] Within each of these categories, he identifies some of the more specific strategies that might be pursued—strategies with a foot in the old, but leading to the new. For example, in considering the need for social ownership, he suggests selective government wage and price controls, government as a final arbiter of corporate decisions when these decisions might otherwise run counter to the public interest, and so on.

Harrington does not develop a perspective on how the mass movement he sees as vital to keeping these reforms in the people's interests will develop, because of his faith in the trade union movement as the vehicle for struggle. The reforms he outlines have the potential he suggests, but, in themselves, they do not lead to the development or nurturance of the movement he sees as necessary. Nonetheless, Harrington's work is important because it indicates some of the directions in which

---

[17] Michael Harrington, *Socialism* (New York: Saturday Review Press, 1970), pp. 291–307.
[18] *Ibid.*

more community-based movements might move and demands they could raise that would escalate their efforts to higher and broader levels of struggle for change.

CHANGING OURSELVES

We have worked our way up the scale from small collectives to encompassing national and international level changes. But there is one more level. We must not leave ourselves, as individuals, out of the picture. Our lives reflect political values and contribute to a pattern of political life. We cannot be exempted from consideration in developing political strategy. Politics concerns all the forces, institutions, and values that shape the dimensions of our society and of our lives. This includes cultural and psychological forces, as well as economic and social forces. Everything that we are and everything that we do and say has a relationship, both as cause and effect, to the overall shape of the society and to everything in it.

The way that people relate to one another in an everyday context illustrates this point. It seems to be common for people to engage one another in a fairly trivial fashion. We discuss our comings and goings, or events of the day, or families and plans in a way that does not get at the essential issues in our lives. We do not engage around our deeper concerns, or try to use interactions with others to build bonds, to explore ourselves, and to explore commonalities that might lead to a deeper awareness of common social issues.

The trivialization of relations with others has political import. It reinforces social isolation which, in turn, contributes to maintenance of the status quo. If we are isolated, we do not have a way to uncover the commonality of our experiences and problems with one another. Consequently, we are not in a position to explore the possibilities of collective solutions. Trivializing our relationships with each other makes us less responsive to each other and must also make us less responsive to our own needs. If we fail to respond fully to the human situation of others, we will not stimulate and develop our feel for what is most human. This pattern is both caused by, and in turn facilitates our acceptance of, a society that in fact does devalue people and that places people in a subordinate relationship to system requirements. The same kind of analysis can be made of other aspects of how we live, where and how we work, the kinds of organizations we join, the importance we attach to them, and so on. As Jerry Rubin wrote in *Do It!*, "Politics is how you live your life, not whom you vote for." [19] He oversimplified, but he made the critical point that politics is not only an "out there" phenomenon.

[19] Jerry Rubin, *Do It!* (New York: Ballantine Books, 1970), p. 250.

This analysis suggests that each of us must consider his or her self as one of our primary targets of change. In part, this requires that we take our own lives more seriously than we usually do. We must come to appreciate that we are the important things in this society. We are what it is about. It is true that we often feel small and powerless and that we come to see ourselves in our roles as consumers and producers and not as whole people. It is also true, however, that our society is nothing but all of us little ones put together and that we do have the power, collectively, to make it more responsive to us. We must not define ourselves in the dominant terms of the society, but must struggle for a more human definition of what we would like to be. The survival of our present society rests on most of us being willing to accept far less for ourselves than might be possible. We can begin to fight this ideological and psychological domination by reasserting, first to ourselves, our own value as people.

This kind of self-analysis and self-change can begin with solitary reflection, but is certainly facilitated by contacts with others. The consciousness-raising groups of the women's movement and, on a smaller scale, the men's consciousness-raising groups that have been developing are illustrations of this process. They have enabled many people to redefine the meaning of their lives, to reinterpret the nature and source of the pains they experience, and to enlarge and transform their own understanding of their needs as people. These groups demonstrate often that heightened consciousness in one area cannot be contained in that area, but generalizes widely, so that a society-wide analysis follows. They facilitate the process of subjecting all of one's life to political analysis and infusing all of one's life with political consciousness.

These groups suggest the desirability of people forming into small collectives to discuss their own lives, in personal, social, and political terms. These collectives can and do take many forms—weekly meetings, action/discussion groups, and communes.[20] We must be active in seeking out such possibilities and, even more important, in creating them. We cannot wait for others to organize us, or until we feel sophisticated enough to be leaders. Everyone is isolated, and all are amateurs in the tasks of recreating themselves. In a real sense there is no one but ourselves to begin this work. One of the consequences of recognizing that we are each enormously important is that it gives each of us an enormous amount of responsibility for ourselves and for each other.

It is true that changed social forms will influence our consciousness.

---

[20] For an example from the social services, see Harvey Finkle, Jeffry Galper, Philip Lichtenberg, and Jack Sternbach, "Social Work Practice as Collective Experience," Unpublished, Philadelphia, Pa., 1974.

It is also true, however, that the nature of the changes we work for and the way we go about working for them will be very much influenced by our sense of who we are, what we need, and how we relate to others. A new society will create new people, but must be brought about by people in the process of becoming new. We must work to change the world outside of ourselves and inside of ourselves simultaneously, with the knowledge that the fullest change in one sphere depends on the fullest change in the next.

Heightened consciousness is also necessary for the practical reason that it is a prerequisite to leading a life committed to creating basic social changes. The most sophisticated intellectual analysis possible will not lead to a commitment to sustained action until it becomes personally and actively painful to continue in the old way. Radical ideals must come to seem not only right, but personally better. They must provide us with a greater sense of meaning in life, of social purpose, and of more rewarding contacts with others. This comes in part with heightened consciousness.[21]

The support of others—psychologically, intellectually, and economically—is essential in the process of transformation. We all respond to the values of those around us and to the reward system of the environment. Those with radical commitment must provide these supports and rewards to each other, as a way to sustain ourselves and to build a movement. Collectives are essential for this. For example, if we are to lead marginal careers, in the usual sense of what is considered a career, we must be prepared to live more cheaply, which collective living can accomplish, and to pool our earnings, either directly or through the creation of an emergency fund held in common. We must be available to one another for political and psychological guidance and support.[22] In these ways we can sustain ourselves and each other as we go about one of the major tasks of creating radical social change, namely, changing ourselves.

SUMMARY

Some general principles have emerged in this discussion of possible forms of revolutionary change in the United States. The key elements, in summary, are these:

[21] A useful discussion is Bruce Brown, "Towards a Method for the Revolutionary Reconstruction of Everyday Life," *Liberation*, 17 (April 1972), pp. 26–41.
[22] One model for a political collective that does not necessarily involve communal living has been developed by Barbara Haber and Al Haber, "Getting by with a Little Help from Our Friends," presented at the Radicals in the Professions Conference, 1968, mimeographed.

1. Revolutionary activity is an ongoing process. There may or may not be a single revolutionary moment in this country. As revolutionary change is conceptualized here, however, that is not a critical concern. The building of collectives and ongoing local work are the bread and butter of revolutionary activity. Revolutionary activity throughout the society may be stimulated by mass dislocations, perhaps brought on by international events, by domestic nonparticipation in the establishment, and by challenge to it. Nonetheless, the form of struggle and of transformation may best be described as the discrediting and delegitimization and eventually the capture and replacement of the old, rather than, in the more classical models, the overthrow of the old. However, this process ought not to be confused with reformist activity which is likewise a process, but which does not build toward structural transformation within the framework of nonreformist or structural reforms.

2. Revolutionary change will come from the bottom up. It will not be centrally dictated. Unity must eventually evolve in the struggle, and national activity should be part of the struggle along with local work. But unity of struggle should emerge from the voluntary association of subunits of the whole.

3. The struggle will involve multiple issues. The next revolution in the United States will be a cultural, social, political, and economic revolution, involving changes in individual consciousness as well as in larger political forms. The diverse, though interlocked, nature of the goals will require diverse targets of change and diverse forms of struggle. These include the development of counterinstitutions, free zones, mass movements, utopian visions, and the challenge to existing institutions within the framework of nonreformist reforms.

4. Changing ourselves, as people, is an important part of the revolutionary process. Political struggle is not only "out there." It is inside as well. This is not an either-or proposition. Both dimensions are critical.

5. Revolutionary change undoubtedly will be, and should be, essentially nonviolent. This does not mean it will necessarily be nonmilitant. It may well involve disruption and conflict. There may even be deaths (there already have been). But it will not be as a result of the planned strategy of revolutionaries and will more commonly be inflicted by establishment forces, as it has been in the past.

Hopefully, this discussion has illustrated the richness of the strategies open to us. Revolutionary struggle is not the fanatical, self-denying, stereotyped work it is all too frequently portrayed to be. It is vital, immediate, long-range, practical, and utopian all at once. It encourages us to believe that we do not have to fear truthful and in-depth analyses of the problems we face because of a fear of the consequences for action they entail. We can pursue our analyses to their furthest logical conclusion and develop appropriate strategy to deal with the issues as we see them. We gain coherence and integrity in our approach through this kind of radical commitment.

11

Practice

"RADICAL" SOCIAL WORK?

Does radical social work imply an impossible contradiction? Some would argue that it does. Radicalism, on the one hand, points toward fundamental, even revolutionary, challenges to the existing social order and to the pursuit of a profoundly altered future. On the other hand, social work is a profession, committed to the more modest goals of helping individuals to cope better with what is and of seeking changes in the social order in a reformist, gradualist fashion. Whether or not we conclude that these commitments are mutually exclusive, we will have to acknowledge that radical social work is surely no description of present practices, at least in the United States.

However, there is a good and, for some, convincing case to be made that a radical social work practice can exist and, in fact, that it already does exist. Even at present, in the face of the relatively low levels of radical political activity in the United States at large and the corresponding lack of radical consciousness among social workers, some social workers with a radical perspective are attempting to bring radical politics to bear on their daily work as professionals. The forms of radical social work are still uncertain and unevenly developed, but they are emerging and are likely to be increasingly important within the profession in coming years.

To explore the extent and the presumed inevitability of the contradiction of radicalism and social work, a definition of radical social work would be helpful. At this point, there is no single definition that would be widely accepted by radical social workers. However, there is some core of agreement on several key aspects of radical social work that can provide the basis for common understanding.

In general, there is strong commitment to the notion that radical social work represents and attempts to define what social work should ideally be about. Radical social work is not conventional social work practiced by people who are otherwise radical. Nor is it a field of practice or a method separate from casework, community organization, or group work. Rather, it is practice that attempts to respond fully both to social work's humanitarian concerns and to the distorted, exploitative realities of this society. Radical social work is little more than social work that has not compromised its own commitments to human welfare. It is social work that takes very seriously the dilemma of a people-serving profession in a people-denying society and tries to resolve that dilemma by finding ways for the profession to be of real service rather than by accommodating itself to conventional arrangements.

Radical social work does not abandon or override concerns for each person in his or her unique situation for the sake of "the revolution" or for a distant, postrevolutionary utopia. It is deeply committed to each person's well-being and pursues that to the absolute maximum. It does so by recognizing that most people will be unable to achieve well-being in this society unless and until there are radical changes in the society. For example, the social work commitment to maximizing individual choices is important, but it is limited in a society in which the choices are limited. Choosing the corporation one will be bound to or the over-priced, self-destructing consumer item one will purchase is a choice, but a choice within a narrow range, given the full spectrum of human possibilities. We may, as part of practice—conventional or radical—help people find work or get money. But radical practice sees those efforts as part of a larger effort to politicize and organize, so that the one change does not simply rationalize an individual's exploitation within a repressive system. Rather, the one change helps to build a base for radical challenge to the social order as a whole. Social work that understands its mission as facilitating the choice of one's own brand of exploitation has lost its way.

A second general characteristic of radical social work is that it is not reformist social work. So obvious a statement is nonetheless important because of the misunderstanding of the meaning of radicalism throughout the society. Despite the fact that the radical is stereotyped as fanatical, extremist, unconcerned with individuals, committed to violence, impractical, and so on, radicalism is adopted as a mantle by all varieties of reformers precisely because that stereotype is so inaccurate; because radical thought does represent hope, idealism, and an uncompromised commitment to human welfare; and because social work has some intention of pursuing those same ends. Reformers mean to tap into the radical spirit, but they are unprepared to throw over their commitments to the established order.

Radical social work is not reformist in that it does not believe that the present structures and values of the society are capable of generating or sustaining the conditions for maximum or even acceptable human growth. This does not mean that those who control or participate in these structures are personally ill-willed, though, of course, they may be. However, the institutions they represent do not respond because they cannot respond within the logic of our present social and economic arrangements. Welfare benefits cannot be made truly adequate because adequate benefits would profoundly disrupt our present wage system. Mental health centers cannot truly promote mental health because mentally healthy citizens would likely become revolutionaries in this society. Work rehabilitation centers cannot truly rehabilitate because the conditions of work in a capitalist society require that workers use small parts of their total beings and let the rest of themselves atrophy.

Radical social work, then, leads to strategies in which requests or demands are made of existing institutions only as a tactic. There is no illusion that creating a "more responsive" institution or changing the leadership of an institution or organization will make the kind of difference that must be made. This does not imply that we ought not to deal with everyday struggles as people understand them. These struggles do represent the real dilemmas that people experience. However, we must try to help people understand the limitations of pursuing the old strategies, based on the old analyses. We must start with people's present situations because the facts of poverty, powerlessness, alienation, and exploitation are the basic issues to address. But we must also help people transcend the present if we are to help them move beyond the limitations of reformism.

A third characteristic of radical social work is that it is unclear about how radical change will occur in the society and about overall strategies for its achievement. As discussed in Chapter 10, there is no consensus in radical thought in general about issues of centralized versus decentralized units of struggle, about what populations in the society have the potential to become revolutionary, about the relationship of cultural revolution, personal politics, and political revolution, and so on. Social workers, hopefully, will join the debate on these issues and will work to develop radical practice within the context of an emerging clarity about its relation to larger strategy. At the same time, they ought not to foreclose options prematurely or become sectarian or dogmatic about the single best approach to radical change.

RADICALISM AND PROFESSIONALISM: CONTRADICTION AND COMPLEMENTARITY

Given this description of the general characteristics of radical social work, it will still be argued by some that social work and radicalism, or social work practice and revolution, are incompatible. As one social work author put it, "the nightmare begins when social work action becomes ideologically transformed into political revolution." [1] While many would defend the appropriateness of social work's engaging in political action and expressing broad concern for social issues and might even agree with the analyses and hopes expressed in this book, most people see a revolutionary ideology as contradictory to social work practice. There are at least three focuses to these objections: social work practice, contrary to revolutionary practice, has a base, weak though it may be, in social and psychological expertise; social work's concern for maximizing the free choice of the individual—that is, its value-free stance—opposes revolutionary discipline; and social work's necessary relationship to established bureaucracies, funding sources, and so on, requires that social work operate within what is. Each of these issues deserves examination.

It is not true that a revolutionary commitment implies the abandonment of the search for deeper human truths and their relevance for daily practice. Revolutionary thought and action are based on rationality. In fact, it can well be argued that the radical commitment is based on a more single-minded pursuit of knowledge than is conventional practice. Conventional practice necessarily denies much of human suffering and of social work's futility to alleviate it, since it must avoid those facts and insights that would lead to a challenge to the status quo. The radical perspective has no such a priori constraints. The argument that radical practice is anti-intellectual or that it violates the profession's commitment to a knowledge base often boils down to an objection to the way in which radicals understand the world—that is, their rejection of system-preserving social and psychological science.

---

[1] Katherine A. Kendall, "Dream or Nightmare? The Future of Social Work Education," *Journal of Education for Social Work*, 9 (Spring 1973), p. 23.

Similarly, radical practice requires a greater expertise than that usually developed in conventional social work since fewer artificial barriers stand between radical practice and the critical judgment of the people served. The radical abandons practice modes based on tradition and authority. The radical's self-imposed legitimation for practice is the extent of his or her ability to be truly useful to others. The radical practitioner will not be validated by an agency, by traditional rewards, or by the social work scriptures. Radical practice either makes a difference to people, or it withers.

The second objection to radical social work is based on social work's commitment to not imposing politics on clients. As we have argued, however, the notion of a nonpolitical social work is a myth. Conventional social work practice is fully political. When these politics are made explicit, it becomes clear that they are conservative. The opposition to radical politics does not become any less real when this is pointed out. But it does become apparent that the underlying opposition is to the particular political content of radical social work and not to the fact of bringing politics per se into social work practice.

It is then sometimes argued that the particular problem with radical politics in social work is that radical politics are coercive. However, radical politics are not necessarily either coercive or noncoercive. In fact, the democratic concerns that inform the radicalism developed in these pages lead to struggle against coercion. They require the kind of growth of insight, consciousness, and human development which is not achieved by force. It is conventional practice that proves to be coercive. It manipulates behavior, while failing to be explicit about the values and politics it represents. This must be so. If conventional practice were explicit, to itself and to its clients, about the political beliefs it represents and the behavioral patterns it encourages, the contradiction of its practice with its humanitarian ideology would be unacceptable to clients and the profession.

Finally, the objection to radical social work based on the threat it represents to social work's existing commitment and sources of support must be acknowledged as absolutely correct. Radical social work is in important ways incompatible with the institutional arrangements social work has maintained to this point. But, after all, that is just the point of radicalism. Its commitment is to fundamental change and that does not occur without change in the forces to which one is accountable. Radical social work practice does imply changes in the bases on which we operate. This will not be easy. But we must recognize and struggle with the fact that the bases of support social work presently enjoys are ideologically and structurally of the same fabric that oppresses those we call clients and ourselves as workers.

Insiders and Outsiders

The broad nature of the struggle that is both necessary and possible has a direct bearing on a question often raised about working for the radical transformation of the society. Is it possible to be a radical "inside the system"? In effect, this is another formulation of the concern about the possibilities of radical social work. Too often, this question really askes another question, which is, "Is it possible to work for radical change in comfort and without struggle?" To this the answer is no, though that answer should be balanced by a consideration of how likely we are to lead lives of comfort in any case (resignation, perhaps, but not comfort).

Taken at its face value, the answer to the question is that, at any particular moment, it may be as possible to work for radical change from inside the system as from outside the system. However, the choice to work within the system is a choice to be made on the basis of where we can find work and of what seems politically and personally most desirable in the particular circumstance. That is, there must be an option in one's thinking to work directly in the movement, and, in fact, the radical may bounce in and out of the system rather than pursue a linear career within it.[2]

To be employed by the social welfare establishment does not mean that one's primary commitment must be to that establishment. The commitment can and must be to the more humane values in which we believe, which sometimes find reflection in the rhetoric, though infrequently the practice, of the social welfare field, and to the movement for radical change. The radical's career in the establishment will not necessarily be a typical career. Nor will the radical in a welfare establishment be free to do the sorts of work a radical outside the establishment would be able to do, though being outside also has its limitations. The radical in a welfare bureaucracy will be influenced in what he or she can do by a variety of factors particular to that situation. Nonetheless, the struggle can be undertaken in a variety of ways from the inside. Inasmuch as the commitment is to issues, the radical on the inside will be concerned with the same matters as will the radical on the outside. This will mean trying to relate inside work to political movements.

It is useful to be somewhat skeptical about the extent to which anyone can really be outside the system and, therefore, about the insider-out-

---

[2] For a useful discussion of the outsider and insider-outsider roles that social workers are playing, see John L. Erlich, "The 'Turned-On' Generation: New Anti-establishment Action Roles," *Social Work*, 16 (October, 1971), pp. 22–27.

sider dichotomy (which is sometimes used by the establishment as a way to bounce radicals out of paid positions: "we sympathize with your position, but it doesn't belong inside the system"). A person's immediate salary may not come from a social welfare bureaucracy, but, in many ways, we are all implicated in the present society. We buy its goods, we use its public roads, we rent or buy houses, and so on. In a real sense, there is no place that is outside the system.

The choice of employment, then, becomes a question of strategy to pursue particular goals at a particular time—and not the reflection of a general dictum that we can or cannot work for radical change inside the system. Our struggle is to change a whole society. Ultimately, such a struggle will have to occur in many places, on many fronts, around many issues, waged by many persons. No location is necessarily excluded.[3]

In countries where there are or have been revolutionary movements, social work has often found a way to be involved in revolutionary activity while maintaining a social work identity. This is an important observation because of the extent to which our understanding of the possibilities for social work is so heavily conditioned by the situation in the United States. For example, in an article reviewing the 1972 International Congress of Schools of Social Work, Katherine Kendall reported that social work was said "to play an outstanding role in the struggle of the Chilean people to gain their liberation."[4] Utilizing the notions of Paulo Freire and the practice of conscientization, Chilean social workers were active in the process of helping to "make the masses aware of their wants and needs and how to demand their satisfaction; of their responsibilities and how to meet them. They must be made conscious of their dignity, liberty and freedom, of social justice and equality."[5]

Similarly, in other Latin American countries, the issues for social work are emerging as those of underdevelopment, which has its roots in imperialism, human liberation, the need for integration of professional practice and political ideology, and "total identification with the oppressed class."[6] As Kendall further pointed out, "on the continent, many students and faculty members in schools of social work regard social responsibility primarily in terms of radical change in the social system and see social

[3] The general dilemma of radical work inside and outside is highlighted in an essay by Staughton Lynd, "Prospects for the New Left," in Staughton Lynd and Gar Alperovitz, *Strategy and Program* (Boston: Beacon Press, 1973), pp. 1–48.
[4] Kendall, "Dream or Nightmare?" p. 15.
[5] *Ibid.*, citing Virginia A. Wolfe, "The Dilemma of Latin American Social Work," *Les Carnets de l'enfance—Assignment Children (UNICEF)*, 19 (July–September 1972), p. 41.
[6] *Ibid.*, p. 18, citing "Cronica del 5° Seminairo Regional Latinoamericano de Servicio Social," *Hoy en El Servicio Social*, 19–20 (Enero–Marzo 1971), pp. 68–73.

work as a means to that end." [7] Austin has also reviewed the emerging role of social work in developing nations as one of support for goals of national level change and struggle.[8]

What emerges from the consideration of these arguments and evidence about the supposed contradiction of radicalism and social work and the insider-outsider debate is that these arguments are themselves part of the ideological struggle within social work. As a consequence, they must be analyzed in political terms. We live in a fundamentally conservative country in a conservative period in its history. This conservatism infuses our profession. It attempts to enlist our support not primarily by representing dissent, though surely this happens. The mode of control is largely the ideological struggle to present the conservative alternative as the only alternative. Our challenge is to see the present as only one possibility—and not the best possibility—and to move beyond that point.

In this chapter, a variety of approaches to radical practice are presented, and examples of practice built on these approaches are described. By and large, however, we do not suggest specific tactics or develop a manual of tactics. Clearly, many of the specific skills and tactics that workers already have at their command may come into play. Radical practice does not involve some heretofore unknown elements of practice, but it does involve some very different notions of direction, purpose, values, roles, and so on. The building blocks are not different from conventional practice in that the community organization skills of working with a committee will be helpful in organizing a radical caucus, the necessity to prepare people and organizations for new directions requires thoughtful and careful work regardless of the nature of the departure, and so on. To a large extent, the task of developing radical strategy is more a task of developing radical analysis, radical commitment, and strategy than it is one of developing a brand new radical technology.

THE SOCIAL AGENCY AS AN ARENA FOR STRUGGLE

Most social workers with a radical commitment work within the traditional range of social agencies and will undoubtedly continue to do so for some time. There are a number of reasons for this. One of the most obvious is the practical necessity of earning money and the absence of opportunities for paid work directly in a political movement. Then, too, there is some part of many of us, even the most politically committed, that main-

---

[7] *Ibid.*
[8] David M. Austin, "Social Work's Relation to National Development in Developing Nations," *Social Work,* 15 (January 1970), pp. 97–106.

tains some traditional career strivings and hopes to integrate professional "success" with political involvement. In addition, the amorphous and transitional situation of the left in the United States leaves many radicals both in and out of the social services unclear about where they would put their full-time energies, were they to leave traditional work settings.

However, the thrust of the analysis developed to this point suggests that working for radical social transformation from within a social agency is not a poor second choice to political work conducted from outside a formal agency structure.[9] Surely there are things that cannot be done from within an agency, and surely the struggle for radical change will eventually require the full-time work of many people. Nonetheless, much valuable work can be done from within. The commitments of the radical bring all parts of life and work into focus as relevant political concerns. A radical stance does not allow one to accept the "professional" position that political work is something one does after 5:00 P.M., on one's own time.[10] For the radical, professional activities, the social agency, and co-workers can be an important part of political work.

The Question of Risk

Surely social agencies can be repressive, and they often are. They attempt to enforce worker conformity through direct coercion, subtle pressures, and ideological indoctrination. Consequently, doing political work in agencies means taking risks. However, social agencies are not as repressive as some other institutions where meaningful political work has occurred and is occurring. For example, important organizing work has taken place in prisons. Social workers sometimes have been a part of this effort.[11] Similarly, the United States Army has felt the impact of radical organizers within its ranks.[12] In comparison with these institutions, the social welfare agencies with their verbal commitments to humanism, their professional associations, and Codes of Ethics are truly the soft underbelly.

The risks to the radical social welfare worker may not be as great as is sometimes assumed. Most social agencies contain a duality in that their stated goals concern equality, democracy, and human service, while their practice contains repressive elements. The radical worker can identify

[9] A parallel view is developed in Robert Knickmeyer, "A Marxist Approach to Social Work," *Social Work,* 17 (July 1972), pp. 58–65.

[10] For example, see Irving Piliavin, "Restructuring The Provision of Social Services," *Social Work,* 13 (January 1968), pp. 34–41.

[11] For a social work perspective that goes to the heart of the matter, see Jack Sternbach, "Organizing Behind Bars," unpublished, Philadelphia, Pa., 1974.

[12] For example, see Andy Stapp, *Up Against the Brass* (New York: Simon and Schuster, 1970).

with the people-serving goals of the agency and can encourage and stimulate them. The stated goals of agencies and the latent sympathies of many social workers with socialist values give a foothold and justification for radical work. They permit the radical greater freedom in refusing to do the dirty work of the agency and in refusing to identify with and lend public support to its less healthy practices.

Furthermore, radical work does not involve some naive, adventuristic notion of bomb throwing or hurling epithets at supervisors. It is not passive or reformist—but it is not self-destructive. It moves beyond where the agency and its workers are at that moment. But if it moves too far beyond, it becomes isolated and therefore ceases to be useful. Consequently, the radical must remain related to what is and have a foot in the old at the same time that he or she is struggling to create the new. By maintaining this duality or tension in a creative way, the radical can avoid unnecessarily precipitous severance from the agency as a consequence of radical work.

Finally, as people become more clear about their radical commitments and begin to organize larger parts of their lives in a fashion that is consistent with these commitments, the definition of a risk changes. In the conventional perspective, loss of a job or jeopardizing movement up the career ladder is greatly feared. With the development of radical consciousness, some of these concerns undergo a modification. Perhaps none of us can be completely free of career strivings in this society, and surely the threat of not having paid work is real and often frightening. But as the limitations of careerism and the artificiality and superficiality of the standard of living we experience become internalized in our consciousnesses, the definition of risk undergoes change. As new commitments modify the commitments to conservatism and materialism, new and freeing possibilities for political work begin to emerge. Challenges that once seemed to pose great risks become a part of everyday functioning.

The Rationale for Political Work in Agencies

The rationale for doing political work within social agencies is multi-faceted. Our previous discussion of new working class theory led us to conclude that social service workers are a potentially important constituency for radicalization and involvement in radical political struggle. The radical social welfare worker is embedded in a rich environment for organizing and is in a situation in which it is unlikely that he or she will be charged with being an outside agitator.

We also suggested that the social services play an important role in the control of resources, in the management of potentially volatile client populations, and in keeping groups with the same long-range interests—for instance, welfare clients and the working poor or welfare workers and welfare clients—from forming coalitions. Furthermore, the social services are important for the role they play as a vehicle for political propaganda. That is, they are one of the responses a capitalist society can make to the charge that it is unresponsive to human welfare. Finally, at the same time that they are an inadequate response to people's needs and are organized to further serve the needs of a corporate society, they also represent one place in the society where some notions of human service reside. A measure of idealism and a sense of possibility keep alive the sparks necessary for mobilization. For these reasons, social agencies are an important arena for political struggle. In the remainder of this section, some of the forms this struggle can and does take are discussed.

The Struggle to Democratize Agencies

Social welfare workers, like workers throughout the society, have little or no say in the determination of agency policies and token say, if any, in planning for the implementation of these policies. In view of the larger purposes that these policies serve, it is not surprising that policy making is not trusted to local groups of workers. If the social services are to fulfill the purposes for which they are designed, they must be organized in a predictable, uniform, and controlled way. The closer that policy making is brought to the point at which people feel the direct impact of services, the more likely it is that considerations of human well-being will come to bear on that policy. Social service workers with little stake in maintaining the repressive functions of social agencies cannot be trusted with the task of policy making. By the same token, the struggle of workers to have an impact on these policies, through their struggle to democratize the internal processes of their agencies, reverberates up the scale. The struggle at the local level connects with and has an impact on the larger political, economic, and social arrangements which the services buttress.

Similarly, social service agencies replicate in their internal structures the same kinds of hierarchy, individualism, competition, and depersonalization that abound in the society at large. The challenge to these values in one place merges with the challenge to them elsewhere and so joins the broader struggles for equality. These challenges are raised by efforts to implement mutual and collective supervision rather than hierarchical individual supervision, collective determination of pay differentials, selection of leadership accountable to the whole, and the inclusion of client groups into the decision-making processes of the agency. In general, radical social service workers, like radicals in other sectors, are concerned about the right of workers to determine the conditions, nature, and purpose of their work.

This concern is not limited to the development of procedures within the prevalent assumptions of the agency, which already occurs in some of the more progressive agencies. It extends also to exploring and establishing the assumptions on which technical work proceeds. Radical workers question the values of the agency. They resist solving its technical problems on its terms, unless they are committed to the social purpose that is represented. Another way in which this same idea has been conceptualized is the necessity of "contesting one's own role," which involves refusing "to see one's work as an isolated technical function and an insistence on seeing it as part of a larger social process."[13] That is, we must try to become more clear about the linkages between the smallest facet of practice and the largest questions of the nature of the social order. Then, we must struggle to organize the conditions and details of practice so that their impact on the larger social order, slight though it may be, points in a direction that is consistent with our overall beliefs.

How shall we achieve, or at the least work toward, these ends? By way of providing guidelines for such a struggle, Lichtenberg has suggested that in opposing the authoritarian behavior of a superior, workers should create appropriate challenges at each instance of autocratic behavior, so as to keep pressure constant, rather than let authoritarian behaviors go unchallenged at some points in favor of some single act of opposition. That is, we must understand that this struggle, like the larger struggle for radical change, is an ongoing process and not a single act of resistance or rebellion. Further, we must oppose autocratic behavior directly as much as possible and should stay as close as possible to the point at which less resistance is passivity and more resistance is self-destruction. It is also important that such struggle not be put on the level of personalities, but be oriented around issues, and that the struggle be brought to bear, to the extent possible, through the worker's involvement with others in similar situations and with similar perspectives.[14] The professional model of individual practice is, therefore, very limited in these kinds of efforts.

Of course, these agendas are easier to identify than to carry out. However, as with any effort to create change, certain principles pertain. Among these are (1) some jobs and some agencies offer more room to maneuver, and these are preferable places to locate oneself; (2) it is necessary to recognize the importance of collective struggle and to form alliances toward that end; (3) not every issue can be fought with the same

[13] Collectively developed by "a group of employees, technicians and political activists in an 'advanced' Italian company," and reprinted as "Technicians and the Capitalist Division of Labor," *Socialist Revolution*, 9 (May–June 1972), pp. 82–83.
[14] Philip Lichtenberg, "Toward Equality—Up and Against," unpublished manuscript, Bryn Mawr College, Bryn Mawr, Pennsylvania, 1973, pp. 13 and 15. Other useful suggestions are found in Rino J. Patti and Herman Resnick, "Changing the Agency from Within," *Social Work*, 17 (July 1972), pp. 48–57.

vigor and in the same way, and one must make strategic choices about points of engagement; (4) we must develop strategy (this means we must concern ourselves with adequate preparation, progressive challenge, alternative tactics, and so on); (5) the manner in which a struggle is waged can be as important as the eventual outcomes (if the struggle builds collectivity and educates politically, it has already met one important objective of radical work).

These kinds of agendas have found expression in some social agencies for shorter or longer periods of time. Some examples may be suggestive. In one important social welfare planning agency in the Philadelphia area, a group of workers in one section of the agency was able to create a partial free zone for themselves. In this zone, an effort was made to equalize pay among the staff, including people who had originally been hired as clerk-secretaries. This could not be done through money transfers, but was accomplished by the unit's arranging for those receiving less pay to work for proportionately fewer hours. The tasks of the section were divided according to the competence of the various workers. Leadership and supervision were collective and mutual. Not surprisingly, the work of that unit had an impact far beyond its numbers or the period of time for which it existed. It provided an exciting and provocative model for workers in that agency and in others, raised many important questions in the agency, and was also able to develop a supportive relationship to movement forces at work in the city at large. The unit was able to create several important, independent, change-oriented organizations in the city and to attract many new people to the movement because of its vitality and clear sense of purpose. As a result of that unit's cohesiveness, energy, competence, and the growing number of allies it had outside the agency, it was able to challenge the more conservative agency definitions of its task and to maintain itself in the agency. It was also able to meet its formal, irreducible agency commitments with sufficient time and energy left over for more vital work. Last, but not least, the workers involved had more plain fun every day than they had had on other jobs, and than other workers were having at that agency.[15]

Internal struggles for democratization can be enhanced when workers are able to form alliances with community groups to organize for worker/community control. This has happened in some hospital settings in conjunction with political struggles in community mental health centers. Two

[15] In this case, as for several of the other examples which will be presented, formal written documentation is not available. Unfortunately, radicals in the social services have not developed sustained facilities for sharing examples of radical practice in writing. Radical practice in the British social services can be reviewed in *Case-Con*, and radical practice in the health field in the United States is discussed in a number of radical health newspapers (although they tend to be located in and limit their focus to single cities).

of these struggles were reviewed in the Spring, 1972, issue of a newspaper published by a radical health organization in Philadelphia, which reported:

> In the past three years, struggles at Lincoln Hospital [New York] and San Francisco General Hospital have shown that community groups and workers, when united, can effectively challenge the priorities and power of health institutions. For example, workers in the Pediatrics Outpatient Department at Lincoln have established a selection committee composed of hospital workers and community people which has a key role in the hiring of hospital staff. This committee interviews applicants and reviews their attitude toward the community and health care.
>
> After a period of struggle that involved strikes by hospital workers and interns, several coalition efforts are emerging at San Francisco General. A group composed of workers, interns and lawyers have succeeded in shaking things up a bit by challenging the accreditation of the hospital. Another group of workers, the Thursday Noon Committee, led a campaign to defeat an unfair billing policy and has made waves by drafting a proposal for emergency room changes.[16]

In a few cases, important because of the examples they provide, workers have been able to take control of their agencies and to run their agencies as collectives. The tenuous hold that such collectives have is matched only by the exciting potential they reveal for agency collectives to provide superior services to clients, to engage in larger political work of all sorts, and to liberate the spirits and energies of their workers.

In one such case in Philadelphia, an agency serving runaway and delinquent youth has been able to capitalize on the accidents of a loose and permissive board structure and the fortuitous (though now planned) coalescence of a politically progressive staff, to develop a collective democratic organizational form. This has permitted the development of a staff network that supports staff in a difficult and close relationship with its client population and encourages the effort to understand the linkages of direct service questions with underlying political dynamics as they relate to youth.

In these ways, the concern for democratizing agency structures and practices can be operationalized. No one model will be universally applicable, and the level and intensity of engagement will naturally vary tremendously from agency to agency. What is important is that the strug-

---

[16] "Health Workers New Focus for Movement," *Philadelphia Health News* (A Publication of the Health Information Project, Philadelphia), 1 (April–May 1972), with contributions from the Medical Committee for Human Rights and the Mental Health Advocacy Association. See also Susan Reverby and Marsha Handleman, "Institutional Organizing: Emancipation of Lincoln," in *Rough Times* (formerly the *Radical Therapist*), 2 (June 1972), pp. 6ff, reprinted from *Health–PAC Bulletin*, 37 (January 1972).

gle be undertaken at some level and that both the theoretical and the organizational relationships between the specific case and the larger efforts be kept firmly in mind.

Caucuses and Unions

If democratization of agency practice is a goal, caucuses and unions can be critical vehicles through which to struggle for its achievement. The kinds of struggles described above must take place in a collective situation. The caucus can be an important starting place for this effort, and struggles within and through unions offer some exciting possibilities.

A caucus can begin simply as a group of like-minded persons who recognize a commonality of perspective in each other. Initially it need have no formal agenda, other than a commitment to exploring points of commonality among its members in an effort to reduce the personal and political isolation often experienced by those who have a left perspective or who feel that a left perspective might make sense. It need have no name, no agreed-upon ideology, and can have as informal a structure as an arrangement to take coffee breaks together once a week.

If a caucus's origins may be humble, its potential is not. Because social agencies leave individual members isolated and often out of sympathy with agency perspectives, a clear and organized alternative source of support, ideological input, and vehicle for challenge to the agency can make a great impact on individuals and the agency. The roles that black caucuses, women's caucuses, and radical or rank-and-file caucuses have already played and are now playing make this clear. Such caucuses can have an important role as a vehicle for the growth and development of its members—as a place where they can share their reactions to the work situation, to social welfare, and to life in general. They can be a combination of consciousness raising, therapy, and political education. At the same time, they can move into professional action as a pressure point in the agency and as a linkage point with other groups in other agencies and other sectors outside the social welfare field.

While to this point we have been discussing caucuses with a focus on organizing within single agencies, we should by no means overlook the development of caucuses within the social welfare sector that has taken place across agency lines. Cross-agency caucuses or radical organizations in the service sector include the Medical Committee for Human Rights, the now-defunct Social Welfare Workers Movement, Radical Action for People (St. Louis), and the various radical therapist groups. These organizations provide an important source of psychological and intellectual support for radical workers, as well as an organizational base for challenging the service sector.

Radical caucuses within agencies can and have been the organizing force for social welfare workers' unions, or have served as the left wing within existing unions. While it is true that unions at the present time tend to be conservative, it is also true that the identification and linkage of welfare workers with organized labor can have a positive impact both on the immediate well-being of these workers and for longer-term political work. As Bertha Reynolds suggested in 1946, as clearly and accurately as anyone has suggested since, social workers

> are increasingly being forced to choose between practicing their profession ethically—that is, refusing to use their clients for the interests of any other group—or becoming slavishly obedient to powerful forces which must in the end destroy every vestige of professional integrity. . . . To resist alone is professional suicide. To resist in a strong protective association inclusive of all who are employed in a given social service and allied with thousands of others in organized labor and professional workers' unions, is to have real effectiveness in the fight for democracy in the whole community. It is to belong to the whole community in a new and real sense.[17]

Within union structures, radicals can and have attempted to move union concerns beyond wages and working conditions for workers (without in any way neglecting or diminishing the importance of these) to questions of the nature of service given to clients and of worker self-management. It has also happened that social service workers, under the aegis of their union organizations, have refused to implement some of the more repressive aspects of social welfare policies. In the 1930s, as reported in the militant journal of the times, *Social Work Today*, welfare workers recognized the commonality of their dilemmas and those of welfare clients. In a number of cases, mass meetings, with both workers and clients present, were organized to protest cutbacks in welfare funding simultaneously harmful to both workers and clients, as well as other repressive welfare measures and regulations. Over 15,000 people attended one such meeting at Madison Square Garden, despite attempts at repression by welfare officials. The platform statements called for both staff retention and for more responsive and adequate government relief programs.[18] In more recent years, welfare workers have refused to implement some of the more repressive welfare policies, for example, the "brownie point system," [19] or the more well-known cases in which wel-

[17] Bertha C. Reynolds, "Re–Thinking Social Case Work," *Social Service Digest* (San Diego: 1946), pp. 30–31.
[18] For a report of this meeting see Mary Siegel, "Worker and Client Join Hands: The Madison Square Garden Meeting in New York," *Social Work Today*, 3 (January 1936), p. 18.
[19] This program is described and discussed in Chapter 4. One report of such union activity is available in "Relief Workers Reject Program," *New York Times* (November 23, 1971), p. 53.

fare workers refused to conduct midnight raids or man-in-the-house searches.[20]

It has long been the case that social welfare workers have individually and privately resisted implementing some of the more repressive policies of their agencies and have sabotaged agency mandates. For example, significant manipulation of rules and regulations takes place, as all workers in such agencies know, around questions of public welfare eligibility and benefit allotment or around parole and probation requirements. Placing such resistance in an organized union context magnifies its importance tremendously by providing an opportunity for general political education and for organizing. It also makes an important difference to the self-image of those who engage in such action, inasmuch as it enriches the act of individual conscience with an explicit dimension of political struggle.

Union efforts, then, ultimately have great potential. They begin to suggest possibilities for collective action to a group of workers heavily conditioned by patterns of individualism. These struggles offer a vehicle for raising questions about, and challenges to, larger social welfare policies, and about worker/client control of services. They also point to linkages with other parts of the working class. These are all potentials. It is true that unionization has not always produced such outcomes. The role of the radical caucus within unions is to help assure that unionization becomes part of the larger struggle for radical social change, rather than a vehicle for the pursuit of a narrow version of self-interest by one section of the new working class.

Linking with the Outside

In addition to working directly in the agency and organizing other workers for direct work, radicals can do propaganda and organizing work in support of outside activity and groups from inside the agency, as their particular positions permit. In some cases, this may involve direct support of client groups, as in the case of welfare workers who have aligned with and found ways to facilitate the work of the National Welfare Rights Asociation.[21] In other cases, it may involve internal or-

[20] The British radical social work journal *Case-Con* regularly reports similar activities. See, for example, Alan Harland,"Urban Guerrillas in Public Service!" *Case-Con*, 9 (October 1972), pp. 3–5; and "No Go in Islington," *Case-Con*, 8 (July 1972), pp. 3–5 (a case of social workers in a housing authority collectively refusing to evict families squatting in vacated housing and joining public demonstrations with them against their department).

[21] For example, the work of the Philadelphia Regional membership of the Pennsylvania Social Service Union, which can be reviewed in their newsletter, *Contact*, is impressive in this respect. They have understood and acted on the commonality of their experiences as welfare workers and the experiences of their clients.

ganizing around broader issues, as in the example of the numerous anti-war groups that grew in social agencies in support of the peace movement of the mid- to late 1960s.

The efforts of social service workers in the early days of the War on Poverty were among the important forces in the creation of rights groups in the social service areas.[22] Working to create such groups was not a part of the official mandate of the Office of Economic Opportunity's agencies, and the political pressures such groups created contributed to the demise of the organizing components of the War on Poverty. Nonetheless, the effort was worthwhile in the sense that the best thing that could have been expected to come from the OEO may have been the creation of independent militant consumer groups.

In more recent, post–Community Action Project times, workers in social agencies have been responsible for the stimulation of clients' rights groups and other radical community groups of some importance. The flexible schedule that some workers have, their organizational and interpersonal skills, and the ambivalence about radical objectives contained in some liberal agencies always permit some workers to be of service to the movement from their positions in the bureaucracy.

Workers in agencies have also been helpful to clients' rights groups by helping them to get a hearing in their agencies. This may facilitate the work of the community group and may also further expose the nature of the agency to its workers as a result of the agency's responses to the community group. For example, several workers in a United Fund welfare planning agency in Philadelphia, pursuing the guidelines recommended in a study commissioned by the United Fund agency, encouraged the Philadelphia Welfare Rights Organization to apply to the United Fund for support. The refusal of the United Fund to act on its own recommendations helped many welfare workers to begin to understand the political role and nature of the United Fund. In turn, this was an important stimulus for the creation of an alternative fund in Philadelphia, the People's Fund, which has subsequently helped support the Philadelphia Welfare Rights Organization and numerous other groups.

Similarly, radical workers have engaged in Nader-like whistle-blowing activities,[23] keeping community groups informed of agency developments that go against their community interests. For example, sympathetic workers in community mental health centers in Philadelphia, through the Mental Health Advocacy Association, maintained an active, if some-

---

[22] For example, see Mary Rabogliati and Ezra Birnbaum, "Organizations of Welfare Clients," in Harold Weissman (ed.), *Community Development in the Mobilization for Youth Experience* (New York: Association Press, 1969), pp. 102–136.
[23] For example, see Joel Freedman, "One Social Worker's Fight for Mental Patients' Rights," *Social Work*, 16 (October 1971), pp. 92–95.

times covert, relationship with local community boards.[24] Further, it has often been possible for workers to find ways to direct agency resources to community and rights groups, for example, in the form of special grants, employment, or the assignment of agency workers as consultants to community groups (which then also permits some of the community group's work to be done in the agency, thereby meeting some of its financial needs).

Another kind of example, directed to the rights of clients, was undertaken by the Ethical Standards Action project. Located in Philadelphia, the project developed a proposed "Bill of Rights for Users of Social Services" which it brought before the delegate assembly of the National Association of Social Workers. The Bill of Rights was rooted in the belief that many social services are coercive to clients and are inappropriate to their needs. To the extent to which clients engage in a fully conscious way in determining the course of their own careers as clients, they will both protect themselves and create an important challenge to social services. To this end, the following sixteen-plank bill was proposed:

1. Users of service have the right to know their rights.

2. People who are users of service are entitled to basic human, legal, and civil rights including full protection of state and federal constitutional and statutory law.

3. Users of service have the right to be treated with dignity, decency and respect.

4. Service is given regardless of the client's race, religion, color, creed, nationality, lifestyle or alienage.

5. Service shall not be withheld, terminated or limited 1) as a punishment for the user's group membership, community or political activity or involvement in social action or 2) for protest or complaint against social worker or agency policy or actions.

6. The client's past or present habits, immoral or illegal actions, diseases, illnesses or personality shall not be grounds for withholding, terminating or limiting appropriate social work service.

7. Clients have the right to the integrity of their minds and bodies. Their right to privacy must be fully respected. No visits or inquiries by third parties may be made without the specific recorded consent of the client for each such visit or inquiry.

8. All information, materials and records regarding a client must be kept in the strictest confidence. Such data is the property of the user of service and must be shared with him or her.

[24] See the issues of the *Mental Health Advocacy Association Newsletter,* Philadelphia.

9. Information, materials and records regarding a client may not be disclosed to any other person or agency, governmental or private, without the specific recorded consent of the client for each such disclosure.

10. Specified information, material or records must, on request, be removed and returned to the user of service.

11. Prior to being evaluated, studied or assisted, the client shall be informed of the nature and purpose of the proposed actions and procedures. An individualized "service plan" shall be formulated and recorded in writing. This shall be reviewed and revised at least every three months.

12. The service plan shall be formulated in full consultation with the user of service.

13. If the client objects to the service plan or actions taken pursuant thereto, he or she will be allowed, without prejudice, to withdraw from the service, to acquire another worker or to transfer to another agency. Where the client is institutionalized and cannot by law withdraw or transfer, he or she shall be advised of his or her legal rights and rights under this Bill of Rights and shall be put in contact with independent legal and social services.

14. Clients have the right not to be subjected to experimental research without the express and informed consent of the client.

15. Users of service have the right to have a specific individual social worker designated as the person with primary responsibility to the client.

16. Users of service as a group shall have major representation in the agency at the policy level. The agency has the responsibility for encouraging the development of user groups within the community.[25]

While only the last item in this plank speaks to the question of the service setting as a base to organize clients, the larger effort is commendable. It represents an attempt by social workers, working in agencies and as members of their professional association, to bring pressures to bear on the social services, through the National Association of Social Workers, consistent with the goals and programs of a number of militant groups of service users.

Political Education and Recruitment

Finally, work in an agency can be oriented toward educating and recruiting others to active participation in the movement. To do so may involve one-to-one conversations, helping to create situations in the agency

---

[25] Proposed Bill of Rights for Users of Social Services, Ethical Standards Action Project, Philadelphia, Pennsylvania, 1972.

that expose its assumptions more clearly, presenting and pushing for more desirable programs in the agency, and engaging other workers in radical activities outside the agency.

It often seems that radicals in social agencies have a more humane and less cynical attitude toward social services, a more integrated analysis of the dilemmas of a given situation, and a more thoughtful perspective than most on their own work and situations. These attitudes of the radical make it more possible for him or her to influence others, in direct and indirect ways, especially if the radical is honest and not manipulative in his or her politics. However, it is useful for radicals, as they go about these efforts, to keep in mind that they may not be as successful in persuasion as they may be in serving as a sounding board for the emerging radicalism in others and for legitimating by their existence and beliefs the radical strivings in others. Educating people and recruiting them for radical work is not a bludgeoning process. It is a process better described as facilitating. Recognizing this fact not only will permit the radical to be more successful in this process, but will free him or her from feelings of failure if each and every co-worker is not converted to radical commitment. The quality of our contact with others and the extent to which we can engage with some in developing radical commitment are more important at this point in the struggle than some grandiose notions of mass conversion to radicalism.

RADICAL CASEWORK AND SERVICE DELIVERY

Can there be a radical casework? It may seem that casework practice, by its very nature, cannot be radical. Some caseworkers feel, for example, that casework is simply unrelated to politics of any sort, despite the personal sympathies they may have with a given political ideology. Others may recognize the theoretical possibilities of radical casework, but may not see a way to pursue such political commitments within existing agency structures and within the orientation of the profession. Still others may recognize full well the political nature of casework practice and may choose to practice within a conservative political framework. Despite these concerns, we suggest in this section that there can be a practice of casework that is consistent with a radical political analysis. Such a practice, we believe, will simultaneously represent an important enrichment of the social work commitment to human service and a meaningful contribution to socialist development.[26]

[26] In key respects, the position developed here parallels that developed by Philip Lichtenberg in "Radicalism and Casework," unpublished paper, Bryn Mawr College, Bryn Mawr, Pennsylvania, 1974. However, the Lichtenberg paper differs from or extends this effort in important areas. While the two analyses were developed independently, the present author readily and happily acknowledges a general intellectual debt to Philip Lichtenberg.

Building on Radical Analysis

It was suggested in Chapter 7 that an important part of the conservatism of casework practice is rooted in a conservative analysis of the social order and of individuals' relationships to the social order. Conventional casework does not build on a sufficiently comprehensive analysis of the extent to which a person's individual well-being is intertwined with the well-being of the social order, nor is it sufficiently critical of the destructive nature of the social order. Rather, it views people in isolation from the most critical institutions and arrangements of the society, and it operates as though one person's private well-being could be achieved in the midst of general public squalor.

As the root of conservative practice is conservative analysis, so the root of radical practice must be radical analysis. At the heart of such analysis is the effort to place the life situation and the particular problems of the individual in their broadest social, political, and economic perspective and to view that larger scene in an uncompromised way. This does not mean that the analysis is diffuse in the sense of not focusing on the particular problem that the client experiences. Radical casework must be of concrete service to individuals; otherwise it will become isolated and will be rightly accused of placing ideology and political commitment above and beyond the needs of individuals. A radical analysis and program must be primarily responsive to people's real needs.

However, the radical analysis does suggest a perspective on the problems of individuals which seeks to relate these problems to the context of the social order in which they occur. A client's depression or disorganization is a reflection of a social order that is isolating, individualistic, competitive, and often assaultive. At the same time, depression has a real, immediate manifestation in the life of the individual. The individual must understand both the psychic manifestations of problems and their social-economic-political components and must learn the ways to struggle against them.[27] To suggest, as some radicals do, that we need not and must not deal with individual personalities is to artificially limit the analysis radicals make about the destructive quality of the social order. To argue, as conventional social work does, that we cannot deal with fundamental questions of the nature of the social order through the casework process is to undermine social work's commitment to human service. An

[27] This point is elaborated in Jeffry Galper, "Personal Politics and Psychoanalysis," *Social Policy*, 4 (November–December 1973), pp. 35–43. See also Norma Campbell, "Radical Therapy and Radical Social Change," unpublished paper, 1972, prepared for seminar in Social Change Strategies, San Francisco State College, 1972.

integrated analysis of the psychic manifestations and the social roots of people's problems is key to the practice of radical casework, and it is the base on which to build the specifics of radical practice.

The nature of the underlying analysis that informs radical practice has direct applicability to the way in which individuals in trouble are assisted in developing an appreciation of the nature of their troubles. In traditional casework practice, that understanding is a conventional psychological one. In the more current varieties of casework, it is broadened into the psychosocial model.[28] Radical practice, in contrast, encourages self-understanding both in the psychological sense and in terms of the individual's relationship to fundamental historical and political processes. That is, it seeks to help the individual locate himself or herself in a psychological, social, economic, political, and historical sense.

This approach has been most clearly illustrated in recent years by the women's movement. Thousands of women, in consciousness-raising groups as well as on their own or with radical feminist therapists, have come to understand the problems they experience from a new perspective.[29] The realities of lack of confidence in oneself, depression, anger, underdeveloped capacities, and isolated lives, and the need for these issues to be confronted in the lives of each woman who experiences them are not denied. At the same time, the larger situation of women in the United States and elsewhere, involving as it does the systematic denial of the full personhood of women, is becoming clear. Women who have engaged this process come to know more fully the way in which these larger patterns are manifested in their personal experiences. Simultaneously, they recognize that the limits to their personal ability to overcome these problems are also broadly set by the conditions of women in society as a whole. A commitment to pursue personal well-being, when it is informed by the feminist perspective, leads to self-understanding in psychological and in historical-political terms and to efforts to create changes at these multiple levels. Efforts to solve one's personal problems and efforts to create fundamental changes in the social order thus become integrated activities.

The model provided by the women's movement, though it has been most broadly developed there, is equally applicable elsewhere. For example, it is hard to imagine that the particular problem of any one black person could be explained without understanding it in relation to the nature and impact of racism as a whole. Similarly, the situation of any one of us can hardly be explained in isolation from an appreciation of the

28 This approach was identified and critiqued in Chapter 7.
29 The literature here is large. A useful discussion from a social work perspective is Barbara Stevens, "The Psychotherapist and Women's Liberation," *Social Work*, 16 (July 1971), pp. 12–18.

impact of a capitalist economy on social relations and on each of our private lives. It might be thought that helping people to place their problems in such broad context leads them to pessimism and despair about the possibility for improvements in their circumstances. In practice, just the opposite tends to occur. This approach creates and releases more energy for creative struggle than does a conventional approach for several reasons.

First, it enables people to modify their self-images in ways that facilitate forward movement. Many of us perceive our problems as evidence of our personal inadequacies. We are encouraged in this view by the ethic of individualism fostered by our society. The radical analysis provides a basis on which we can broaden our understanding so that our problems are seen not solely as inadequacies—which they may in part be—but also as a reflection of the dehumanizing nature of the social order. One initial reaction to gaining this insight is frequently the release of tremendous anger, so characteristic of the early stages of liberation movements. The experience of anger is itself often therapeutic. It feels better than debilitating depression and self-flagellation, and it opens the door to concrete actions in the world.

Second, an appreciation of the political and historical nature of personal issues reduces the isolation we tend to feel in our personal situations. Whether or not the appreciation leads to collective efforts to seek solutions, the experience of recognizing the commonalities can be helpful and freeing.

Finally, we need to compare the outcomes of this process, in terms of hopefulness and despair, with the outcomes of conventional practice. Typically, casework practice suggests that a particular intervention will solve a given problem in some specific and limited way. If the client is fortunate, some solution will be achieved. The caseworker and the social agency can then be self-congratulatory about having solved a given problem. But, how can the client who has been helped not feel let down in some critical way? The client has come to some understanding of a problem he or she faces. This understanding or interpretation of the problem is, of course, very much conditioned by larger social processes and often by the casework process in particular. Generally the client's understanding of the problem is such that it permits a solution to the problem within conventional social arrangements. Consequently, the solution itself contributes to conventionality and, therefore, from a radical perspective, to limited life possibilities. The client has been motivated to seek help and has gotten help successfully. Yet, though the problem is solved, at a deeper level the client has a perception that something still remains basically wrong in his or her life. And, of course, something is basically wrong, though it is not generally given a name in the casework process. The radical alternative does not lead to this dilemma. It tries to take immediate solutions as far as possible, but it is realistic and straightforward about the requirements for full solution.

We all experience a confusing and frustrating discongruence in our lives. On the one hand, we are encouraged to believe that our society represents the pinnacle of successful social organization and that we, its citizens, are the wealthiest, freest, most developed people in the world. On the other hand, our daily experience reinforces the view that we are a destructive and demoralized society. This discongruence is reduced when it is understood through political education. The resulting clarity is energizing in that it helps us to focus our thoughts and actions even though the magnitude of the tasks before us expands tremendously.

How does this kind of analysis emerge from the helping process? A critical factor is the intervention of the worker. In every interaction in which we engage, we encourage certain responses in others and discourage other responses. Workers who are themselves politicized will naturally look for and reinforce those occasions in which clients touch on the social-political nature of their own lives. At the same time, they will offer suggestions and interpretations from this perspective—just as all workers make such interpretations from whatever perspective they themselves utilize to understand the world. It is important that these interpretations be neither imposed nor forced. The social-political context and explanation must elaborate or clarify, and not be substituted for, the psychological perspective. And it must clearly be offered in service to the client and not in service to political ends that are somehow separate from the situation and well-being of the client.

The Use of Groups

If it is true, as we believe, that the lives and problems of each of us must be understood in a political and social context, then we will recognize that the kind of diagnosis and analysis we have been discussing must take place in conjunction with others. This suggests the desirability of practice occurring in group situations. For the worker and client to analyze the political determinants of a problem and to intellectually posit the extent to which the problem is widely shared will not be as real or as powerful an experience as if the commonality emerges from the interaction of people who had previously seen their problems as idiosyncratic. Nor will it set the stage, in itself, for collective activity toward solution. The group basis of practice more nearly meets these requirements.

The fact that practice occurs in groups does not in itself make casework any more or less radical. When caseworkers work in groups, in the absence of a radical political analysis, group activity tends to be simply individual casework in groups and tends to use group pressure to enforce standards of behavior on individuals.[30] On the other hand, given a political perspective, a group framework can enhance practice since it brings the power of a collectivity immediately to bear on the lives of individuals. It may well be that some persons cannot easily use groups in approaching their problems, especially in the initial stages of confronting the issues in their lives. However, at some point, it is important for all of us to experience the power of a mutual, collective exploration of the dilemmas we face.

In the same way, the group context of practice goes further than the individual context in pointing toward solutions. It is true that a radical analysis does not lead one to believe that a complete solution to our problems will be immediately forthcoming. However, it does point to a wide variety of steps we can take on the way. These tend to involve collective struggle. If the therapy group or consciousness-raising group does not itself become a unit for ongoing political struggle, it can be a laboratory for its participants to learn about the issues involved in collective effort, to experiment in working in groups, and, hopefully, to observe and experience one model of a group that attends simultaneously to the internal psychological needs of its members, to issues of group process and cohesion, and to the external task issues before it.

Who Will Be Clients?

A further way in which the radical practitioner can bring practice and politics together is through the selection of clients. All casework selection processes involve some kind of discrimination according to the capabilities and goals of the particular school of thought that is represented by the worker and/or agency. Radical caseworkers ought to try to be as clear as possible about the clients toward whom they should address themselves and with whom they can be most effective.

Caseworkers in social agencies often have some discretion about the composition of their caseloads. This gives some opportunity for the radical worker to make discriminations according to political criteria. In fact, some radical social workers have suggested that caseworkers can engage in "client refusal." [31] That is, where the goals of casework are to coerce particular behaviors not necessarily in the clients' best interests, caseworkers ought not to deal with clients for whom the casework process can only mean repression by finding ways to keep those

---

[30] See Helen M. Levinson, "Use and Misuse of Groups," *Social Work*, 18 (January 1973), pp. 66–73.
[31] Ian Taylor, "Client Refusal: A Political Strategy for Radical Social Work," *Case-Con*, 7 (April 1972), pp. 5–10.

persons out of the service network altogether. This is one way to reverse the negative control elements in casework practice.

The flip side of client refusal is politically self-conscious client selection. The radical can select clients on the basis of his or her ability to do effective personal/political work with them. On what basis would a radical implement a political selection process? One category of people we might place in high priority for service is people who are already active in the movement for social change. Workers in agencies, depending on what services their agencies offer, can help keep already committed people in action. A second important group would include those not active in the movement, but demonstrating a broader awareness or having potential to develop such awareness. This group would be selected on what must be imprecise criteria at this point, since there is relatively little clarity about the forces that lead people to a politicized interpretation of their lives.[32] Furthermore, the relevant group might vary, depending on the nature of the agency and the services it offers. The radical worker, however, will experiment with various possibilities.

At least two objections to this procedure will come to some minds. First, it may be argued that to use political criteria is to violate the professional ethic of political neutrality. However, as we argued in Chapter 6, the so-called political neutrality of professionalism is, in reality, a conservative politics. Agencies select clients according to what they consider to be clients' abilities to use service or their formal eligibility for service. The client who defines his or her problem as the kind amenable to the usual social service solutions and seeks out those solutions thereby reinforces conservative problem-solving modes and, in turn, is further conservatized by engaging in that process. In other words, the typical processes of client selection reflect political considerations. The radical worker attempts to establish different criteria from those that exist. Radical workers should be clear that the issue concerns differing political perspectives, not politics on the one hand and nonpolitical professionalism on the other.

The second objection to an explicitly political selection process is that it is unfair to engage in such selection in the face of the enormous pool of unmet client need every agency faces. With so many people in so much need, how can the worker play politics? However, we need only reflect on the enormous amount of unmet needs that exists in our society. By whatever process we select clients, we will barely make an impact on those needs. And if every client already known to every agency were served, an equal or larger number of persons unknown to agencies would still not be served. The most reasonable and committed way to

---

[32] For a discussion of this point see David Shapiro, "On Psychological Liberation," *Social Policy*, 3 (July–August 1972), pp. 9–15.

act on a deep concern for helping people is, therefore, to think and work politically. If we stay locked into current procedures of existing agencies, we will do very little. Trying to help every client who comes to us, on the basis of a selection process dictated by agencies, is not a serious way to deal with the current issues in this society. The worker who rejects this process and struggles toward a new process is not cold-hearted or a political adventurer, but realistic and humane.

Worker–Client Relations

A radical commitment carries implications for the way in which workers and clients relate to one another. An important component of the relationship is the stress on equalitarianism. In our earlier analysis of the politics of professionalism, we identified the destructive consequences for worker and client of the "professional" role with its hierarchy and inequality. In addition to being the optimal stance for therapeutic psychological processes and outcomes, equality is also the stance most consistent with the political concerns of the radical. Further, in a strategic sense, a radical analysis and strategy place the caseworker not only in the role of therapist but also in the role of political ally. The worker is as implicated and involved in the social situation as is the client, and the solutions which the client must seek are the same solutions that the worker must pursue in his or her life. An equalitarian casework relationship sets the stage for political unity and integrated struggle.

Of course, the worker will have some skills and insights that the client does not have. However, an important underlying assumption that needs to pervade the relationship is that the situations of the worker and client are more alike than not in their fundamental characteristics. This assumption can be operationalized through the understandings the worker and client reach about those problems with which the worker can help the client and those with which the worker and client must ultimately struggle jointly to achieve solutions for both. The worker must make conscious efforts to dispel any myths of "expert" solutions to fundamental problems or about the transferability of the worker's technical skills and abilities to broader or deeper issues.

This suggests that radical workers will be more open than conventional wisdom advises to sharing their personal lives and experiences. The relationship is not totally reciprocal in that the situations of the client and worker are not identical. But the ultimate goal is reciprocity, or a casework relationship that is therapeutic and supportive for all parties. In this way, the particular tasks of the casework process and the larger tasks of building a radical political community and movement blend in to one.

This requires that the worker not act in a superior, haughty, or "professional" way. Of course, acting in a superior or haughty way is a criterion of good practice in general, not solely for practice that specifically attempts to be radical. This is neither surprising nor undermining of the notion of radical practice. In arguing for radical casework in particular and radical social work in general we stated that radical practice is simply conventional practice that does not compromise itself by accommodation to a repressive social order. When social work practice acts more in conformity to its own best ideals, it more nearly approximates a style of practice consistent with radical commitments.

Finally, equalitarianism is fostered through the worker's efforts to demystify the casework situation itself. Radical practice ought to not only help clients in whatever ways possible with specific problems, but should also arm them with the tools to deal with their problems and with the problems of others in the future. This means that radical workers share with those they help the knowledge they have about helping people. They are not possessive about their skills, and they see making such skills more broadly available to people at large as part of their job. Helping clients to become more aware of the nature of helping processes and encouraging them in the appropriate use of these processes elsewhere are the themes of radical practice.

Goals and Outcomes

The radical caseworker must try to be of maximum service to clients and to the movement for radical change at the same time and as part of the same process. If these become opposing processes, it means either that casework practice has been conservatized or artificially depoliticized or that the political movement has placed itself over and above or against the very people for and with whom it struggles.

We have suggested that radical workers will attempt to help clients to the fullest possible extent with the problems clients experience. This will not mean helping clients adjust more comfortably to repressive situations. Helping a welfare client live more comfortably by arranging for a higher monthly benefit is important work, but, if the process ends there and the client is not encouraged to see and eventually to act on the exploitative nature of welfare status as a whole, then the worker has served the best interests of neither the client nor the political movement. In this conception, therapy, direct service, education, politicization, and involvement in collective political struggle are all part of the same process and are all goals of the radical worker.

The radical worker also should have in mind changing himself or herself through the casework process. If we focus away from client illness and difference and on commonality, we are in a better position to learn from clients. As we come out from behind the shield of pro-fessionalism, we can better solicit and hear feedback about our skills and our personalities. In some ways, professional social workers, by virtue of the discipline we impose on ourselves to become professional workers and the values we absorb in social work schools on the way to becoming professionals, have more need to change than do those with less formal education who tend to be our clients. We are encouraged to have distorted notions of our importance, we are trained to be emotionally repressed, we have lingering or strong faith in "the American way of life," and so on. Many clients are way ahead of us in those respects, and if we are attuned to them and to ourselves in human ways, we will have an opportunity to become more real and healthy.

These, then, are some notions of a radical casework practice. Surely it is not a polished model. Hopefully, however, it will be provocative to some in their efforts to more fully develop the role of casework in the development of a radical social movement.

ORGANIZING AND PLANNING

Few social workers are being hired specifically to do organizing work in the context of welfare state programs. The philosophical and financial support for such work conducted within the auspices of the welfare state reached its height in the mid-1960s, through the Office of Economic Opportunity's Community Action Programs. It tapered off in the late 1960s and early 1970s through the vehicle of the Model Cities Program (defined as a mayor's program, in contrast to the Community Action Programs which stressed grass-roots activity and control), and is now virtually absent from official policy and programming. As a consequence, it is necessary to discuss organizing, and its radical potential, less as a formal assignment which some workers will be hired to fulfill than as a stance toward any social service activity. In one sense, the virtual death of a formal welfare state organizing role is a benefit because it forces us to develop the organizing role for persons in all service-delivery positions.

Social planners and social administrators have, to some extent, taken the positions once filled by organizers in the welfare state bureaucracies. They tend to be concerned with creating, maintaining, and further rationalizing some part of the superstructure within which social services operate from their positions in social agencies, planning councils, or de-partments of government. There is nothing inherently progressive about the social planning or administration role, though the radicals of the 1930s saw in their demand for government planning a critical handle on destructive private activity. However, it has become clear that private interests have made good use of the rationality and predictability that increased social planning has accomplished. The planner or administrator may be in a position to facilitate radical activity, though his or her possibilities are limited by higher general visibility and remoteness from grass-roots forces. Hopefully, this discussion will be of some use to persons in those positions who are developing a radical commitment.

In the previous chapter, we discussed the notion of nonreformist or structural reforms. This notion can be useful to radical workers in developing an orientation to organizing work. The criteria for nonreformist reforms will be recalled here for the light they can shed on the specifics of practice. These criteria suggest ways to analyze and develop change strategies so as to circumvent the dilemmas of practice from within the liberal reformist position. They keep us alert to the dual concerns of practicing to further immediate well-being and to build toward the realization of a fundamentally transformed society.

Decentralizing Power and Control

The first characteristic of a structural reform, as we identified it in the previous chapter, is that it encourages the decentralization of power and control and the simultaneous restriction of centralized power and control. That is, it tends to disperse power to local groups, collectives, and communities at the same time it weakens centralized power. The administrative decentralization of functions, as represented by some school decentralization plans and, in some measure, by revenue sharing, does not really meet this criterion since the final say about the overall shape of policy remains fairly centralized, though implementation of policy may be somewhat dispersed.

This criterion creates some dilemma for the planner-administrator in his or her traditional role. The assumptions of the planning-administration task tend to encourage faith in and pursuit of increased centralization of power and control. These assumptions may be based, in part, on decent motives, for example, on the notion that centralized rationality can produce more humane outcomes than can decentralized, disjointed, and perhaps somewhat less efficient efforts. Wtihin the framework of liberal assumptions, this may be true. For example, in the public assistance program as it now exists, centralized control assures some uniformity and in the past has prevented local governments from instituting more repressive rules and regulations concerning client eligibility, standards of behavior, and so on.

However, our analysis has suggested that central control, while possibly more progressive in the short run, reinforces the welfare state superstructure within which it functions and, therefore, strengthens an inadequate and undesirable social mechanism. Central control may produce short-run gains within the boundaries of what is and simultaneously help ensure that those boundaries will be less easily transcended. The principle, therefore, is to struggle for the empowerment of local units. If we believe that we will achieve a decent arrangement for social services only in a transformed society and that the society should and can only be transformed from the bottom up, then all our actions must be directed to facilitating struggle at the local level. This guideline suggests a reasoning process for the social service worker, if not a specific set of tactics. It helps to identify the nature of most of the change or reform activity that organizers and planners are often called on to implement, namely, changes that call for some improved benefit schemes within the framework of centralized power and control.

Problems of developing a political strategy around the federal government's periodic retrenchment in levels of spending for social programs may be clarified by applying this criterion. In the effort to counter reductions in social spending that occurred in the early 1970s, coalitions of liberal and progressive forces struggled for a return to what would be, in effect, the Great Society days. They argued the "more is better" position. The lack of radical analysis and radical organization prior to those cuts left little alternative but for the liberal political forces to respond from the conservative position of calling for a return to the good old days. In so doing, their major allies were service providers. In building their case this way, they let the terms of political debate be set in a way that aided conservative forces. After all, the good old days were not so good; and Nixon, then President, was correct in suggesting that welfare state programming in the 1960s did not much help those for whom it was created (though his analysis of the reasons for this failure was faulty). He was also correct in identifying the self-serving nature of the objections raised by social service workers and organizations.

The struggle to enlarge social spending may be more or less successful in any period. To the extent to which it is more successful, more social service jobs will be saved. However, no more stable or meaningful organization to prevent the next round of reductions will have been created, nor will the reinstated programs, whatever their extent, be able to go beyond the earlier generation of programs in their impact on social problems.

This suggests a dual focus for activity around social service budget cuts. On the one hand, it is important to struggle for increased government spending for people in need. It is also important, however, to raise questions about the locus of control of these programs and the underlying purposes they serve. Admittedly, social service cuts tend to occur in periods that are generally repressive, yet it is precisely at such times that a more aggressive stance is called for. A liberal stance plays into the criticism of self-interest on the part of service providers which politicians can level so successfully at the social service professions. That debate will be partially transcended and important political, educational, and organizing work will be done when the issue expands beyond more or less money to control at the grass-roots level. The social service professions have not stood for this, by and large. Their failure to do so has led to their vulnerability to political attack, and their effort to do so now could lead to a meaningful basis for long-term struggle in the future.

Building Alternative Institutions

A second characteristic of nonreformist reforms is that they model and help build, in the present, the social units and values that would characterize the kind of society in which we would ultimately hope to live. This means that we must struggle to create, here and now, some examples, however modest, of a better way. This can help to show larger numbers of people what is possible, can renew our own faith in our ability to make a difference in the world, and can begin to build some units to serve as a nucleus for much-expanded activity in a more propitious period. As part of our work, we must attempt to create collective, communal, democratic organizations that function to meet the needs of people in the community and that are joyous and growth-producing for those who live and work in them. While we must struggle with the institutions that exist and attempt to move them forward, we must also try to create alternatives here and now. Increasing numbers of social service workers are discovering these possibilities.

One set of examples, from the health field, is the variety of people's health clinics that have sprung up in the United States in the last five years or so. One such effort, focusing on health care for women, is in Seattle, Washington. It is distinguished from traditional services in its provision of service free of charge to poor and working women; in its control by the women of the local community; in its antiprofessional stance (in the sense of being concerned with demystifying gynecology and making self-knowledge and self-help a reality); by putting a major emphasis on teaching-learning relationships among patients, staff, and doctors; and by a major emphasis on preventive medicine. While separate from major existing institutions, the free clinic relates to such institutions in several ways and thereby avoids isolation and containment that could unwittingly place the clinic in the role of alleviating pressures for change on conventional institutions. For example, it is active in seeking allies within existing institutions, both for help with the clinic and to encourage workers to raise challenges in their institutions along the lines suggested

by the free clinic's operation. Also, it uses the clinic as a locus for organizing in the community among patient groups and with health-care
workers to raise challenges to existing institutions about the cost, quality
and control of traditional services.[33] This activity is being duplicated in
many settings across the United States.

Counterinstitutions are also being developed in other areas of service.
For example, a wide variety of services have sprung up for youth and
counterculture people, generally organized and operated from the bottom. These centers not only provide service, but, again, serve as a locus
for other organizing work. In one case of a free clinic in Long Beach,
California, a group of workers organized a service for street people on
the basis of a democratic communal form of organization. This clinic
provided medical treatment, drug counseling, informal therapy, and a
chance to pull together groups of people to think about and work on a
variety of political issues, for example, draft counseling.[34]

Another exciting model of alternative services is the Women-in-Transition project, located in Philadelphia. This project was a response to the
enormous number of requests for help the Philadelphia Women's Liberation Center was receiving from separated and divorced women. The
project provides a variety of services to women. One of these is to engage
women in small-group, support and consciousness-raising sessions which
are run by women trained by the project. Other services are legal assistance, referral to needed psychological-legal services, and outreach to
already separated women, especially low-income women, about their
legal rights. Several of the project's staff have social work training, but
find they have been best able to integrate their social work skills and
their feminist orientation outside of a traditional agency structure. The
staff functions as a collective and works in consultation with a project
planning group. The Women-in-Transition project not only provides a
much-needed service, but does so in a way that orients and involves
many "clients" to the women's movement. In addition, by teaching
women to conduct their own divorce proceedings, the project is challenging both the Pennsylvania Bar Association and the laws of the State
of Pennsylvania, which have attempted to impose legal hegemony on
divorce proceedings to the enrichment of lawyers and at the expense of
women.[35]

In a number of cities, alternatives to the local United Ways and United

---

[33] See "An Approach to Women's Health Care," *The People's Health* (voice of
the Seattle, Washington, Health Movement), 9 (April–May 1972), pp. 2 ff.

[34] See Gerald R. Wheeler, "America's New Street People: Implications for Human
Services," *Social Work*, 16 (July 1971), pp. 19–21.

[35] The project has developed an important resource for divorced and separated
women (which has proven useful to other women as well) entitled *Women in
Transition: A Feminist Handbook on Separation and Divorce*, New York: Charles
Scribners Sons, 1975.

Funds have been created by radicals to serve as funding sources to movement groups. In Philadelphia, the People's Fund is such an organization. Organized in 1970 by radical social welfare professionals, the People's Fund raises money through a broad-based community fund-raising drive and distributes this money to grass-roots community groups working for radical social change. The People's Fund helps support over thirty groups, including the Welfare Rights Organization, the Addicts' Rights Organization, the Barbwire Society, the Black Panther Party, the Puerto Rican Revolutionary Workers' Party, the Philadelphia Resistance, the Women's Liberation Center, the United Farm Workers' Organizing Committee, the Black United Liberation Front, the Lawyer's Guild, and the Pennsylvania Abortion Rights Association. While the amount of money raised has not been large in comparison with the United Fund's efforts, even the smaller amounts of money have made a difference to a number of the recipient groups which operate on small, hard-to-come-by budgets. The People's Fund has been important in other ways as well. It has served as an information clearinghouse for some parts of the movement in Philadelphia and has been useful in educating people about the movement and about the shortcomings of the traditional fund-raising mechanisms. By its nature, it also lends support to the notion that radical forces must engage in a kind of internal community development process. This means getting to know one another, pooling information and resources, and learning to work cooperatively.[36] Alternative institutions like the People's Fund mobilize the energies and commitments of radicals who may also continue to work in "straight" agencies.

Many radicals with a social service background prefer to develop possibilities for full-time movement commitment. While not all their members are social service workers, the Movement for a New Society offers one model for full-time engagement in political work. The Movement for a New Society is a development of the Quaker Action Group and is now located in centers throughout the United States and in other countries.[37] By living collectively (in over a dozen homes in the Philadelphia area, for example); by conscious attention to reducing the cost of living (though by no means the quality); and by collective approaches to buying consumer goods, purchasing services, and so on; members of MNS are able to live quite inexpensively. For many,

---

[36] The People's Fund can be contacted at Box 1225, Philadelphia, Pennsylvania 19105. Information on other alternative funds is available in C. Simpson, "This Is Not a History Book: Some Information About Sustaining Funds in the U.S.," printed by Common Sense, 1802 Belmont Road, N.W., Washington, D.C. 20009, May 1974.

[37] Contact can be made with Movement for a New Society at 4722 Baltimore Avenue, Philadelphia, Pennsylvania 19143.

this means that a few days of straight work each month frees the rest of their time for direct political work.

Members of the MNS may engage in radical political activities as a collectivity or as individuals in other groups, as each person sees fit. There is no strict party line, although there is a point of view, of course. Part of what the MNS is able to do is to provide internal and external educational seminars on radical analysis and nonviolent radical change strategies. Members of this group have also been active in antiwar and anti-imperialist work, ecology, education, Indian rights, and other issues. For those involved, affiliation with MNS provides emotional support, intellectual stimulation, and the opportunity to work directly on the issues they have come to see as critical to both personal and social survival. They suggest, by their nature, how far radicals can go in developing alternative institutions as they struggle within and against existing institutions.

Each of the examples in this section illustrates some of the possibilities for building new institutions within the old society.[38] Radicals in the social services have been attracted to these possibilities in the past. Hopefully, more will become involved in the future, as the awareness of the personal rewards and the political potency of this approach becomes more widely shared.

Working with Mobilized Populations

A further characteristic of nonreformist reforms is that they recognize that basic change occurs only when people are mobilized. This characteristic suggests, therefore, that radical organizers look for ways to provide resources to people who are already mobilized or have the potential to be mobilized. These resources may be money, personnel, or organizing skill and other expertise.

This does not imply that we should abandon the concept of providing resources where there is human need. It does mean that we take seriously the fact that our society will never truly meet people's needs unless it is basically changed. Therefore, orienting resources only on the basis of need may be humane in the short run, but self-defeating in the long run. This is, it will be recalled, the same argument we developed in defending the morality and political soundness of the radical caseworker's selection of client populations on political grounds. If resources can be used not only to meet need, but to facilitate political organization, a larger purpose is met.

If it became a choice, for example, of allocating resources for a deprived but unmobilized population (for example, alcoholics) or to a per-

---

[38] A useful journal on such alternatives is % *The Journal of Alternative Human Services* (621 Fourth Avenue, San Diego, California 92101).

haps less deprived but mobilized group (the forces active around day care), the choice would have to be made on the basis of the long-range concerns for facilitating political activity. While the radical organizer may help to start activity in various settings, it is well to remember that, contrary to the liberal image of organizing, the radical worker does not see himself or herself primarily as a person with a bag of skills, capable of application through a problem-solving model. Given the sorts of problems that concern the radical, political mobilization or readiness for mobilization is critical, and no single or simple or traditional professional expertise or intervention technology can produce that readiness. The radical operates, therefore, where the action is.

Political Education

An ongoing part of all practice must be political education. The opportunity to do education and propaganda work further transforms what might be self-contained liberal efforts into an effort with larger potential. The radical practitioner must try to help more people understand the immediate situation in its larger light. This can involve discussion of all sorts and, at present, is leading to growing amounts of collective, organized, and self-conscious study. In practice situations, without manipulating situations for such purposes, it may well happen that efforts to create changes reveal underlying repressive dynamics, and these should be fully explored and interpreted by all participants.

These, then, are some of the ways in which the notion of nonreformist reforms can serve as guides to radical organizing practice. As a final note on such practice, we stress that the radical organizer, like the radical caseworker, needs to strive for mutuality in relations with those we have been accustomed to calling clients. This means that the worker is as ready to be influenced as to influence and to see himself or herself as an agent to be used in a common struggle rather than as a central figure in a larger plan of his or her own making. When the agenda is radical change, the worker is primarily an ally and a colleague, not a professional technician of the welfare state solving other people's problems within the framework of welfare state rationality.

A CODE OF ETHICS FOR RADICAL SOCIAL SERVICE WORKERS

As an effort to contribute to the development of a radical ideology and commitment capable of informing radical practice, we close by returning to the Code of Ethics of the professional social work association, the National Association of Social Workers. In an earlier chapter we argued, point by point, that this Code contains a conservative bias that serves the best interests of neither client, worker, nor social well-being in general. We will consider each item of this Code, therefore, and suggest how it might be revised were it organized in service of the development of the kind of society we hope to build. In a sense, the following point-by-point comparison summarizes this book. As the existing Code encapsulates the analysis and goals of conventional practice, so our modifications encapsulate the analysis and goals of the radical social service worker. Our Code will have fourteen planks.

1. I regard as my primary obligation the welfare of all human kind.

The existing Code suggests that the social welfare worker regards as a primary obligation the welfare of the individual or group served. The limiting and destructive nature of the individualistic and pluralistic strategies that follow from this obligation have been documented numerous times in this book. The well-being of any one of us is inseparable from the well-being of all of us, and this awareness must be reflected in radical practice.

2. I will work toward the development of a society that is committed to the dictum, "From each according to his or her ability, to each according to his or her need."

The existing Code is concerned with nondiscrimination, in the civil libertarian sense, and commits the worker to serving all persons without bias. We have described the limitations inherent in the notion of equality of opportunity, which this plank reflects, and have suggested that our focus must be on outcomes as well as processes.

3. I will struggle for the realization of a society in which my personal interests and my personal actions are consistent with my interests and actions as a worker.

At present, the Code suggests that personal interests be subordinated to professional responsibility and that statements and actions as a professional be kept apart from statements and actions as a private person. The personal fragmentation and politically conservative implications of this arrangement received attention elsewhere in this book. Our work and our lives must become increasingly integrated.

4. I will consider my self accountable to all who join in the struggle for social change and will consider them accountable to me for the quality and extent of the work we perform and the society we create.

The current Code commits the worker to be responsible to himself or herself for this work. The need for collective accountability and struggle, however, is paramount. While personal standards are always desirable, we must add to them the critical collective concern.

5. I will work to achieve the kind of world in which all people can be free and open with one another in all matters.

The existing Code's commitment is to respect the privacy of all persons served. Without suggesting that one violate the trust of others, the emphasis on privacy must be counteracted inasmuch as our society is adept at using privacy to control us by keeping us apart. Openness is critical to the development of a society organized around positive mutual commitments.

6. I will use information gained from my work to facilitate humanistic, revolutionary change in the society.

The Code's commitment to the responsible use of information gained in professional work on the one hand implies a desirable concern for integrity. On the other hand, it suggests commitment to professional practice above a commitment to radical social change. This is not acceptable in radical practice.

7. I will treat the findings, views, and actions of colleagues with the respect due them. This respect is conditioned by their demonstrated concern for revolutionary values and radical social change.

This plank in the old Code argues for respect of colleagues per se. No commitment can be made to professional colleagues that is not in the context of a commitment to larger social values. Inasmuch as they do not have such a commitment, their findings, views, and actions must be rejected and challenged, though their humanity must always be acknowledged.

8. I will use all the knowledge and skill available to me in bringing about a radically transformed society.

The old Code's concern is that practice be conducted within the recognized knowledge and competence of the profession. This does not facilitate the kind of total engagement and total use of all resources which is required in the struggle for radical change.

9. I recognize my responsibility to add my ideas and findings to our society's knowledge and practice.

The existing Code's concern for adding such ideas and findings to social welfare knowledge and practice is worthy but limiting. Social work is a vehicle and servant. It is neither the temple nor the master.

10. I accept my responsibility to help protect the community against unethical practice by any individuals or organizations in the society.

The present Code asks for protection against such practices in the social welfare field. This is not enough. Our commitment is to struggle against the destructive elements of the whole.

11. **I commit myself to use myself fully in the struggle for revolutionary change.**

The existing Code urges readiness to provide services in public emergencies. Our society, at this time, is experiencing an emergency in an ongoing way. There is no more appropriate time for us to engage. Earthquakes, floods, and fires are minor happenings compared to the daily destruction wreaked by our institutions in the normal course of events.

12. **I support the principle that all persons can and must contribute to the realization of a humanized society.**

The old Code stresses the need for professional education for professional practice. Inasmuch as radical work is concerned with the fundamental reorganization of our society, all persons are potentially equally qualified and engaged students and particpants.

13. **I accept responsibility for working toward the creation and maintenance of conditions in society that enable all people to live by this Code.**

The present Code's stress on enabling social workers in agencies to live by that Code is isolating and limiting in view of the tasks before us.

14. **I contribute my knowledge, skills, and support to the accomplishment of a humanistic, democratic, communal socialist society.**

The Code's suggestion that we contribute knowledge, skills, and support to programs of human welfare is desirable but limited. We must be clear about our goals and courageous in putting the notion of a radically altered society on the agenda.

It seems likely that, for any one of us, if there is a will, there is not necessarily a way. Acting collectively, however, the possibilities of what we can create are very exciting. While radicals are more given to manifestos than Codes of Ethics, we need to find ways to think together about how we can proceed. If this Code, and this book, serve any useful political purpose, it will be to facilitate that thinking.

Index